The Rakhine State Violence

Vol. 2: The Rohingya

Shwe Lu Maung

A publication of
Shahnawaz Khan
USA

Printed and Published in USA by Shahnawaz Khan.
The covers and interior designed and edited by the Khan
Publication team. Proof date: November 26, 2014.

Website: http://www.shwelumaung.org

Library of Congress Control Number: 2014902841

The Rakhine State Violence, Vol. 1: The Rakhaing Revolution

ISBN 13: 978-1928840-09-1
ISBN 10: 1-928840-09-4

The Rakhine State Violence, Vol. 2: The Rohingya

ISBN 13: 978-1928840-10-7
ISBN 10: 1-928840-10-8

MADE IN USA

To my Comrades

in Revolution

The Rakhine State Violence
Vol. 2: The Rohingya

Table of Contents

Acknowledgements
Special Acknowledgements to the Volume II
Preface
Preface to Vol. II
Introduction by Dr. Habib Siddiqui to the Vol. II
Introduction by Dr. Muhammad Firdaus to the Vol. II

Prologue 1
1. The Rohingya   3
2. Rohing-ya Anthropology 4-8
3. The Touchstone 9-30
4. Pure Gold 31-40
5. 1982 Citizenship Act – Ne Win   41-57
6. The Rohing-ya
        Linguistic Manifestation   58-75
7. The Aborigines   76-111
8. Myanmar mtDNA   112-140
9. Self-Alienation   141-159
10. Crimes Against Humanity   160-169
11. The Victims of Civilization   170-183
12. Citizenship and Beyond   184-205
(A historical materialism)
13. Bangladesh and International 206-218
Epilogue   219-220

Appendix-1 Open Letter to Dr. Dip Moni   221-226
Appendix-2 Roshang 227-244
Appendix-3 Table of Contents (Vol. 1) 245
Appendix-4 Books by Shwe Lu Maung 246-250
Index 251-257

Acknowledgements

I **AM** deeply grateful to my friends who always render sincere support to me, with encouragement to boldly present my views and experience to the global audience. They are Minrammar (Ko Tin Maung, a poet and activist), Chairman Kyaw Hlaing of AIO and NUFA (deceased), Red Comrade Oo Khin Maung (Politburo of ACP), Khaing Arnani (Secretary of NUFA), Dr. Khine Maung (Chairman, NUPA), Khaing Saw Tun (Arakan Army, deceased), Maung Tin (Mohd. Yacoob, Secretary, Arakanese Muslim Association), Kyaw Hla (M. Kamal, Chairman, MLOB), Maung Sein (Mohd. Mohiuddin), and Kyaw Soe Aung (MSK Jilani), and Khaing Mrat Kyaw (Chief Editor, Narinjara News), from the political arena of Burma, and Professor Zillur Rahman Khan (USA), Professor Abdul Mahbud Khan (Bangladesh), Dr. Habib Siddiqui (Ph.D., USA), and Dr. Muhammad Firdaus (M.D., USA), who are the academics and professionals. The members of the Arakan Democratic Forces (ADF) are also among those whom I ever remain grateful to for their support. I am equally grateful to other friends whose names I fail to mention here.

I am also grateful to all who oppose me and try to silence me with threats because the threats give me one more reason to be vocal.

With great appreciation, I would also like to express my thanks to the Khan publication team for their help with the cover and interior designs and formats, making this book more presentable.

Thank you all.
SLM

Special Acknowledgements to the Volume II

IN addition to the Acknowledgements I have mentioned earlier, I owe special thanks to U Bodhinyana, a banker-turned-Bikkhu, and the Arakanese Research Society of Bangladesh (ARSB) for giving me the complimentary copies of their journal Vol. III (2001), and to Maung Sein Pru for his translation of *Arakan Rajsabhay Bangala Sahitya* from Bengali to English (Appendix-2).

I am also indebted to Dr. Habib Siddiqui, Ph.D., Ph.D., (i.e. double Ph.D.) who is a Chemical Engineer by profession and foremost human rights activist, and to Dr. Muhammad Firdaus, M.D., FACP, an American physician of Rohingya ancestry. They tediously read the manuscripts and gave valuable feedback, making the presentation clearer and the flow smoother. I am deeply grateful to them for writing introductions to this volume, adding new and valuable dimensions to the book.

Most sincere thanks are due to Professor Zillur Rahman Khan, Ph.D., Professor Emeritus of the University of Wisconsin, Chairman of RC 37 of International Political Science Association, President of Bangladesh Foundation and Adjunct Professor at Rollins College in USA. He has been my mentor beginning with my first book on Burma, published in 1989.

Last, not the least, I would like to thank the Khan publication team for helping me with the designing, reviewing, editing, analyzing, validating and computer logistics.

Thank you, again.
SLM

Preface

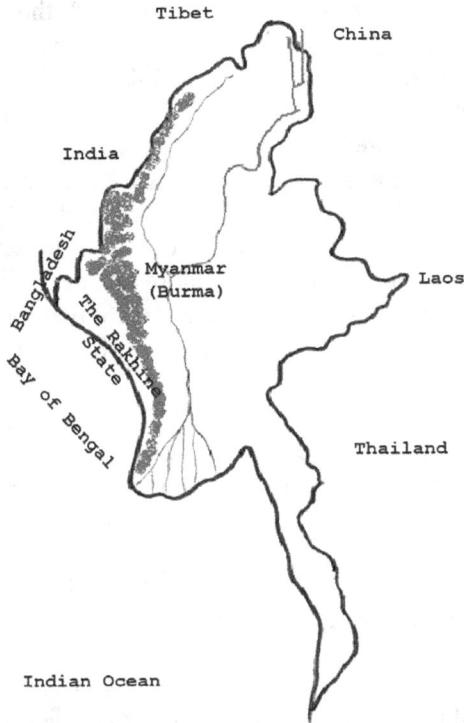

OBVIOUSLY, it is visible that *the Rakhine State violence* has not only regional but also global ramification and the causes of violence must be urgently addressed. Some concerns expressed by the world leaders are given below.

➢ Indonesian foreign minister Marty Natalegawa said that Myanmar Buddhist-Muslim violence has regional impact during the meeting of the ASEAN Foreign Ministers, held in Myanmar in January 2014.[1]

➢ The UN Resident and Humanitarian Coordinator and UNDP Resident Representative, Ms. Renata Lok-Dessallien said that the March 2014 Sittwe attack at the United Nations, World Food Programs, and other Non-Governmental Organizations

---

[1] http://www.irrawaddy.org/burma/sectarian-violence-burma-regional-impact-says-indonesian-foreign-minister.html

(NGOs) that are helping the displaced people was "an attack on the entire humanitarian response in Rakhine State."[2]

➤ In the 12 March 2014 "Report of the Special Rapporteur on the situation of human rights in Myanmar," the Special Rapporteur Tomás Ojea Quintana "concludes that the pattern of widespread and systematic human rights violations in Rakhine State may constitute crimes against humanity as defined under the Rome Statute of the International Criminal Court."[3]

➤ In April, 2014, the Assistant Secretary of State for East Asian and Pacific Affairs Daniel Russ told Myanmar government "to take a more active role in resolving these issues, to work toward a durable solution that addresses the underlying causes of conflict in Rakhine State, and to create the conditions for sustainable peace and development, with which the United States is prepared to assist"[4]

➤ Again, on April 17, 2014, the U.S. ambassador to the United Nations Samantha Power asked Myanmar government "to intervene in Rakhine State to stop violence between ethnic Rakhine Buddhists and Rohingya Muslims and ensure the delivery of humanitarian aid."[5] Her message came after her hearing the briefing on Myanmar crisis, at the UN Security Council, by Vijay Nambiar who is the U.N. special adviser on Myanmar.

In the year 2012, the world was shocked and saddened by the news of the Rakhine State violence that displaced 140,000 people with an unknown number of deaths, from both Rohingya Muslim and Rakhine Buddhist communities. The ongoing violence has created tens of thousands of Rohingya boat people who attempted to escape from Myanmar terrorism. The violence continues to date and while this book is being finalized the violence occurred on 13 January 2014 in Du Chee Yar Tan (Ducheertan, Middle) village, Maungdaw Township. According to the United Nations more than 40 Rohingya were killed, but the Myanmar government denied the killing. The violence was also

---

[2] http://www.un.org/apps/news/story.asp?
NewsID=47486&Cr=myanmar&Cr1=#.Uz8WBBD_mbg
[3] Report of the Special Rapporteur on the situation of human rights in Myanmar, Tomás Ojea Quintana, A/HRC/25/64 at *www.ohchr.org*
[4] Press Release, US embassy, Rangoon, Myanmar, April 10, 2014.
[5] http://www.reuters.com/article/2014/04/17/us-myanmar-usa-un-idUSBREA3G2DN20140417

inflicted upon the UN and NGO humanitarian services and personnel in Sittwe, the capital of the Rakhine State, in the last week of March 2014. The Arakan National Conference, which was held in Kyaukpyu, Rakhine State, from April 27 to May 01, 2014, ended with a demand for the formation of the Arakan National Defense Army and effective segregation of the Rohingya Muslim and Rakhine Buddhist communities. It is a war cry with a policy of apartheid.

The Rakhaing revolution began with King Bering in 1784 at the advent of Burmese occupation of the Rakhaing Kingdom. The revolution took a modern turn under the leadership of Bikkhu U Uttama towards the end of the 19th century, but armed insurrection was reborn in 1948 when the British left Burma. The Rakhaing Revolution failed. The failure marked the rise of the extremists who fermented the Rakhine State violence.

The Rakhaing revolutionaries, in contrast to *the Rakhaing reactionaries and conservatives*, have struggled against the odds to make Myanmar an equitable republic in the philosophy of "we-the-people". I have been involved in the revolution since 2nd March 1962, the day General Ne Win's Revolutionary Council staged the coup d'état. I was a strategist and theoretician in the revolution. This is an account of the development and application of the thoughts, philosophy, strategies, and tactics in the Rakhaing revolution in view of an equitable republic of Burma. But, our revolution failed and an equitable republic of Burma still remains a dream.

Today, the world is intertwined and connected more than ever before. Injustice in one place has *Tsunamic* effect all over the world. The poverty and zero purchasing power at one corner of the world has given birth to the global financial crisis. Civil war in a place like Somalia has created civil unrests in Europe. Myanmar and Afghanistan opium have crippled law and order situation in many countries. Myanmar refugees are putting enormous pressure on every country of the globe. Above all Myanmar gross human rights violations, ethnic wars, racial and religious violence, symptoms of genocide and ethnic cleansing are dehumanizing humanity.

Against the odds, the world is putting investment in

Myanmar pseudo-democracy with the hope of emergence of a civil society in the land of atrocities. However, my experience in the Rakhaing revolution highlights major faults in the Myanmar society. We need to make revolutionary changes in the fundamentals of the Myanmar society and polity in view of a civil society. Otherwise, it is very likely that a sinkhole will undo the weak and cracked foundation of Myanmar pseudo-democracy, sooner or later. Any superstructure will simply crumble down.

The objective of this book, *The Rakhine State Violence*, in two volumes, is to tell the world the untold story of the Rakhine State. Earlier, I have presented the world with two books *Burma Nationalism and Ideology* (1989) and *The Price of Silence* (2005), all based on my own experience. In this book, I again present my experience, from my days in the student politics (1962-66), in the guerrilla politics working with the leaders like President Kra Hla Aung and Chairman Red Comrade Kyaw Zan Rhee, and from the later days in my capacity of the Diplomatic Representative of ALD (in exile) and the Patron and CEO of the Arakan Democratic Forces. The special emphasis is put on the etiology of the Rakhine State violence so that the world may judge the right from the wrong and work for a better future in the interest of common humanity. We do not want to be the prisoners of the past.

The presentation is in the form of narration and is supported with 101 exhibits and 2 maps, in 341 pages, in the Vol. 1, and with 76 exhibits that include illustrations, maps, graphs, and tables, in 281 pages, in the Vol. 2, laden with scholarly references and footnotes whenever relevant. *Some classified documents* are also presented for the better understanding of the situation. Some materials of the chapters 3 and 5-10 have been published under the heading of "the Arakanese Student and Youth Movements" in Arakanpost between 2001 and 2006. Major part of the writing is in American English, but there is a good amount of British English, especially the quotes. There will also be some broken English. The Burmese names could be a challenge to the reader. Nevertheless, I am confident that the reader will find the book informative, enjoyable and delightful.

SLM
May 07, 2014

Preface to the Volume II

ON July 27, 2014, the au.news.yahoo.com[6] reported that "Myanmar's plans for the future of a western region torn apart by Buddhist-Muslim unrest could result in "permanent segregation" of the two religious groups," as per assessment of the UN Special Rapporteur on human rights in Myanmar, Yanghee Lee. If the permanent segregation sets in creating East and West Arakan, in the fashion of East and West Bengal, it will be detrimental to the regional stability.

The Rakhine State violence and the Rohingya issue are complicated simply because we are looking at each other with green or blue glasses. If we were to see one another through the crystalline clear eyes of 'common humanity' things would be simpler. Keeping this fact in mind, the presentation is designed to give the reader a panoramic overview of the various facets of the issue.

Hopefully, this book will help Myanmar *rethink* and *advance* to the age of human rights and common humanity, sailing high on the global tides of science and technology.

With due thanks, I here include the introductions to this volume by Dr. Habib Siddiqui and Dr. Muhammad Firdaus. Their introductions also serve as the windows to the current affairs in Myanmar. Originally, this volume was planned to be published as a "standalone" edition in 2013. However, due to the death threats and intimidations I delayed the publication and redrafted the manuscript in the line of the prevailing circumstances to date. Although it is published as the Volume II of the Rakhine State Violence, it can still 'standalone.'

---

[6] https://au.news.yahoo.com/world/a/24558338/un-envoy-warns-of-permanent-segregation-in-west-myanmar/

Introduction

The Rohingya people of Myanmar (formerly Burma) who mostly live in the western part - the Rakhine (formerly Arakan) state, bordering the Muslim-majority Bangladesh, are undoubtedly the most persecuted people on earth. Denied citizenship in the Buddhist majority country, the Rohingyas have simply become the most unwanted people in our planet. Not a single of the 30 clauses of the Universal Declaration of Human Rights is honored by the Myanmar regime when it comes to its treatment of this unfortunate people. The nearby Bangladesh does not want the persecuted Rohingyas to settle there either. In desperate attempts to save their lives, many Rohingyas have become now the 'boat people' of our time!

Yet Myanmar has gone through a change in recent years. The former military general Thein Sein is the poster-boy of reform inside the country. With him as the head of the state, there is a quasi-civil-military government in place that runs the fractured country. Myanmar had its election – albeit a limited one, which some political observers may complain about – in which many politicians with grass root support within the masses have managed to win the limited seats available in the parliament. The new regime has also released many political prisoners (mostly Buddhists) who were once rotting in many of Myanmar's notorious dungeons. In reaction to such positive image-building initiatives, the western world has reciprocated by lifting its political and economic sanctions against the once hated military dictatorship, which has ruled the country for almost its entire life since earning independence from Britain in January 4 of 1948.

There was much expectation – probably too unrealistic and too premature – that the Thein Sein government was serious about 'real' reform and that the Rohingyas will be integrated as citizens at par with other ethnic/national groups inside Myanmar. What we have witnessed instead is worsening of their situations. They are now victims of a highly organized genocidal campaign in which even Buddhists like Aung San Suu Kyi – touted one-time as the democracy icon – are sadly, either silent or willing partners in this gross violation of human rights. Since May of 2012, an estimated 150,000 Rohingyas are internally displaced in the Rakhine state. Tens of thousands of Muslims living in other parts of Myanmar have also seen organized mob violence, lynching, and wholesale destruction of their homes, schools, mosques and businesses, which have resulted in some 250,000 internally displaced persons (IDPs) all across Myanmar.

What is worse, the international NGOs, esp. from the Muslim countries, were barred from helping out the Muslim victims. In the face of reported protests from the Rakhine Buddhist community, the

Organization of Islamic Countries (OIC) could not even open an office to carry out its much needed humanitarian relief work in the troubled region.

This year (2014), the Myanmar authorities have cracked down even harder, making the situation worse. First, the government expelled **Doctors Without Borders** (MSF), which had been providing health care for the Rohingya. Then orchestrated mobs attacked the offices of humanitarian organizations, forcing them out. While some kinds of aid are resuming, but not the health care! As noted by award-winning journalist Nicholas Kristof, expected mothers and their children are dying for lack of doctors. They need doctors desperately to save their lives, but the Myanmar government has confined them to quasi-concentration camps outside towns, and it blocks aid workers from entering to provide medical help. They are on their own in Myanmar, where democratic progress is being swamped by crimes against humanity toward the Rohingya. [1]

Many of the Muslim IDPs now live in squalid camps with no provisions and are counting their days hopelessly to be relocated to their burned homes. And yet, such a provision seems unlikely. In recent months, Rakhine Buddhists have organized demonstrations protesting any resettlement of the Rohingya and other Muslims. Bottom line – they want the Rohingya and other Muslims out of Myanmar, if not totally annihilated. [2]

Many international observers and some experts, including human rights activists, were surprised by such outbreaks of ethnic cleansing drives last year against the Muslims, in general, and the Rohingya people, in particular, let alone the level of Buddhist intolerance against non-Buddhists everywhere inside Myanmar. However, such sad episodes were no surprise to many keen readers and researchers of the Myanmar's problematic history.

In 2007, when I was invited as the chief guest and keynote speaker in an international conference on the Rohingyas of Burma, held in Tokyo, Japan, its theme was the prevalent xenophobia in Myanmar and how to address the issue so that people of all ethnic and religious backgrounds could live harmoniously. One after another the speakers spoke at length about the danger that they foresaw. The proceedings of the Tokyo Conference later appeared in a book form. [3]

We all knew that simply a transition to democracy would not and could not solve the Rohingya problem. Instead of a much-needed

---

[1] *Myanmar's Appalling Apartheid* by Nicholas Kristof, New York Times, May 28, 2014.

[2] For a summary of the current unrest see, e.g., Habib Siddiqui, **U.S. Congressional Hearing on Burma**, New Age, October 4, 2013, http://www.newagebd.com/detail.php?date=2013-10-04&nid=67845#.Uk5Bd9Ia7oc; see also: Eurasia Review.

[3] *Problems of Democratic Development in Burma & the Rohingya People*, eds. Habib Siddiqui and Abid Bahar, pub. JARO, Tokyo, Japan (2007).

dialogue for reconciliation and confidence-building between ethnic/national and religious groups, what we recognized was appalling Buddhist chauvinism - outright rejection of the 'other' people from such processes by the so-called 'democracy' leaders within the Burmese and Rakhine Diaspora. As if, their so-called struggle for democracy against the hated military regime was a purely Buddhist one, the Rohingya Muslims were unwelcome in those dialogues between ethnic/national groups.

The level of Buddhist intolerance, hatred and xenophobia has simply no parallel in our time! The chauvinist Buddhists are in denial of the very existence of the Rohingya people, in spite of the fact that the latter group comprised almost half the population of the Rakhine State and that the ancestors of the Rohingya were the first settlers in the crescent of Arakan before others moved in. While the vast majority of the late comers to the contested territory were Buddhists, the Rohingyas, much like the people living next door – on the other side of the Naaf River – in today's Bangladesh had embraced Islam voluntarily. Their conversion had also much to do with the history of the entire region, esp. in the post-13th century when the Sultans and the great Mughal Emperors ruled vast territories of the South Asia from the foothills of the Himalayas to the shores of the Indian Ocean.

As a matter of fact, the history of Arakan, sandwiched then between Muslim-dominated India and Buddhist-dominated Burma, would have been much different had it not been for the crucial decision made by the Muslim Sultan of Bengal who reinstalled the fleeing Buddhist king Narameikhtla to the throne of Arakan in 1430 with a massive Muslim force of nearly 60,000 soldiers – sent in two campaigns. Interestingly, the Muslim General Wali Khan – leading a force of 25,000 soldiers, who was instructed to put the fleeing monarch to the throne of Arakan –claimed it for himself. He was subsequently uprooted in a new campaign - again at the directive of the Sultan of Muslim Bengal, by General Sandi Khan who led a force of 35,000 soldiers. What would be Arakan's history today if the Muslim Sultan of Bengal had let General Wali Khan rule the country as his client?

The so-called democracy leaders in the opposition had very little, if any, in common with values and ideals of democracy but more with hard-core fascism. Their behavior showed that they were closet fascists and were no democrats. Thus, all the efforts of the Rohingya and other non-Buddhist minority groups to reach out to the Buddhist-dominated opposition leadership simply failed. It was an ominous warning for the coming days!

So, in 2012 when the region witnessed a series of highly orchestrated ethnic cleansing drives against the Rohingya and other Muslim groups not just within the Rakhine state but all across

Myanmar, like some keen observers of the political developments I was not too surprised. Nor was I surprised with the poisonous role played by leaders of the so-called democracy movement. They showed their real fascist color. But the level of ferocity, savagery and inhumanity simply shocked me. It showed that the Theravada Buddhists of Myanmar, like their co-religionists in Sri Lanka and Cambodia, have unmistakably become one of the most racists and bigots in our world. With the evolving incendiary role of Buddhist monks like Wirathu - the abbot of historically influential Mandalay Ma-soe-yein monastery and his 969 Fascist Movement, which sanctifies eliminationist policies against the Muslims, surely, the teachings of Gautama Buddha have miserably failed to enlighten them and/or put a lid on their all too obvious savagery and monstrosity.

On June 20, 2013 twelve Nobel Peace Laureates called upon the Myanmar government for ending violence against Muslims in Burma. They also called for an international independent investigation of the anti-Muslim violence.[4] Yet, the Myanmar regime continues to ignore international plea for integration of the Rohingya and other minorities. It proclaims – "There are no people called Rohingya in Myanmar." This narrative is absurd, as well as racist. A document as far back as 1799 refers to the Rohingya population in Arakan, and an 1826 report estimates that 30 percent of the population of this region was Muslim.[5]

Is there a solution to the Rohingya problem? How?

Dr. Shahnawaz Khan (Shwe Lu Maung), author of the book – *The Price of Silence: Muslim-Buddhist War of Bangladesh and Myanmar* – is a well-known authority on Myanmar.[6] He is a scientist by training and profession and claims to be a social Darwinist. He has written and spoken many times on the sensitive issues of Myanmar. Interestingly, he is also a native of Arakan, who before settling in the USA spent decades living both in Burma and Bangladesh.

In this book, Dr. Khan reviews the controversy surrounding the Rohingya case and recommends ways that may facilitate their integration inside the bigotry-ridden Myanmar. He opines that the national politics around the Rohingya people of Arakan who are dumped as the 'Bengali illegal Muslim immigrants' is not mere bigotry but a viable toxic fruit of Myanmar ultra-nationalism⇉ *Bhumi Rakkhita Putra Principle*; it is a deliberate act of provocative target-marking in line with YMBA's (Young Men Buddhist Association)

[4] For the full report see: http://nobelwomensinitiative.org/wp-content/uploads/2013/06/NobelWomen_Burma-Statement-June-20-2013_FINAL.pdf

[5] *A Comparative Vocabulary of Some of the Languages Spoken in the Burma Empire* by Francis Buchanan, 5th Volume, Asiatic Researches (1799); SOAS Bulletin of Burma Research, Vol. 1, No. 1, Spring 2003; http://www.soas.ac.uk/sbbr/editions/file64276.pdf

[6] Shwe Lu Maung, *The Price of Silence: Muslim-Buddhist War of Bangladesh and Myanmar – A Social Darwinist's Analysis*, DewDrop Arts & Technology, USA, 2005

amyo-batha-tharthana (race-language-religion) and is *the foundation* of the Burma Citizenship Act 1982. It is strong, powerful, and ultra-toxic. This apartheid law allows a Rakhine Buddhist like Aye Maung – an MP and chairman of the RNDP (a religio-racist Rakhine political party) whose parents only emigrated to Arakan state in 1953-54 from Bangladesh (erstwhile East Pakistan) – to be automatically recognized as a Burmese citizen while denying the same privilege to millions of Rohingya and other Muslims whose ancestors had lived in the territory for centuries.

Dr. Khan argues that Myanmarism – the noxious cocktail of Buddhism, ultra-nationalism, racism and bigotry – is hardened with fear of Pan-Islam. Whether one likes it or not, there is no denying that the Rohingya issue is no longer a local issue. It has become an international one with serious implications especially for the entire South Asia and Southeast Asia. Dr. Khan opines that without a concerted international cooperation, especially from Bangladesh, Myanmar cannot solve the Rohingya crisis, the potential Islamic extremism, and the growing Buddhist radicalism which is increasingly becoming genocidal. He argues that even if the Rohingya people were given the Myanmar citizenship today the problem will not go away any time soon. For genuine integration with equal rights and privileges the Buddhist and other peoples of various races, religions, ethnicities and nationalities must think 'citizenship and beyond.' He argues that ethnic identities are feudal in nature and serve no purpose other than creating division and deprivation in the 21st century when citizenship defines one's identity and root in a state. Based on well researched scientific works on human DNA, he maintains that the so-called dark-and-ugly-like-ogre Rohingyas and 'fair-and-beautiful' Burmese Consulate-General Ye Myint Aung[7] both came from a single common ancestry. It is, thus, absolutely illogical to deny the Rohingya people their due rights of citizenship in Myanmar. Will the Myanmar regime listen and will its Buddhist people modify their racist views?

I pray and hope that Dr. Khan's book will go a long way to challenging our current paradigms and finding alternative solutions to one of the saddest chapters of human suffering of our time, failing which, I am afraid that we should all be guilty of allowing a genocide to succeed which would eliminate the Rohingya people from the place of their origin.

Habib Siddiqui
Philadelphia, USA
July 29, 2014

---

[7] Consulate-General Ye Myint Aung of Myanmar made some highly racist comments about the Rohingya people comparing them to ugly looking ogres vis-à-vis Burmese people. (The comment can be found on the pages 85, 109, 135, and 222 in this book, SLM).

INTRODUCTION TO "The Rakhine State Violence, Vol. 2: The Rohingya"

Myanmar President Thein Sein, on 11th of July 2012, stated to a visiting delegation led by Antonio Guterres from the United Nation's High Commissioner for Refugees that (1) the "Bengalis (Rohingyas) were brought into Burma to work as farmhands by the English colonialists before the country's independence in 1948 from the British Empire (2) the government will not recognize the Rohingya as Myanmar citizens and are considering handing over the ethnic group to the UNHCR, and would set up refugee camps for the group so that they can eventually be settled in any third country that are willing to take them, and (3) the 800,000 Rohingyas posed a threat to Myanmar national security.[1] These statements result from the naïvety of the President about the Rohingya people, who are of dark-skinned Indo-Aryan stock as opposed to fair-complexioned Tibeto-Burmans. Historical and archeological evidence indicates that Indo-Aryans (similar to today's Rohingyas) lived in Arakan from time immemorial. According to Dr. Emil Forchhammer, a Swiss Professor of Pali at Rangoon College, and Superintendent of the Archaeological Survey (1881) "The earliest dawn of the history of Arakan reveals the base of the hills, which divide the lowest courses of the Kaladan and Lemro rivers, inhabited by sojourners from India... Their subjects are divided into the four castes of the older Hindu communities...". M.S. Collis, who did extensive research work on Arakan's history, including studying its coinage and old manuscripts, similarly concluded that "that Wesali was an easterly Hindu kingdom of Bengal" and that "both government and people were Indian as the Mongolian influx had not yet occurred." As to the origin of the ancestors of Tibeto-Burman Rakhines, historian D.G.E. Hall states "Burmese do not seem to have settled in Arakan until possibly as late as the tenth century A.D. Hence earlier dynasties are thought to have been Indian, ruling over a population similar to that of Bengal."[2]

1http://www.dvb.no/news/gov't-will-not-recognise-rohingya-thein-sein/22875. Accessed on August 11, 2014.

2Siddiqui, Habib, Muslim Identity and Demography in the Arakan State of Burma (October 26, 2011). Available at SSRN: http://ssrn.com/abstract=1949971 or

The expansion of the Muslim Rohingya in Arakan took place in the aftermath of the Burmese invasion of Arakan Kingdom in1404 CE, when the King of Arakan, Narameikhla *alias* Solaiman Shah (1404-1434), was expelled from his kingdom by the Burmese; he took refuge in Muslim Sultanate of Bengal, ruled by Sultan Ahmed Shah of Gaur. His successor Jalaluddin Mohammad Shah reinstalled the fleeing Buddhist King Narameikhla to the throne of Arakan in 1430 with a Muslim army of nearly 60,000 soldiers in two successive campaigns: the Muslim General Wali Khan, leading a force of 25,000 soldiers, successfully freed Arakan from Burmese occupation, but instead of putting King Narameikhla to the throne of Arakan, he became the ruler of Arakan. General Wali Khan was subsequently removed in a new campaign at the directive of the Sultan of Muslim Bengal, by *General Sandi Khan* who led a force of 35,000 soldiers. Narameikhla, thus became the founder and first king (reigned 1404–34) of the Mrohaung (Mrauk-U) dynasty in Arakan.[3] (3).The Muslim armies of the Sultan of Bengal accompanying Narameikhla (Solaiman Shah) were mostly of Turkish, Iranian and Afghan origin. They settled in a village near Mrohaung and, built the Sandi Khan Mosque (named after General Sandi Khan) *in 1430*.They also introduced Persian Language in the court of Arakan. King Narameikhla held his kingdom as the vassal of Gaur. For the next hundred years from 1430 to 1531, Arakan was ruled by Buddhist Arakanese kings who also assumed Muslim titles, following the tradition of Narameikhla; they issued coins bearing the Kalima, the Muslim confession of faith. *These Muslims of Mrohaung subsequently identified themselves as Rohing-ya.* This is how the term Rohingya was coined.

As the Sultanate of Bengal became weak, Chittagong was ruled by Arakanese kings until 1666 CE. With the annexation of Chittagong into Arakan Kingdom, Chittagonian Muslims freely settled in (M)rohaung (or Rohang as they called it) over the course of centuries. They interbred with both the Arakanese and Burmese. Subsequent generations no longer remained purely Bengalis; they proclaimed themselves as *Rohingya*. This is evident from the observations of Francis Buchanan-Hamilton. In his 1799 article "A

http://dx.doi.org/10.2139/ssrn.1949971. Accessed on August 11, 2014.
3http://www.britannica.com/EBchecked/topic/403403/Narameikhla. Accessed on August 12, 2014.

Comparative Vocabulary of Some of the Languages Spoken in the Burma Empire," Buchanan-Hamilton stated: "I shall now add three dialects, spoken in the Burma Empire, but evidently derived from the language of the Hindu nation. The first is that spoken by the Mohammedans, who have long settled in Arakan, and who call themselves *Rooinga, or natives of Arakan*."[4]

I have personally reviewed this dialect; it is similar to the language spoken by the Rohingyas of today. This is one of several unbiased historical evidences that the Rohingya or Rooinga had lived in Arakan (Rakhine) Kingdom before Arakan was annexed by the British to India 1824 CE. Therefore, according to Myanmar Constitution, they are one of the original races of the Union of Myanmar. The Rohingyas are, thus, neither the recent-era Bengalis, who came illegally to Myanmar after its independence from Great Britain in 1948, nor the term Rohingya was invented by Bengali immigrants in 1950s. The natives of Arakan, who were of Mohammedan (or Islamic) faith, used the term Rohingya in 1799 to identify themselves apart from other races of Arakan.

My friend Dr Shwe Lu Maung is an outstanding zoological scientist, who is well-versed in genetics and has published many scholarly research papers in prestigious scientific journals; he is also a self-designated Social Darwinist. He has authored two prominent books on the background and future of Myanmar politics, i.e. *Burma Nationalism and Ideology* (1989) and *The Price of Silence Muslim-Buddhist War of Bangladesh and Myanmar* (2005), respectively. He is indeed the most important unbiased authority on the politics of Myanmar Rohingyas. Dr Maung spent his prime youth in the guerrilla politics (1962-66). He also served as the Diplomatic Representative of Arakan League for Democracy (in exile) and the Patron and CEO of the Arakan Democratic Forces.

Dr Maung gives his purpose behind writing this volume of recent book: *The Rakhine State Violence,* by telling a true love story of two Rangoon University students, when he was a senior at Rangoon University in 1965. Both the girl and the boy were high-

---

4 http://www.scribd.com/doc/
99047980/1799-Rohingya-or-Rooinga-Name-in-Fifth-Volume-of-A-Comparative-
Vocabulary-of-Some-of-the-Languages-Spoken-in-the-Burma-Empire, pages 237-240

school sweethearts and belonged to the aristocracy. The girl found egalitarianism and started social work, teaching the children of hawkers in the slums of the university reading, writing, and arithmetic (known as the 3R). However, the boy found her work incompatible with their background of aristocracy, and warned her that he would be compelled to leave her if she did not stop her work helping the under-privileged. She told him, "Perhaps, I am like water that naturally flows from high to low. I am not letting myself down but I am simply providing water to those who are badly in need of it. You have to take me as I am." The boy was not satisfied and left her. The girl, however, continued her social work. Dr Maung states "Similarly, I consider that 'I am simply providing water to those who are badly in need of it'" when he supports the Rohingya people in their struggle for human rights and an equitable place in the society.

Dr Maung is an extremely compassionate human being, who being a zoologist, firmly believes, based on recent advances in the anthropological, population, and evolutionary genetics, that all human beings belong to one species known as Homo sapiens, and that *all humans (Homo sapiens), being the members of the same big family, are equal brethren, transcending the boundaries of race, religion and region. He makes a convincing use of profound scientific advances in molecular genetics and the population (anthropological) genetics to unite us through strong scientific bond of our "common humanity". Latest scientific evidence proves that the entire Asian population (Myanmar, Bengalis and Indians) shares a common genetic tree, signifying our "common humanity", despite our diversities in phenotypes and genotypes. Thus our genetic, cultural and religious diversities impart in us varying unique qualities and talents, which, when combined together make us stronger as a nation, and therefore are sources of strength of our mankind as a whole.* At DNA level, all Homo sapiens are entitled to equal rights, responsibilities and privileges; the politics, religion, patriotism and nationalism become illogical and incomprehensible to a scientist. There is evidence in all successful democracies of the world that these disciplines can be operated positively to advance our "common humanity" for a better life of all human beings.

Furthermore, Dr Maung has used elaborate scientific methods to prove conclusively that *Rohing-ya is a synonym of Rakhaing-thá*: Rohing-ya is a variant of Ra(k)h(a)ing-thá where 'k' and 'a' sound become silent and 'Ra' is rounded to 'Ro', and 'thá' is replaced by 'ya' due to the variation of pronunciation of different syllables and words by Indo- Aryan Rohingyas.

Dr Maung successfully argues that the root cause of catastrophic Myanmar political problems lie in the power vested in 'we-ethnic-people' in Myanmar Constitution instead of 'we-the-people'. In Myanmar, the political rights, responsibilities and powers do not come from the people but from their specific ethnicities, which is highly hierarchal, and effectively divides the entire Myanmar society into a *caste system*, which is extremely discriminatory. Myanmar was constitutionally divided, even before independence, into 135 races or castes; each race or caste is given political rights and powers based upon the size of its population. According to this unequal hierarchy, the Bama race or caste becomes the supreme ruling race and the Rakhine, the Chin, the Kachin, the Shan, the Kaya (Karenni), the Karen (Kawthoolei), and the Mon become subservient races, and the rest of the 127 races are merely slaves to the foregoing superior races. Myanmar will not become a peaceful and progressive nation until it gets rid of this unethical and inhumane caste system and amends its constitution, vesting all powers in 'we-the-people', and asserts "We hold these truths to be self-evident, that *all men are created equal*, that they are endowed by their Creator with certain unalienable Rights, that among these are Life, Liberty, and the Pursuit of Happiness. That to secure these rights, Governments *are instituted among Men, deriving their just powers from the consent of the governed*".[5]

Once it is settled that the Rohingya Muslims are not Bengalis, and are actually victims of organized pogroms, Myanmar government should work with Bangladesh and solve the Rohingya crisis through a sincere dialogue and mutual brotherly cooperation of a good neighbor.

In my humble opinion Dr. Maung's current book will help people of Myanmar in general and Rakhine State in particular understand the various aspects of the Rohingya crisis, and create a

---

5 United States Declaration of Independence. Thomas Jefferson. July 4, 1776.

humane and soft spot in their hearts. This will in turn lead to a change in the attitude of the Myanmar people towards the Rohingya, and a pathway to Myanmar citizenship for the Rohingya people, who can then contribute immensely to the development of Myanmar economy with their skills in farming, fishing and livestock breeding. They can become even more productive if the Rohingya are given education and trained in highly technical skills. Their integration, population growth, and religious fanaticism can be managed with specifically-targeted programs.

Muhammad Firdaus, MD, FACP
Edmond, Oklahoma, USA
August 25, 2014

The Rakhine State Violence

Vol. 2: The Rohingya

Prologue

IN THE 2014 Myanmar census more than 1.3 million identified themselves Rohingya.[1] The self-identification is a birthright that every human has. Therefore, the identity of Rohingya is no more to be questioned. The world is the witness and as an example, a news clip from the guardian.com[2] is given below.

"all of them are saying that they are Rohingya"

Source:
http://www.theguardian.com/world/video/2014/mar/31/r
ohingya-anger-at-burma-census-video

---

theguardian

News | US | World | Sports | Comment | Culture | Business | Money | Environment | Science

News › World news › Burma

Burma census: Rohingya anger at snub – video

"There's no problem here, but all of them are saying that they are Rohingya."

Nevertheless, in the real world the grass is not green all the time. The Myanmar authorities did not accept their identity "Rohingya" and excluded them from the 2014 census. The Myanmar authorities are firm that the "Rohingya" will be included in the census only if the "Rohingya" accept the identity "Bengali." The Rohingya, more than one million, defy the injustice and brave to live a "stateless life" in the concentration camps. Now they are known as the 'internally displaced persons' or IDP. Keeping this in mind, I explore various aspects of the Rohingya.

The Rohingya issues are examined from the following angles.

---

[1] http://www.theguardian.com/world/video/2014/mar/31/rohingya-anger-at-burma-census-video and https://www.dvb.no/dvb-video/census-will-try-to-count-arakan-muslims-burma-myanmar/40462

[2] http://www.theguardian.com/world/video/2014/mar/31/rohingya-anger-at-burma-census-video

1. The 'out-of-Africa' human migration.
2. The population genetics
3. The Anthropological approach
4. The history
5. The traditions
6. The historical materialism
7. The politics
8. The human rights
9. The common humanity

I present the reader what I find and understand. I am confident that the reader will find it helpful.

1
The Rohingya

THE Rohingya people have been facing a hidden slow genocide since Myanmar gained independence in 1948 from the British colonialism.

Why?

I have attempted to find answers with one article "The sociology of Rohingya persecution" that was published in Holiday Weekly, Dhaka, Friday January 3, 1992, with an introduction by Chief Editor Enayetullah Khan himself. The article was an analysis of the 1991-1992 situation when Bangladesh and Myanmar border tension was at its peak. Famous journalist Enayetullah Khan was also a former cabinet minister and ambassador to China and Myanmar. He was stationed at Rangoon during the 1988 Myanmar Uprising. In 1991, he completed his diplomatic mission and returned Dhaka and back to his influential editorial desk at Holiday Weekly. I have presented the article in the Chapter 18, Volume 1 of *The Rakhine State Violence* so that the reader may understand the particular (or rather peculiar) situation of 1991-1992. Again, in 2005, I presented the faces of Pan-Islam and Rakhine Nazism in my earlier book–*The Price of Silence.*[3]

In those 1992 and 2005 presentations I had emphasized the probability of "communal elimination," at both east and west of Naaf River. The 2012 events of tit-for-tat retaliation in the Rakhine State and Chittagong District and Hill Tracts of Bangladesh call for urgent international action to enforce "Responsibility to Protect."

In this book I try to present a different aspect of the communal conflict, with the hope that the spirit of "common humanity" will have a chance to go for reconciliation.

---

[3] Shwe Lu Maung, *The Price of Silence: Muslim-Buddhist War of Bangladesh and Myanmar – A Social Darwinist's Analysis*, DewDrop Arts & Technology, USA, 2005.

2
Rohing-ya Anthropology

The Rohingya could be the direct descendants of the earliest *Homo sapiens* who settled along the India-Bengal-Myanmar coastal area some 100,000 years ago as per evidence of "out-of-Africa" migration.

Exhibit-R1: Map showing out-of-Africa early human migration

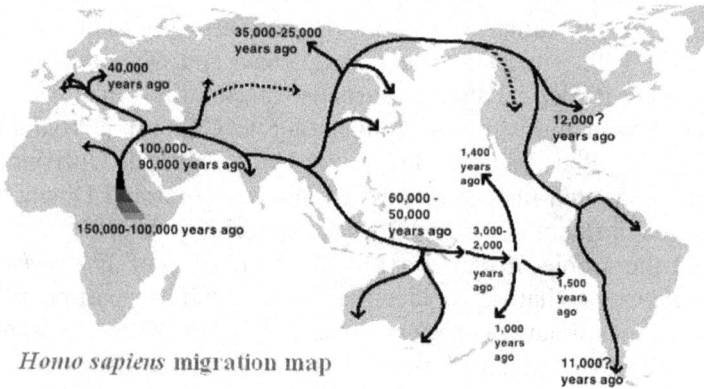

Homo sapiens migration map

http://en.wikipedia.org/wiki/File:Human_migration_out_of_Africa.png
The file is licensed under the Creative Common

At the very beginning, my interest was drawn into the Rohingya for its anthropology, which I studied as a minor subject in zoology honors courses at Rangoon University. I view that Rohingya community is the live laboratory, demonstrating the evolution of the clades, tribes, and clans. When I was in Great Britain (1972-1976) and also in the United States I found that the academicians show keen interest in Rohingya with reference to their anthropology and language. No doubt, the Rohingya community is a gold mine of the anthropologists and linguists.

In my later days of scientific career I was fortunate to be a member of the team of gene hunters and gene testers led by Dr. Gary

Johnson[4]. Evolutionary genetics and molecular genetics have been subjects of interest to me from the time I read Charles Darwin's "On the origin of species" in 1963. Profound advances in the science of molecular genetics have made the population (anthropological) genetics capable of tracing "common humanity" on a strong scientific platform.

"Mapping Human Genetic Diversity in Asia[5]," a landmark scientific research carried out by the HUGO Pan-Asian SNP Consortium[6] and published in the world authoritative journal "Science[7]" in 2009, clearly shows that the entire Asian population shares a common genetic tree, manifesting "common humanity". The paper was authored by 92 scientists of the HUGO Pan-Asian SNP Consortium plus Indian Genome Variation Consortium. The authors concluded their research report as follow.

"Although this study does not disprove a two-wave model of migration, the evidence from our autosomal data and the accompanying simulation studies...point toward a history that unites the Negrito and non-Negrito populations of Southeast and East Asia via a single primary wave of entry of humans into the continent."

The scientists, through their scientific research, have shown that we belong to "common genetic tree" or "common humanity" despite having diversities in phenotype and genotype. We have to realize that cultural as well as genetic "diversity" is what makes us human and therefore is the strength of our mankind.

It is not Rohin-gya but Rohing-ya. It is a synonym of Rakhaing-thá. Rohing is a variant of Rakhaing where 'k' and 'a' sound become silent and 'Ra' is rounded to 'Ro'. I believe the changes in phonetic and syntax took place as a result of transliteration as the speakers of the Austro-Asian, Negrito, Indo-Aryan, and Tibeto-Burman languages happened to mix up in the Bay of Bengal southeastern region that includes the Arakan coastal strip. In spite of having an apparent phonetics and syntax differences the words have

---

[4] Dr. Gary Johnson, Ph.D., DVM, Associate Professor, Department of Pathobiology, College of Veterinary Medicine, University of Missouri, Columbia, Missouri, USA.

[5] Paper can be read at http://humpopgenfudan.cn/p/A/A1.pdf

[6] http://www.hugo-international.org/; SNP stands for single nucleotide polymorphism, very important genetic marker.

[7] www.sciencemag.org

a common origin. You will find the explanation of the word in the coming sections.

In the present English language it is commonly written and pronounced "Rohingya". In Burmese it is written ရိုဟင်းဂျာ and pronounced differently at different locality as described below.

1. Yo-hin-gya, Bama pronunciation
2. Ro-hun-gya, Sittwe Rakhine pronunciation
3. Ro-han-gya, Rambree Rakhine pronunciation

A trip from Yangon (Rangoon) to Bandarban in Bangladesh will help our understanding of the geopolitics and cultural commonness as well as diversities. if an interested reader may like to make the trip I will recommend the following itinerary. A sketch of the suggested trip is given in theExhibit-R2.

Below is the cultural research trip plan.

1. Yangon to Pyay
2. Pyay to Taungup by car across the Rakhaing Yoma.
3. Taungup to Man Aung by the coastal waterway.
4. Man Aung to Kyaukpyu via Rambree Myo and Rambree Township.
5. Kyaukpyu to Myaypon by coastal water. You will sail across famous Naungdaw Gri and Naungdaw Chay[8] seas, which are famous (notorious) for unexpected rough high waves. I believe the unexpected rough high waves occur due to the frequent earthquakes beneath the ocean. Arakan is on the collision zone of the Indian and Burma tectonic plates.
6. Myaypon to Minbya; also visit Myaungbwe that is about twelve miles north to Minbya. Minbya (Bama pronunciation) Munbra (Rakhaing pronunciation) means "King's Mangrove[9]". During the Era of Four Cities Dynasties of Rakkhapura Kingdom the locality was part of the area known as Kyaing-Taite or Kyaing Province. In the days of Mrauk-U Era it was the seat of Crown

---

[8] Naungdaw Gri and Naungdaw Chay seas mean Big Royal Brother and Young Royal Brother seas.

[9] People who are not familiar with Kyaing Province history and Rakhaing language wrongly translate Minbya as "Flattened King". Yes, in Burman language, Minbya literally means 'Flattened King'. As a matter of fact it not 'Bya' or "Bra" but it is "Pra", a tidal mangrove. "Min" or "Mun" is a king in Burman and Rakhaing languages respectively.

Prince. With my parents,[10] I frequently visited the palace of the Crown Prince at the foot of Kyaing Hills in 1950s. I just hope that it is still there.

    7. Minbya to Mrauk-U

    8. Mrauk-U to Sittwe

    9. Sittwe to Paletwa

    10. Paletwa (Myanmar) to Bandarban (Ramu) in the Chittagong Hill Tracts of Bangladesh.

    11. Bandarban to Chittagong.

During the trip please try to meet as many tribes as you can and think where all these tribes come from. You will be able to discover the prevailing cultural segregation and variation that lead to prevalence of hostile socio-political environment. It is important to understand that the Rohingya issue is the Myanmar failure in advancing tribalism to nationalism. The emphasis of "we-the-national-races" rather than "we-the-people" in the present Myanmar 2008 constitution is a systematic error that strongly manifests Myanmar retrogressive metamorphosis into tribalism.

Please conclude the trip with visits to Chittagong Ethnological Museum and Chittagong University Museum. Wonderful anthropological and historical artifacts of the people will take you to a world of the "people-without-borders", highlighting "common humanity". The multicultural facets of the Arakanese gold coins treasured at the Chittagong University Museum will tell you the "common heritage" of the people transcending the political borders.

---

[10] My maternal ancestry belongs to the Kyaing Province. Please see Shwe Lu Maung, *The Price of Silence: Muslim-Buddhist War of Bangladesh and Myanmar – A Social Darwinist's Analysis*, DewDrop Arts & Technology, USA, 2005, pp 173-175.

Exhibit-R2: Map showing the recommended trip from Yangon to Chittagong

Take an anthropological and linguistic trip from Yangon to Chittagong as per given direction in the map

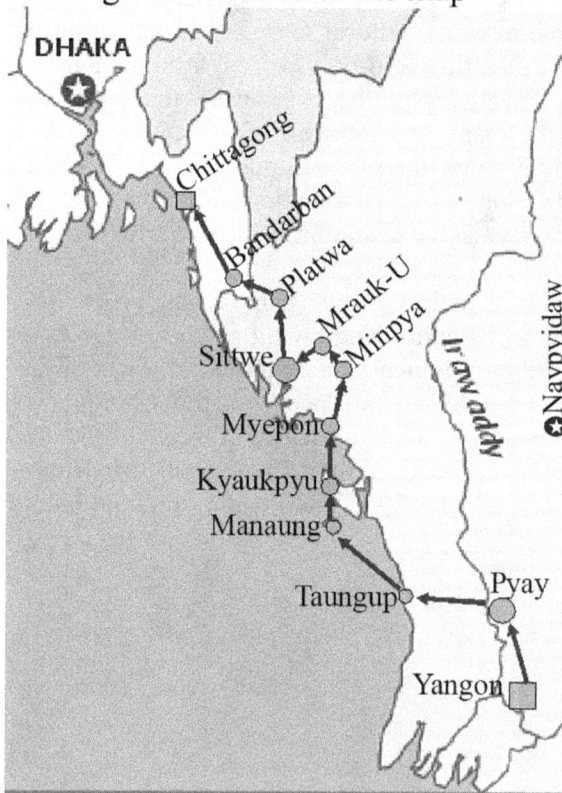

3
The Touchstone

The emergence of the Rohingya is more of an anthropological interest than a political interest to me. This may be due to my profession. I read Charles Darwin's *On the Origin of Species* (1859) and became a Zoology Honours student at the Rangoon University in 1963.[11] To a zoologist, all humans are *Homo sapiens*, belonging to one species in the Genus Homo. Race, religion, culture *et cetera* are nothing more than a designer apparel to a zoologist. As a minor subject, I also studied anthropology, a science that studies the origin, formation, development and culture of human society. It is in the interest of the anthropological science that my attention fell on the Rohingya. Today, I keep up with the advances in the anthropological, population, and evolutionary genetics that reassure us again and again that we, today's humans, all belong to one species known as *Homo sapiens*. However, politics is filled with weird and illogical views and practices that are beyond the comprehension of the scientific disciplines. For example, patriotism and nationalism are totally meaningless to a zoologist, except in the context of the "struggle for existence" and the "survival of the fittest".[12] At the same time, I happen to agree with Aristotle when he said "man is by nature a political animal," in his book, *Politics*.[13] Therefore, I view that 'patriotism and nationalism' belong to the primitive politics of *a group's or an individual's* 'struggle for existence' and as such, the patriotism and nationalism should not be given a place in the politics of modern 'common humanity' when we are working for the advancement of humanity and humankind as a whole. Today, a country or so-called a nation is nothing but an

---

[11] In addition, I have my master degree (1973) in Embryology and Mammalian Reproduction, and doctoral degree (1976) in the Reproductive Endocrinology, under the guidance of Sir Brian K Follett (Ph.D., D.Sc., FRS), at the University College of North Wales (now Bangor University), Bangor, Gwynedd, United Kingdom. Gwynedd is the native land of Thomas Edward Lawrence (Lawrence of Saudi Arabia).

[12] See Shwe Lu Maung, *The Price of Silence: Muslim-Buddhist War of Bangladesh and Myanmar – A Social Darwinist's Analysis*, DewDrop Arts & Technology, USA, 2005, p 12-14

[13] http://www.perseus.tufts.edu/hopper/text?
doc=Perseus:text:1999.01.0058:book=1:section=1253a

administrative unit of a geopolitical area where the people work and live together under the fluidity of multiculturalism and common humanity, for the well-being of one and all. In light of a planetary or global economic system,[14] I am also of opinion that the citizenship tied to a country is no longer relevant in the 21st century and beyond, and all we may need is an international tax ID so that we may go and work anywhere depending on the job opportunity and economic fluidity. Why should one be confined in a geopolitical unit?

Accordingly, I view that the issues that surround the Rohingya people is a political perversion, which resulted from the Myanmar politics of Myanmar colonialism and primitive nationalism.[15] In the independent Burma, which was born out of the 1947 Nu-Attalee Agreement, the politics of 'we-the-people' failed and the politics of 'we-ethnic-people' came into prominence. Thus, in Burma, the political rights do not emanate from the people but from the ethnicity. Burma was effectively divided into 135 races and each race is given certain political rights based upon the size of the population. For example, the Bama becomes the ruling race and the Rakhine, the Chin, the Kachin, the Shan, the Kaya (Karenni), the Karen (Kawthoolei), and the Mon become deputy ruling races, and the rest of the 127 races become the insignificant subordinates.[16] The question that the proportional representation in the general election system, which is being considered and discussed in the Upper House (Amyothar Hluttaw), will or will not make any meaning to the small people of the 127 national races has to wait and see.[17] To be somebody, a person must belong to a well-defined Myanmar ethnic group that can exert political leverage. It is in this ultranationalistic scenario that the Arakanese Muslims, upon the failure of the armed insurrection, picked up the most inconspicuous name 'Rohingya' and

---

[14] The global economy, natural resources, and technology are so much intertwined that free movement of the skilled workers and investment have to be liberalized for the sustainable global development.

[15] Please see Shwe Lu Maung, *Burma Nationalism and Ideology*, University Press Ltd., Dhaka, 1989, and *The Price of Silence: Muslim-Buddhist War of Bangladesh and Myanmar – A Social Darwinist's Analysis*, DewDrop Arts & Technology, USA, 2005.

[16] See Shwe Lu Maung, *The Price of Silence: Muslim-Buddhist War of Bangladesh and Myanmar – A Social Darwinist's Analysis*, DewDrop Arts & Technology, USA, 2005, p 159

[17] http://www.mmtimes.com/index.php/national-news/10667-parliament-forms-commission-to-probe-voting-system.html and also see http://www.networkmyanmar.org/images/stories/PDF14/CPPF-Myanmar-Proportional-Representation.pdf and Myanmar's Electoral System-Towards Proportional Representation at http://www.eduinitiatives.org.

armed it with the Islamic fervor and catapulted into the Myanmar politics in 1958. By saying so, I do not mean that the Rohingya did not exist before 1958. They do exist and are among the most indigenous people of the region. In support of this statement, I shall present my findings in this book.

In my earlier book *The Price of Silence*,[18] I have described that the "launching of the Rohingya nationalism is the Burmese Muslim's struggle to escape from the modern slavery [known] as *the Kala*." They were and are still being discriminated as the Kala, or "despised foreigners," or "nigger" by the Burmese, with a view that they do not belong to the Mongolian tribes. While I do not approve the use of ethnicity and religious color in politics, I accept it as a phenomenon in Burmese politics. Unless Burmese ethnic-based ulranationalistic politics is revolutionized into modern day's politics of "we-the-people" race, ethnicity, and religion will retain their power in the foundation of Burmese polity, hence in politics. It is true that if the Rohingya is officially recognized as an ethnic group it will have rights to demand for a separate statehood, thus dividing the existing Rakhine State into two. In light of the Myanmar Census 2014 estimates, there are at least 1.3 million Rohingya[19] among the total 3 million people, (i.e. 43.33%) of the Rakhine State. Earlier in 2005, I estimated the Rohingya to be up to 48% of the Rakhine State population.[20] Therefore, if the Rohingya demands for a separate statehood, it would carry substance and legitimacy. Even if, the Rohingya remains within the Rakhine State the Rakhine power base in the Rakhine State government will be significantly compromised. At present, the Rohingya are with the Union Solidarity and Development Party (USDP) or the National League for Democracy (NLD). With due realization of such Rohingya political clout the Rakhine people alienate the Rohingya with a program of ultimate elimination of Rohingya from Burma once for all. The Buddhist majority of Burma renders a hand of support to Rakhine ultranationalists with a philosophy of Buddhist Brotherhood and

---

[18] Shwe Lu Maung, *The Price of Silence: Muslim-Buddhist War of Bangladesh and Myanmar – A Social Darwinist's Analysis*, DewDrop Arts & Technology, USA, 2005, p 250.

[19] https://www.dvb.no/dvb-video/census-will-try-to-count-arakan-muslims-burma-myanmar/40462, and http://www.theguardian.com/world/video/2014/mar/31/rohingya-anger-at-burma-census-video

[20] See Shwe Lu Maung, *The Price of Silence: Muslim-Buddhist War of Bangladesh and Myanmar – A Social Darwinist's Analysis*, DewDrop Arts & Technology, USA, 2005, p 252.

anti-Islam.

In light of the above discussion, the Myanmar's negation of the Rohingya existence, Rohingya identity, and Rohingya citizenship is a campaign of *political perversion*, encoded with racial and religious hatred.

It began with the expulsion of more than two hundred thousand Arakanese Muslims into Bangladesh in 1978. The alienation of the Rohingya was constitutionalized by the adoption of "Burma Citizenship Act 1982". Myanmar persecution of the Rohingya people continues with vigor and cruelty, and today, in the aftermath of the 2012 Rakhine State racio-religious pogrom, the entire Rohingya population is displaced and concentrated in the dire refugee camps, which are isolated and blockaded with restricted food and medical supply. Such treatment with slow death could be seen as a crime against humanity. Reportedly, as per estimates of the United Nations Refugee Agency, more than 86,000 Rohingya people have become boat-people, in the period from June 2012 and June 2014, in their struggle for existence.[21]

There are four points of Myanmar violent attack on the Rohingya; these are:

1. Historical alienation
The Rohingya never existed in Myanmar and it is a name invented in 1958 by the *Mujahideens*. Therefore, they are not a Myanmar ethnic group. Therefore, they are not Myanmar citizens.

2. Illegal immigrants
a. The Rohingya are the British era illegal immigrants to the British Burma, in the period from 1826-1947.

b. The Rohingya are the Bengali illegal immigrants from East Pakistan, and later from Bangladesh, in the period from 1948 to date. (Note: Burma became independent on the 4th of January, 1948).

Therefore, they do not belong to Myanmar.

---

[21] http://www.huffingtonpost.com/2014/06/26/myanmar-rohingya-persecution_n_5473724.html. And more than 100,000 Rohingya has escaped Myanmar as of October 15, 2014, as per estimate of Chris Lewa, director of the Arakan Project (http://abcnews.go.com/International/wireStory/expert-8000-rohingya-flee-myanmar-26446748)

3. Religious animosity

The Rohingya are the Muslims, a danger to Myanmar Buddhism.

4. Racial animosity

The Rohingya belong to a *kala* or dark skin race, and thus are inferior to the light skin Tibeto-Burman race.

All the above four points of attack are encapsulated in the Burma Citizenship Act 1982. As a matter of fact, the Burma Citizenship Act 1982 and its enforcement violate the very fundamental principle of humanity and every article of the Universal Declaration of Human Rights (UDHR), which was adopted by the UN General Assembly on 10 December 1948.[22] Myanmar was among the foremost countries that adopted the UDHR. Laws are made on the foundation of the principles of justice for all. Justice for all is constituted in the United Nations Charter. Myanmar is a member of the United Nations since 1948. Therefore, she is obliged to follow the principles mandated by the UN Charter and other international conventions. For example, the United Nations Charter Article 55:3 says a member nation is obliged to "universal respect for, and observance of, human rights and fundamental freedoms for all without distinction as to race, sex, language, or religion." Human rights are defined by the Universal Declaration of Human Rights, which I downloaded on June 26, 2014 from the http://www.un.org/en/documents/udhr/ and is given below for easy reference, especially for those who lack internet access.

The Universal Declaration of Human Rights

PREAMBLE

Whereas recognition of the inherent dignity and of the equal and inalienable rights of all members of the human family is the foundation of freedom, justice and peace in the world,

Whereas disregard and contempt for human rights have resulted in barbarous acts which have outraged the conscience of mankind, and the advent of a world in which human beings shall enjoy

---

[22] http://www.un.org/en/documents/udhr/history.shtml

freedom of speech and belief and freedom from fear and want has been proclaimed as the highest aspiration of the common people,

Whereas it is essential, if man is not to be compelled to have recourse, as a last resort, to rebellion against tyranny and oppression, that human rights should be protected by the rule of law,

Whereas it is essential to promote the development of friendly relations between nations,

Whereas the peoples of the United Nations have in the Charter reaffirmed their faith in fundamental human rights, in the dignity and worth of the human person and in the equal rights of men and women and have determined to promote social progress and better standards of life in larger freedom,

Whereas Member States have pledged themselves to achieve, in co-operation with the United Nations, the promotion of universal respect for and observance of human rights and fundamental freedoms,

Whereas a common understanding of these rights and freedoms is of the greatest importance for the full realization of this pledge,

Now, Therefore THE GENERAL ASSEMBLY proclaims THIS UNIVERSAL DECLARATION OF HUMAN RIGHTS as a common standard of achievement for all peoples and all nations, to the end that every individual and every organ of society, keeping this Declaration constantly in mind, shall strive by teaching and education to promote respect for these rights and freedoms and by progressive measures, national and international, to secure their universal and effective recognition and observance, both among the peoples of Member States themselves and among the peoples of territories under their jurisdiction.

Article 1.

• All human beings are born free and equal in dignity and rights. They are endowed with reason and conscience and should act towards one another in a spirit of brotherhood.

Article 2.

• Everyone is entitled to all the rights and freedoms set forth in this Declaration, without distinction of any kind, such as race, colour, sex, language, religion, political or other opinion, national or social origin, property, birth or other status. Furthermore, no distinction shall be made on the basis of the political, jurisdictional or international status of the country or territory to which a person belongs, whether it be independent, trust, non-self-governing or under any other limitation of sovereignty.

Article 3.

• Everyone has the right to life, liberty and security of person.

Article 4.

• No one shall be held in slavery or servitude; slavery and the slave trade shall be prohibited in all their forms.

Article 5.

• No one shall be subjected to torture or to cruel, inhuman or degrading treatment or punishment.

Article 6.

• Everyone has the right to recognition everywhere as a person before the law.

Article 7.

• All are equal before the law and are entitled without any discrimination to equal protection of the law. All are entitled to equal protection against any discrimination in violation of this Declaration and against any incitement to such discrimination.

Article 8.

• Everyone has the right to an effective remedy by the competent national tribunals for acts violating the fundamental rights granted him by the constitution or by law.

Article 9.

• No one shall be subjected to arbitrary arrest, detention or exile.

Article 10.

• Everyone is entitled in full equality to a fair and public hearing by an independent and impartial tribunal, in the determination of his rights and obligations and of any criminal charge against him.

Article 11.

• (1) Everyone charged with a penal offence has the right to be presumed innocent until proved guilty according to law in a public trial at which he has had all the guarantees necessary for his defence.

• (2) No one shall be held guilty of any penal offence on account of any act or omission which did not constitute a penal offence, under national or international law, at the time when it was committed. Nor shall a heavier penalty be imposed than the one that was applicable at the time the penal offence was committed.

Article 12.

• No one shall be subjected to arbitrary interference with his privacy, family, home or correspondence, nor to attacks upon his honour and reputation. Everyone has the right to the protection of the law against such interference or attacks.

Article 13.

• (1) Everyone has the right to freedom of movement and residence within the borders of each state.

• (2) Everyone has the right to leave any country, including his own, and to return to his country.

Article 14.

• (1) Everyone has the right to seek and to enjoy in other countries asylum from persecution.

• (2) This right may not be invoked in the case of prosecutions genuinely arising from non-political crimes or from acts contrary to the purposes and principles of the United Nations.

Article 15.

• (1) Everyone has the right to a nationality.

• (2) No one shall be arbitrarily deprived of his nationality nor denied the right to change his nationality.

Article 16.

• (1) Men and women of full age, without any limitation due to race, nationality or religion, have the right to marry and to found a family. They are entitled to equal rights as to marriage, during marriage and at its dissolution.

• (2) Marriage shall be entered into only with the free and full consent of the intending spouses.

• (3) The family is the natural and fundamental group unit of society and is entitled to protection by society and the State.

Article 17.

• (1) Everyone has the right to own property alone as well as in association with others.

• (2) No one shall be arbitrarily deprived of his property.

Article 18.

• Everyone has the right to freedom of thought, conscience and religion; this right includes freedom to change his religion or belief, and freedom, either alone or in community with others and in public or private, to manifest his religion or belief in teaching, practice, worship and observance.

Article 19.

• Everyone has the right to freedom of opinion and expression; this right includes freedom to hold opinions without interference and to seek, receive and impart information and ideas through any media and regardless of frontiers.

Article 20.

• (1) Everyone has the right to freedom of peaceful assembly and association.

• (2) No one may be compelled to belong to an association.

Article 21.

• (1) Everyone has the right to take part in the government of his country, directly or through freely chosen representatives.

• (2) Everyone has the right of equal access to public service in his country.

• (3) The will of the people shall be the basis of the authority of government; this will shall be expressed in periodic and genuine elections which shall be by universal and equal suffrage and shall be held by secret vote or by equivalent free voting procedures.

Article 22.

• Everyone, as a member of society, has the right to social security and is entitled to realization, through national effort and international co-operation and in accordance with the organization and resources of each State, of the economic, social and cultural rights indispensable for his dignity and the free development of his personality.

Article 23.

• (1) Everyone has the right to work, to free choice of employment, to just and favourable conditions of work and to protection against unemployment.

• (2) Everyone, without any discrimination, has the right to equal pay for equal work.

• (3) Everyone who works has the right to just and favourable remuneration ensuring for himself and his family an existence worthy of human dignity, and supplemented, if necessary, by other means of social protection.

• (4) Everyone has the right to form and to join trade unions for the protection of his interests.

Article 24.
• Everyone has the right to rest and leisure, including reasonable limitation of working hours and periodic holidays with pay.
Article 25.
• (1) Everyone has the right to a standard of living adequate for the health and well-being of himself and of his family, including food, clothing, housing and medical care and necessary social services, and the right to security in the event of unemployment, sickness, disability, widowhood, old age or other lack of livelihood in circumstances beyond his control.
• (2) Motherhood and childhood are entitled to special care and assistance. All children, whether born in or out of wedlock, shall enjoy the same social protection.
Article 26.
• (1) Everyone has the right to education. Education shall be free, at least in the elementary and fundamental stages. Elementary education shall be compulsory. Technical and professional education shall be made generally available and higher education shall be equally accessible to all on the basis of merit.
• (2) Education shall be directed to the full development of the human personality and to the strengthening of respect for human rights and fundamental freedoms. It shall promote understanding, tolerance and friendship among all nations, racial or religious groups, and shall further the activities of the United Nations for the maintenance of peace.
• (3) Parents have a prior right to choose the kind of education that shall be given to their children.
Article 27.
• (1) Everyone has the right freely to participate in the cultural life of the community, to enjoy the arts and to share in scientific advancement and its benefits.
• (2) Everyone has the right to the protection of the moral and material interests resulting from any scientific, literary or artistic production of which he is the author.
Article 28.
• Everyone is entitled to a social and international order in which the rights and freedoms set forth in this Declaration can be fully realized.

Article 29.

• (1) Everyone has duties to the community in which alone the free and full development of his personality is possible.

• (2) In the exercise of his rights and freedoms, everyone shall be subject only to such limitations as are determined by law solely for the purpose of securing due recognition and respect for the rights and freedoms of others and of meeting the just requirements of morality, public order and the general welfare in a democratic society.

• (3) These rights and freedoms may in no case be exercised contrary to the purposes and principles of the United Nations.

Article 30.

• Nothing in this Declaration may be interpreted as implying for any State, group or person any right to engage in any activity or to perform any act aimed at the destruction of any of the rights and freedoms set forth herein.

Exhibit-R3

http://www.ohchr.org/en/udhr/pages/Language.aspx?LangID=bms

United Nations **Human Rights**
Office of the High Commissioner for Human Rights

ENGLISH FR

| Home | Your human rights | Countries | Human rights bodies | News and events | Human rights - New York | Publications and |

English > Universal declaration > **Language**

Introduction
Search by Translation
UDHR in sign languages
UDHR materials
Contact the UDHR Team

Universal Declaration of Human Rights

PDF Version

Burmese/Myanmar

Source: United Nations Information Centre, Myanmar

The official Myanmar version is given below, for easy reference. It is downloaded on July 8, 2014 from–
http://www.ohchr.org/EN/UDHR/Documents/UDHR_Translations/bms.pdf (Exhibit-R3).

အပြည်ပြည်ဆိုင်ရာ လူ့အခွင့်အရေး ကြေညာစာတမ်း

၁၉၄၈ ခုနှစ်၊ဒီဇင်ဘာလ ၁၀ ရက်နေ့တွင် ကမ္ဘာ့ကုလသမဂ္ဂအဖွဲ့ညီလာခံ အစည်းအဝေးကြီးက လူ့အခွင့်အရေး ကြေညာစာတမ်းကြီးကို အတည်ပြု၍ ကြေညာလိုက်ရာထိုကြေညာစာတမ်းကြီး၏ စာသားသည်နောက်စာမျက်နှာများ တွင် အပြည့်အစုံပါရှိသည်။ ဤကဲ့သို့ရာဇဝင်တင်မည့် ကြေညာချက်ကို ပြုလုပ်ပြီးနောက် ဤညီလာခံအစည်းအဝေးကြီးက ကမ္ဘာ့ကုလသမဂ္ဂအဖွဲ့ဝင် နိုင်ငံ အားလုံးအား ထိုကြေညာစာတမ်းကြီး၏ စာသားကိုအများပြည်သူတို့ ကြားသိစေရန် ကြေညာပါမည့်အကြောင်းကိုလည်းကောင်း၊ ထိုပြင်နိုင်ငံများ၊ သို့တည်းမဟုတ် နယ်မြေများ၏ နိုင်ငံရေး အဆင့်အတန်းကို လိုက်၍ ခွဲခြားခြင်း မပြုဘဲအဓိကအားဖြင့် စာသင်ကျောင်းများနှင့် အခြားပညာရေး အဖွဲ့အစည်းများတွင် ထိုကြေညာစာတမ်းကြီးကို ဖြန့်ချီ ဝေငှ စေရန် မြင်သာအောင် ပြသထားစေရန်၊ဖတ်ကြားစေရန်နှင့် အဓိပ္ပါယ်ရှင်းလင်း ဖော်ပြစေရန် ဆောင်ရွက်ပါမည့် အကြောင်းဖြင့် လည်းကောင်း ဆင့်ဆို လိုက်သည်။

စကားချီး . . .

လူ့ခပ်သိမ်း၏ မျိုးရိုးဂုဏ်သိက္ခာနှင့်တကွ လူတိုင်းအညီအမျှခံစားခွင့်ရှိသည့် အခွင့်အရေးများကို အသိအမှတ် ပြုခြင်းသည် လူ့ခပ်သိမ်း၏ လွတ်လပ်မှု၊ တရားမျှတမှု၊ငြိမ်းချမ်းမှုတို့၏ အခြေခံအုတ်မြစ်ဖြစ်သောကြောင့်လည်းကောင်း၊

လူ့အခွင့်ရေးများကို အရေးမထား မထီလေးစား ပြုခြင်းသည် လူ့ခပ်သိမ်း၏ အကျင့်သိက္ခာကို ချိုးဖောက် ဖျက်ဆီးတတ်သည့် ရက်စက် ကြမ်းကြုတ်သော အပြုအမူများကို ဖြစ်ပေါ်စေခဲ့သော ကြောင့်လည်းကောင်း၊ လွတ်လပ်စွာ ဖွင့်ဟပြောဆိုနိုင်မှု လွတ်လပ်စွာ သက်ဝင် ယုံကြည်နိုင်မှု ကြောက်ရွံ့ခြင်း၊ ချို့ငဲ့ခြင်းတို့မှ ကင်းလွတ်စွာ အသက်မွေးနိုင်မှုတို့ကို ခံစားရယူနိုင်စေမည့် လောကတစ်ခု ပေါ်ပေါက်လာရန်အရေးကို လူ့ခပ်သိမ်းတို့က မိမိတို့၏ အထက်သန်ဆုံးသော လိုလားချက်ဆန္ဒကြီးအဖြစ်ဖြင့် ကြေးကြော် ကြေညာပြီးဖြစ် သောကြောင့်လည်းကောင်း၊

လူခပ်သိမ်းတို့သည်၊ တရားလက်လွတ် နှိပ်စက်က လူပုန်မှု၊ အုပ်စိုးမှုနှင့် ဖိစီးညှင်းပန်းမှု တို့ကို နောက်ဆုံး မလွဲသာ မရှောင်သာ လက်နက် စွဲကိုင်ကာ တော်လှန်ခြင်း၊ ပုန်ကန်ခြင်းမပြုစေရန်၊ လူ့အခွင့်ရေး များကိုဥပဒေဖြင့် ထိန်းသိမ်းကာကွယ် ပေးရမည်ဖြစ်သောကြောင့် လည်းကောင်း၊

နိုင်ငံ အချင်းချင်း ချစ်ခင် ရင်းနှီးစွာ ဆက်ဆံရေးကို ပိုမိုတိုးတက်စေရန် ကြိုဆောင်ရမည် ဖြစ်သောကြောင့် လည်းကောင်း၊ ကမ္ဘာ့ကုလသမဂ္ဂအဖွဲ့ဝင်တို့သည် မူလလူ့အခွင့် ရေးများကို လည်းကောင်း၊ လူ့၏ ဂုဏ်သိက္ခာကို လည်းကောင်း၊ ယောက်ျား မိန်းမတို့၏ တူညီသည့် အခွင့်အရေးများကိုလည်းကောင်း၊လေးစားယုံကြည်ပါသည်ဟု ကုလသမဂ္ဂတွင်ထပ်မံ၍ အတည်ပြု ပြီးသည့်ပြင်၊ လူမှုကြီးပွား တိုးတက်ရေးနှင့်တကွ ပိုမို လွတ်လပ် ကောင်းမွန်သော လူ့ဘဝ အဆင့်အတန်းတို့ကို မြှင့်တင်ရန် သန္နိဋ္ဌာန်ချပြီး ဖြစ်သောကြောင့် လည်းကောင်း၊

ကမ္ဘာ့ကုလသမဂ္ဂ အဖွဲ့ဝင်နိုင်ငံတို့သည် ကုလသမဂ္ဂအဖွဲ့နှင့်ပူပေါင်း၍ လူ့အခွင့်အရေးများကိုလည်ကောင်း၊ အခြေခံလွတ်လပ်ခွင့်၊ အခွင့်အရေးများကို လည်းကောင်း၊ ကမ္ဘာ့တဝှမ်းလုံးတွင် ရှိသေလေးစားကျင့်သုံး စောင့်စည်း ကြခြင်းကို အားပေးမည်ဟု ကတိပြုပြီးဖြစ်သောကြောင့် လည်းကောင်း၊

ထိုကြောင့်

အထွေထွေညီလာခံ က

အပြည်ပြည်ဆိုင်ရာလူ့အခွင့်ရေးကြေညာစာတမ်းကိုလူတိုင်းအဖွဲ့ အစည်းတိုင်းသည် အစဉ် နှလုံးသွင်းလျက် ကမ္ဘာ့တဝှမ်းလုံးတွင် အဆိုပါ အခွင့်အရေးများနှင့် လွတ်လပ် ခွင့်များကို ရှိသေလေးစားကြစေရန် ဆုံးမ သွန်သင်ခြင်းဖြင့် အားထုတ်
ကြရမည်ဟုလည်းကောင်း၊ ကုလသမဂ္ဂအဖွဲ့ဝင်နိုင်ငံများနှင့် ထိုနိုင်ငံတို့၏ အာဏာပိုင်အတွင်းရှိ နယ်ပယ်ဆိုင်ရာ တိုင်းသူပြည်သား များအား အဆိုပါ အခွင့်အရေးနှင့် လွတ်လပ်ခွင့်များကို ကျယ်ကျယ်ပြန့်ပြန့် ထိရောက်စွာ သိမှတ်ကျင့်သုံး စောင့်စည်းကြစေရန် ပြည်တွင်းပြည်ပဆိုင်ရာ တိုးတက်သော ဆောင်ရွက်ချက်များဖြင့် အားထုတ်ကြရမည်ဟုလည်းကောင်း ရည်ရွယ်ပြီးလျှင် လူ့အခွင့်အရေး များဆိုင်ရာ အပြည်ပြည်ဆိုင်ရာ ကြေညာစာတမ်းကို နိုင်ငံခပ်သိမ်း၊ လူခပ်သိမ်းတို့ တပြေးညီစွာ ဆောင်ရွက် နိုင်ကြစိမ့်သောငှာ ယခုထုတ်ပြန် ကြေညာလိုက်သည်။

အပိုဒ် ၁

လူတိုင်းသည် တူညီ လွတ်လပ်သော ဂုဏ်သိက္ခာဖြင့် လည်းကောင်း၊ တူညီလွတ်လပ်သော အခွင့်အရေးများဖြင့် လည်းကောင်း၊ မွေးဖွားလာသူများ ဖြစ်သည်။ ထိုသူတို့၌ ပိုင်းခြား ဝေဖန်တတ်သော ဉာဏ်နှင့် ကျင့်ဝတ် သိတတ်သော စိတ်တို့ရှိကြ၍ ထိုသူတို့သည် အချင်းချင်း မေတ္တာထား၍ ဆက်ဆံကျင့်သုံးသင့်၏။

အပိုဒ် ၂

လူတိုင်းသည် လူ့အခွင့် အရေး ကြေညာစာတမ်းတွင် ဖော်ပြထားသည့် အခွင့်အရေး အားလုံး၊ လွတ်လပ်ခွင့် အားလုံးတို့ကို ပိုင်ဆိုင် ခံစားခွင့်ရှိသည်။ လူမျိုးနွယ်အားဖြင့် ဖြစ်စေ၊ အသားအရောင်အားဖြင့် ဖြစ်စေ၊ ကျား ၊ မ ၊ သဘာဝအားဖြင့် ဖြစ်စေ၊ ဘာသာစကားအားဖြင့် ဖြစ်စေ၊ ကိုးကွယ်သည့် ဘာသာအားဖြင့် ဖြစ်စေ၊ နိုင်ငံရေးယူဆချက်၊ သို့တည်းမဟုတ် အခြားယူဆချက်အားဖြင့် ဖြစ်စေ၊ နိုင်ငံနှင့် ဆိုင်သော၊ သို့တည်းမဟုတ် လူမှုအဆင့်အတန်းနှင့် ဆိုင်သော ဇစ်မြစ် အားဖြင့်ဖြစ်စေ၊ ပစ္စည်း ဥစ္စာ ဂုဏ်အားဖြင့် ဖြစ်စေ၊ မျိုးရိုးဇာတိအားဖြင့် ဖြစ်စေ၊ အခြား အဆင့်အတန်း အားဖြင့် ဖြစ်စေ ခွဲခြားခြင်းမရှိစေရ။

ထိုပြင် လူတစ်ဦး တစ်ယောက် နေထိုင်ရာ နိုင်ငံ၏ သို့တည်းမဟုတ် နယ်မြေဒေသ၏ နိုင်ငံရေးဆိုင်ရာ ဖြစ်စေ စီရင် ပိုင်ခွင့်ဆိုင်ရာ ဖြစ်စေ တိုင်းပြည် အချင်းချင်း ဆိုင်ရာဖြစ်စေ၊ အဆင့်အတန်း တစ်ခုခုကို အခြေပြု၍ သော်လည်းကောင်း၊ ဒေသနယ်မြေတစ်ခုသည် အချုပ်အခြာ အာဏာပိုင် လွတ်လပ်သည့် နယ်မြေ၊ သို့တည်းမဟုတ် ကုလသမဂ္ဂ ထိန်းသိမ်း စောင့်ရှောက် ထားရသည့် နယ်မြေ၊ သို့တည်းမဟုတ် ကိုယ်ပိုင် အုပ်ချုပ်ခွင့် အာဏာကို တစ်စိတ်တဒေသလောက်သာ ရရှိသည့် နယ်မြေ စသဖြင့် ယင်းသို့ သော နယ်မြေများ ဖြစ်သည်၊ဖြစ်သည် ဟူသော အကြောင်းကို အထောက်အထား ပြု၍ သော်လည်းကောင်း ခွဲခြားခြင်း လုံးဝ မရှိစေရ။

အပိုဒ် ၃

လူတိုင်း၌ အသက်ရှင်ရန်လွတ်လပ်မှုခွင့်နှင့် လုံခြုံစိတ်ချခွင့် ရှိသည်။

အပိုဒ် ၄

မည်သူကိုမျှ ကျေးကျွန်အဖြစ်၊ သို့တည်းမဟုတ် အစေအပါးအဖြစ် နိုင်ထက်စီးနင်း စေခိုင်းခြင်း မပြုရ၊ လူကို ကျေးကျွန် သဖွယ် အဓမ္မ စေခိုင်းခြင်း၊ အရောင်းအဝယ် ပြုခြင်းနှင့် ထိုသဘော သက်ရောက်သော လုပ်ငန်းဟူသမျှကို ပိတ်ပင် တားမြစ် ရမည်။

အပိုဒ် ၅

မည်သူကိုမျှ ညှဉ်းပန်း နှိပ်စက်ခြင်း၊ သို့တည်းမဟုတ် ရက်စက်ကြမ်းကြုတ်စွာ လူမဆန်စွာ ဂုဏ်ငယ်စေသောဆက်ဆံမှု မပြုရ၊ သို့တည်းမဟုတ် အပြစ်ဒဏ် ပေးခြင်းမပြုရ။

အပိုဒ် ၆

လူတိုင်းတွင် ဥပဒေအရာ၌ လူပုဂ္ဂိုလ်တစ်ဦး အဖြစ်ဖြင့် အရာခပ်သိမ်းတွင် အသိအမှတ် ပြုခြင်းကို ခံယူပိုင်ခွင့်ရှိသည်။

အပိုဒ် ၇

လူအားလုံးတို့သည် ဥပဒေအရာ၌ တူညီကြသည့်အပြင်၊ ဥပဒေ၏ အကာအကွယ်ကို ခြားနားခြင်း မခံရစေဘဲ တူညီစွာ ခံစားပိုင်ခွင့်ရှိသည်။ ၍ကြေညာ စာတမ်းပါ သဘောတရားများကို ဖီဆန်၍ ခွဲခြားခြင်းမှ လည်းကောင်း၊ ထိုသို့ခွဲခြားခြင်းကို လှုံ့ဆော်ခြင်းမှ လည်းကောင်း၊ ကင်းလွတ် စေရန် အကာအကွယ်ကို တူညီစွာ ခံစားပိုင်ခွင့် ရှိသည်။

အပိုဒ် ၈

ဖွဲ့စည်းပုံ အခြေခံဥပဒေက သော်လည်းကောင်း အခြား ဥပဒေက သော်လည်းကောင်း လူတိုင်းအတွက် ပေးထားသည့် အခြေခံ အခွင့်အရေး များသည် ချိုးဖောက် ဖျက်ဆီးခြင်းခံခဲ့ရလျှင် ထိုသို့ ချိုးဖောက်ဖျက်ဆီးသော ပြုလုပ်မှုကြောင့် ဖြစ်ပေါ်လာသော နစ်နာချက် အတွက် ထိုသူသည် နိုင်ငံဆိုင်ရာ အာဏာပိုင်တရားရုံးတွင် ထိရောက်စွာ သက်သာ ခွင့်ရနိုင်စေရမည်။

အပိုဒ် ၉

မည်သူမျှ ဥပဒေအရ မဟုတ်သော ဖမ်းဆီးခြင်းကို ဖြစ်စေ၊ ချုပ်နှောင်ခြင်းကို ဖြစ်စေ၊ ပြည်နှင်ခြင်းကိုဖြစ်စေ မခံစေရ။

အပိုဒ် ၁၀

အခွင့်အရေးများနှင့် တာဝန် ဝတ္တရားများကို အဆုံးအဖြတ်ခံရာတွင် လည်းကောင်း၊ ပြစ်မှုကြောင့် တရားစွဲဆိုစီရင် ဆုံးဖြတ်ခံရာတွင် လည်းကောင်း၊ လူတိုင်းသည် လွတ်လပ်၍ ဘက်မလိုက်သော တရားရုံးတော်၏ လူအများ ရှေ့မှောက်တွင် မျှတစွာ ကြားနာစစ်ဆေးခြင်းကို တူညီစွာ ခံစား ပိုင်ခွင့်ရှိသည်။

အပိုဒ် ၁၁

(၁) လူအများ ရှေ့မှောက်၌၌ ဥပဒေအတိုင်း စစ်ဆေး၍ ပြစ်မှုကျူးလွန်သည်ဟု ထင်ရှား စီရင်ခြင်းခံရသည့် အချိန်အထိ ပြစ်မှုနှင့် တရားစွဲဆိုခြင်း ခံရသူတိုင်းသည် အပြစ်မဲ့သူဟု၍ ယူဆခြင်းခံထိုက်သည်၊ အခွင့်အရေးရှိသည်။ ထိုအမှုကို ကြားနာစစ်ဆေးရာဝယ် စွပ်စွဲခံရသည့် ပြစ်မှုအတွက် ခုခံချေပနိုင်ရန် လိုအပ်သော အခွင့်အရေးများကို ထိုသူအား ပေးပြီး ဖြစ်စေရမည်။

(၂) လူတစ်ဦးတစ်ယောက်အား နိုင်ငံဥပဒေအရဖြစ်စေ၊ အပြည်ပြည်ဆိုင်ရာ ဥပဒေအရ ဖြစ်စေ၊ ပြစ်မှုမမြောက်သော လုပ်ရပ် သို့မဟုတ် ပျက်ကွက်မှုအရ ဆွဲဆိုပြစ်ပေးခြင်း မပြုရ။ ထို့အပြင် ပြစ်မှုကျူးလွန်စဉ်အခါက ထိုက်သင့်စေနိုင်သော အပြစ်ဒဏ်ထက်ပိုမိုကြီးလေးသော အပြစ်ဒဏ်ကို ထိုက်သင့်ခြင်းမရှိစေရ။

အပိုဒ် ၁၂

မည်သူမျှ မိမိသဘောအတိုင်း အေးချမ်းလွတ်လပ်စွာ နေထိုင်ခြင်းကို သော်လည်းကောင်း၊ မိမိ၏ မိသားစုကို သော်လည်းကောင်း၊ မိမိ၏ နေအိမ် အသိုက်အဝန်းကို သော်လည်းကောင်း၊ စာပေးစာယူကို သော်လည်းကောင်း၊ ဥပဒေအရ မဟုတ်သော ဝင်ရောက် စွက်ဖက်ခြင်း မခံစေရ။ ထို့ပြင် မိမိ၏ဂုဏ်သိက္ခာ ကိုလည်း အထက်ပါအတိုင်း ပုတ်ခတ်ခြင်း မခံစေရ။ လူတိုင်းတွင် ထိုသို့ ဝင်ရောက်စွက်ဖက်ခြင်းမှ သော်လည်းကောင်း ပုတ်ခတ်ခြင်းမှ သော်လည်းကောင်း ဥပဒေအရ ကာကွယ် ပိုင်ခွင့်ရှိသည်။

အပိုဒ် ၁၃

(၁) လူတိုင်းတွင် မိမိ၏နိုင်ငံ နယ်နိမိတ် အတွင်း၌၌ လွတ်လပ်စွာ သွားလာ ရွှေ့ပြောင်း နိုင်ခွင့်၊ နေထိုင်ခွင့်ရှိသည်။

(၂) လူတိုင်းတွင် မိမိနေထိုင်ရာ တိုင်းပြည်မှ လည်းကောင်း၊ အခြားတိုင်းပြည်မှလည်းကောင်း ထွက်စွာ သွားပိုင်ခွင့်ရှိသည့်အပြင်၊ မိမိ၏ တိုင်းပြည်သို့ ပြန်လာ ပိုင်ခွင့်လည်းရှိသည်။

အပိုဒ် ၁၄

(၁) လူတိုင်းသည် ညှဉ်းပန်း နှိပ်စက် ခံနေရခြင်းမှ လွတ်ကင်းရန် အခြားတိုင်းပြည် များ၌ အေးချမ်းစွာ ခိုလှုံနေနိုင်ခွင့်ရှိသည်။

(၂) နိုင်ငံရေးနှင့် မပတ်သက်သည့် ပြစ်မှုများမှ သော်လည်းကောင်း၊ ကုလသမဂ္ဂ၏ ရည်ရွယ်ချက်နှင့် သဘောတရား မူများကို ဖီဆန်သော အမှုများမှ သော်လည်းကောင်း၊ အမှန် ပေါ်ပေါက် လာသော ပြစ်မှုကြောင့် တရားစွဲဆိုခြင်း ခံရသည့် အမှုအခင်များတွင် အထက်ပါ အခွင့်အရေးကို အသုံးမပြုနိုင်စေရ။

အပိုဒ် ၁၅

(၁) လူတိုင်းသည်၊ နိုင်ငံ တစ်နိုင်ငံ၏ နိုင်ငံသားအဖြစ် ခံယူခွင့်ရှိသည်။

(၂) ဥပဒေအရ မဟုတ်လျှင် မည်သူမျှ မိမိ၏ နိုင်ငံသားအဖြစ်ကို စွန့်လွှတ်ခြင်း မခံစေရ၊ နိုင်ငံသားအဖြစ် ပြောင်းလဲနိုင်သော အခွင့်အရေးကို လည်း ငြင်းပယ်ခြင်း မခံစေရ။

အပိုဒ် ၁၆

(၁) အရွယ်ရောက် ပြီးသော ယောကျ်ား နှင့် မိန်းမတို့တွင် လူမျိုးကို သော်လည်းကောင်း၊ နိုင်ငံသားအဖြစ်ကို သော်လည်းကောင်း ကိုးကွယ်သည့် ဘာသာကို သော်လည်းကောင်း၊ အကြောင်းပြု၍ ချုပ်ချယ် ကန့်သတ်ခြင်း မရှိဘဲ၊ ထိမ်းမြားနိုင်ခွင့် နှင့် မိသားစု ထူထောင်နိုင်ခွင့်ရှိသည်။ အဆိုပါ ယောကျ်ားနှင့် မိန်းမ တို့သည် လင်မယားအဖြစ် ပေါင်းသင်းနေစဉ် အချိန် အတွင်း၌ သော်လည်းကောင်း၊ အိမ်ထောင်ကို ဖျက်သိမ်း၍ ကွာရှင်းကြသည့် အခါ၌လည်းကောင်း၊ လက်ထပ် ပေါင်းသင်း အိမ်ထောင် ပြုခြင်းနှင့် စပ်လျဉ်းသော တူညီသည့် အခွင့်အရေးများကို ရရှိထိုက်သည်။

(၂) သတို့သား နှင့် သတို့သမီး နှစ်ဦးနှစ်ဘက်၏ လွတ်လပ်သော သဘောဆန္ဒရှိမှသာလျှင် ထိမ်းမြားခြင်းကို ပြုရမည်။

(၃) မိသားစု တစ်ခုသည် လူ့အဖွဲ့အစည်း၏ သဘာဝကျသော အခြေခံအဖွဲ့တစ်ရပ်ဖြစ်သည်၊ ထိုမိသားစုသည် လူ့ အဖွဲ့အစည်းနှင့် အစိုးရတို့၏ ကာကွယ်စောင့်ရှောက်ခြင်းကို ခံယူခွင့်ရှိသည်။

အပိုဒ် ၁၇

လူတိုင်းတွင် မိမိတစ်ဦး ချင်းသော်လည်းကောင်း ၊ အခြားသူများနှင့် ဖက်စပ်၍ သော်လည်းကောင်း၊ ပစ္စည်းဥစ္စာ တို့ကို ပိုင်ဆိုင်ရန် အခွင့်အရေးရှိရမည်။

ဥပဒေအရ မဟုတ်လျှင်၊ မည်သူမျှ မိမိ၏ ပစ္စည်းဥစ္စာပိုင်ဆိုင်ခွင့်ကို စွန့်လွှတ်ခြင်း မခံစေရ။

အပိုဒ် ၁၈

လူတိုင်းတွင် လွတ်လပ်စွာ တွေးခေါ် ကြံဆနိုင်ခွင့်၊ လွတ်လပ်စွာ ခံယူရပ်တည်နိုင်ခွင့် နှင့် လွတ်လပ်စွာ သက်ဝင် ကိုးကွယ်နိုင်ခွင့်ရှိသည်။ အဆိုပါ အခွင့်အရေးများ၌ မိမိကိုးကွယ်သည့် ဘာသာကို သို့တည်းမဟုတ် သက်ဝင်ယုံကြည်ချက်ကို လွတ်လပ်စွာ ပြောင်းလဲနိုင်ခွင့်၊ ပါဝင်သည့် အပြင် မိမိတစ်ယောက် ချင်းဖြစ်စေ၊ အခြားသူများနှင့် စုပေါင်း၍ဖြစ်စေ၊ ပြည်သူအများ ရှေ့မှောက်တွင် သော်လည်းကောင်း၊ ရှေ့မှောက်တွင် မဟုတ်ဘဲ သော်လည်းကောင်း၊ မိမိ ကိုးကွယ်သော ဘာသာကို သို့တည်းမဟုတ် သက်ဝင် ယုံကြည်ချက်ကို လွတ်လပ်စွာ သင်ပြနိုင်ခွင့်၊ ကျင့်သုံးနိုင်ခွင့်၊ ဝတ်ပြုကိုးကွယ်နိုင်ခွင့်နှင့် ဆောက်တည် နိုင်ခွင့်တို့လည်း ပါဝင်သည်။

အပိုဒ် ၁၉

လူတိုင်းတွင် လွတ်လပ်စွာ ထင်မြင် ယူဆနိုင်ခွင့်နှင့် လွတ်လပ်စွာ ဖွင့်ဟ ဖော်ပြနိုင်ခွင့်ရှိသည်။ အဆိုပါ အခွင့်အရေးများ၌ အနှောင့် အယှက်မရှိဘဲ လွတ်လပ်စွာ ထင်မြင်ယူဆနိုင်ခွင့် ပါဝင် သည့်အပြင်၊ နိုင်ငံနယ်နိမိတ်များကို ထောက်ထားရန် မလိုဘဲ သတင်းအကြောင်းအရာနှင့် သဘောတရားများကို တနည်းနည်းဖြင့် လွတ်လပ်စွာ ရှာယူဆည်းပူးနိုင်ခွင့်၊ လက်ခံနိုင်ခွင့်နှင့် ဝေ၍ ဖြန့်ချိခွင့်တို့လည်း ပါဝင်သည်။

အပိုဒ် ၂၀

(၁) လူတိုင်းတွင် လွတ်လပ် အေးချမ်းစွာ စုဝေးနိုင်ခွင့် နှင့် ဖွဲ့စည်းနိုင်ခွင့် တို့ ရှိသည်။
(၂) မည်သူကိုမျှ အဖွဲ့.အစည်းတစ်ခုသို့ ဝင်စေရန် အတင်းအကျပ်မပြုရ။

အပိုဒ် ၂၁

(၁) လူတိုင်းတွင် မိမိနိုင်ငံ၏ အုပ်ချုပ်ရေး၌ ကိုယ်တိုင်ဖြစ်စေ၊ လွတ်လပ်စွာ ရွေးချယ်လိုက်သည့် ကိုယ်စားလှယ်များမှ တစ်ဆင့်ဖြစ်စေ ပါဝင် ဆောင်ရွက်နိုင်ခွင့် ရှိသည်။
(၂) လူတိုင်းတွင် မိမိ၏နိုင်ငံရှိ ပြည်သူ့ ဝန်ထမ်းအဖွဲ့၌ ဝင်ရောက်နိုင်ရန် တူညီသည့် အခွင့် အရေးရှိသည်။

(၃) ပြည်သူပြည်သားတို့၏ ဆန္ဒသည် အုပ်ချုပ် အာဏာ၏ အခြေခံဖြစ်ရမည်၊ အဆိုပါ ဆန္ဒကို အချိန်ကာလပိုင်းခြားလျက် စစ်မှန်သောရွေးကောက်ပွဲများဖြင့် ထင်ရှားစေရမည်။ ရွေးကောက် ပွဲများတွင်လည်း လူတိုင်းအညီအမျှ ဆန္ဒမဲ ပေးနိုင်ခွင့် ရှိရမည်အပြင် ၊ ထိုရွေးကောက်ပွဲများကို လျှို့ဝှက် မဲပေး စနစ်ဖြင့် ဖြစ်စေ၊ အလားတူ လွတ်လပ်သော မဲပေးစနစ် ဖြင့်ဖြစ်စေ၊ ကျင်းပရမည်။

အပိုဒ် ၂၂

လူတိုင်းတွင် လူ့အဖွဲ့အစည်း၏ အဖွဲ့ဝင်တစ်ဦးအနေနှင့်၊ လူမှုရေးလုံခြုံခွင့် ရယူပိုင်ခွင့်ရှိသည့်အပြင်နိုင်ငံရေးကြိုးပမ်းမှုဖြင့်ဖြစ်စေ၊ နိုင်ငံတကာ ပူးပေါင်း ဆောင်ရွက်မှုဖြင့်ဖြစ်စေ၊ နိုင်ငံအသီးသီး၏ ဖွဲ့စည်းပုံနှင့် လည်းကောင်း၊ သယံဇာတအင်အားနှင့်လည်းကောင်း ထိုလူ၏ ဂုဏ်သိက္ခာနှင့် စရိုက်လက္ခဏာ လွတ်လပ်စွာ တိုးတက်မြင့်မားရေးအတွက် မရှိမဖြစ်လိုအပ်သော စီးပွားရေး၊လူမှုရေးနှင့် ယဉ်ကျေးမှု အခွင့်အရေးများကို သုံးစွဲပိုင်ခွင့်ရှိသည်။

အပိုဒ် ၂၃

(၁) လူတိုင်းတွင် အလုပ်လုပ် ရန်လည်းကောင်း၊ မိမိနှစ်သက်ရာ အသက်မွေးမှု အလုပ် အကိုင်ကို လွတ်လပ်စွာရွေးချယ်ရန် လည်းကောင်း၊ တရား မျှတ၍ လုပ်ပျော်သော အလုပ်ခွင်၏ အခြေအနေကို ရရှိရန် လည်းကောင်း၊ အလုပ်လက်မဲ့ ဖြစ်ရခြင်းမှ အကာအကွယ် ရရှိရန် လည်းကောင်း အခွင့်အရေးရှိသည်။
(၂) လူတိုင်းတွင် ခွဲခြားခြင်းမခံရစေဘဲ၊ တူညီသော အလုပ်အတွက် တူညီသော အခကြေးငွေ ရနိုင်ခွင့်ရှိသည်။
(၃) အလုပ်လုပ်ကိုင်သည့် လူတိုင်းတွင်၊ မိမိနှင့် မိမိ၏ မိသားစုအတွက် လူ့ဂုဏ်သိက္ခာ နှင့် ညီအောင် နေထိုင် စားသောက်နိုင်ရန်၊ စိတ်ချလောက်သည်ပြင်၊ တရား မျှတ၍ လုပ်ပျော်သည့် လစာကြေးငွေ ရပိုင်ခွင့်ရှိသည်။ လိုအပ်ခဲ့လျှင်အခြား နည်းလမ်းများမှ လူမှုရေး အထောက်အပံ့ကိုလည်း ထပ်မံ၍ ရနိုင်ခွင့် ရှိသည်။
(၄) လူတိုင်းတွင် မိမိအကျိုး ခံစားခွင့်ကို ကာကွယ်ရန် အလုပ်သမား အစည်းအရုံးများ ဖွဲ့စည်းခွင့်၊ ပါဝင် ဆောင်ရွက်ခွင့် ရှိသည်။

အပိုဒ် ၂၄

လူတိုင်းတွင် သင့်မြတ်လျော်ကန်စွာ ကန့်သတ်ထားသည့် အလုပ်လုပ်ချိန် အပြင်၊ လစာနှင့်တကွ အခါကာလအားလျော်စွာ သတ်မှတ် ထားသည့် အလုပ်

အားလပ်ရက်များပါဝင်သည့် အနားယူခွင့်နှင့် အားလပ်ခွင့် ခံစားပိုင်ခွင့် ရှိသည်။

အပိုဒ် ၂၅

(၁) လူတိုင်းတွင် မိမိနှင့်တကွ မိမိ၏ မိသားစု ကျန်းမာရေးနှင့်တကွ ကိုယ်စိတ်နှစ်ဖြာ အေးချမ်းစွာ နေထိုင်နိုင်ရေး အတွက် အစာအဟာရ၊ အဝတ်အထည် နေအိမ်၊ ဆေးဝါး အကူအညီနှင့် လိုအပ်သည့် လူမှု အထောက်အပံ့များ ပါဝင်သော သင့်တော် လျှောက်ပတ်သည့် လူမှု အဆင့်အတန်းကို ရယူခံစားခွင့် ရှိသည်။ ထို့ပြင် အလုပ်လက်မဲ့ဖြစ်သော အခါ၌ သော်လည်းကောင်း၊ မကျန်းမမာဖြစ်သော အခါ၌ သော်လည်းကောင်း၊ ကိုယ်အင်္ဂါ မစွမ်း မသန်ဖြစ်သော အခါ၌ သော်လည်းကောင်း၊ မုဆိုးမဖြစ်သော်အခါ၌ သော်လည်းကောင်း၊ အသက်အရွယ်အိုမင်းသော အခါ၌ သော်လည်းကောင်း၊ မိမိကိုယ်တိုင်က မတတ်နိုင်သော အကြောင်းကြောင့် ဝမ်းစာ ရှာမှီးနိုင်သော နည်းလမ်း မရှိသော အခါ၌ သော်လည်းကောင်း၊ နေထိုင်စားသောက်ရေးအတွက် လုံခြုံစိတ်ချရမှု အခွင့်အရေးရှိသည်။

(၂) သားသည် မိခင်များနှင့် ကလေးများသည် အထူးစောင့်ရှောက်ခြင်းနှင့် အကူအညီပေးခြင်းကို ရခွင့် ရှိသည်။ ဥပဒေအရ ထိမ်းမြားခြင်းဖြင့်ဖြစ်စေ အခြား နည်းဖြင့် ဖြစ်စေ မွေးဖွားသော ကလေးအားလုံးသည် တူညီသော လူမှု ကာကွယ်
စောင့်ရှောက်ရေးကို ရယူ ခံစားကြရမည်။

အပိုဒ် ၂၆

(၁) လူတိုင်းသည် ပညာသင် ယူနိုင်ခွင့်ရှိသည်၊ အနည်းဆုံးမူလတန်းနှင့်၊ အခြေခံ အဆင့် အတန်းများတွင် ပညာ သင်ကြားရေးသည် အခမဲ့ဖြစ်ရမည်။ မူလတန်းပညာသည် မသင်မနေရ ပညာ ဖြစ်ရမည်။ စက်မှုလက်မှုပညာနှင့်၊ အသက်မွေးမှု ပညာများကို ယေဘုယျအားဖြင့် သင်ကြားရယူနိုင်စေရမည်။ ထို့ပြင် အထက်တန်းပညာအတွက် အရည်အချင်းကို အခြေခံပြု၍ တူညီသော အခွင့်အရေး ရရှိစေရမည်။

(၂) ပညာသင်ကြားရေးကို လူသားတို့၏ စရိုက်လက္ခဏာအပြည့်အဝတိုးတက်မှု အပြင်၊ လူ့အခွင့်အရေးနှင့်၊ အခြေခံလွတ်လပ်ခွင့် ရှိသေ လေးစားမှု တို့ကို ရှင်သန်ဖွံ့ဖြိုးလာစေရန် ရည်ရွယ်၍ သင်ကြား စေရမည်။ ပညာသင်ကြားရေးသည် နိုင်ငံ အားလုံး တို့တွင် လည်းကောင်း၊ လူမျိုးစုများ တွင်လည်းကောင်း၊ ဘာသာရေးအသင်းအဖွဲ့များတွင် လည်းကောင်း၊ အချင်းချင်းနားလည်မှု၊ သည်းခံ မှုနှင့် ခင်မင်ရင်းနှီးမှုတို့ကို အားပေးရမည်။

ထို့ပြင် ငြိမ်းချမ်းရေး တည်တံ့အောင် ဆောင်ရွက်ရန် အလို့ငှါ၊ ကုလသမဂ္ဂ၏ ဆောင်ရွက်မှုများကိုလည်း ဖြစ်မြောက် အောင် အားပေးရမည်။

(၃) မိဘတို့တွင်၊ မိမိတို့၏ ကလေးများ သင်ယူရမည့် ပညာ အမျိုးအစားကို ရွေးချယ်နိုင်သော လက်ဦး အခွင့်အရေးရှိသည်။

အပိုဒ် ၂၇

(၁) လူတိုင်းတွင် သက်ဆိုင်ရာ ယဉ်ကျေးမှု လောကဒ္ဒ လွတ်လပ်စွာ ပါဝင်ဆောင် ရွက်နိုင်ခွင့်၊ သုခမပညာရပ် များကို လွတ်လပ်စွာလိုက်စား မွေ့လျော်နိုင်ခွင့်၊ သိပ္ပံ ပညာထွန်းကားရေး လုပ်ငန်းများတွင် လွတ်လပ်စွာ ဝင်ရောက် လုပ်ကိုင် နိုင်ခွင့်နှင့်၊ ထိုပညာ၏ အကျိုး အာနိသင်များကို လွတ်လပ်စွာ ခံစားသုံးစွဲနိုင်ခွင့် ရှိသည်။

(၂) လူတိုင်းတွင် သိပ္ပံမှ ဖြစ်စေ၊ စာပေမှဖြစ်စေ၊ သုခမပညာမှ ဖြစ်စေ၊ မိမိကိုယ်ပိုင်ဉာဏ်ဖြင့်ကြံစည်ဖန်တီးမှုမှဖြစ်ထွန်းလာသည့် ဂုဏ်နှင့်၊ ငွေကြေး အကျိုးအမြတ်များကို ခံစားရယူနိုင်ရန် အခွင့်အရေးအတွက် ကာကွယ်မှုကို ရရှိရန် အခွင့်အရေး ရှိသည်။

အပိုဒ် ၂၈

လူတိုင်းသည် ဤကြေညာ စာတမ်းတွင် ဖော်ပြထားသည့် အခွင့်အရေးများ နှင့်၊ လွတ်လပ်ခွင့်များကို အပြည့်အစုံ ရယူနိုင်သော လူမှု ဆက်ဆံရေး အခြေအနေနှင့်၊ အပြည်ပြည်ဆိုင်ရာ ဆက်ဆံရေး အခြေအနေတို့၏ အကျိုးကျေးဇူးကို ခံစားနိုင်ခွင့် ရှိသည်။

အပိုဒ် ၂၉

(၁) မိမိ၏ စရိုက်လက္ခဏာ လွတ်လပ်စွာ ဖွံ့ဖြိုးတိုးတက်နိုင်သည့် တစ်ခုတည်းသော လူ့အသိုက်အဝန်း အတွက်လူတိုင်း၌ တာဝန် ရှိသည်။

(၂) မိမိ၏ အခွင့်အရေးများနှင့်၊ လွတ်လပ် ခွင့်များကို သုံးစွဲရာတွင် လူတိုင်းသည်၊ အခြားသူများ၏ အခွင့်အရေးများနှင့်၊ လွတ်လပ်ခွင့်များကိုအသိအမှတ်ပြု၍ ရှိသေလေးစားစေရန်အလို့ငှာ လည်းကောင်း၊ ဒီမိုကရေစီ ကျင့်သုံးသော လူ့အဖွဲ့အစည်းတွင် ကိုယ်ကျင့်တရားအပြင်၊ ရပ်ရွာအေးချမ်းသာယာရေးနှင့်၊ ပြည်သူ့ အကျိုး စီးပွား ဖြစ်ထွန်းရေးတို့ အတွက်၊ တရားမျှတစွာကျင့် ဆောင်ရန် အလို့ငှာ လည်းကောင်း၊ ဥပဒေက ပြဋ္ဌာန်းထားသည့် ချုပ်ချယ်မှုများဖြင့်သာ ကန့်သတ်ခြင်းခံရမည်။

(၃) အဆိုပါ အခွင့်အရေးများနှင့် လွတ်လပ် ခွင့်များကို မည်သည့် အမှုကိစ္စတွင်မျှ ကုလသမဂ္ဂ၏ ရည်ရွယ်ချက်များနှင့် လည်းကောင်း၊ အခြေခံမူများနှင့် လည်းကောင်း ဆန့်ကျင်၍ မသုံးစွဲရ။

အပိုဒ် ၃၀

ဤကြေညာစာတမ်းပါ အခွင့်အရေးနှင့်တကွ လွတ်လပ်ခွင့်များ ပျက်စီးရာပျက်စီးကြောင်းတို့ကိုရည်ရွယ်၍၊ နိုင်ငံ တစ်နိုင်ငံ အတွက် ဖြစ်စေ၊ လူတစ်စု အတွက်ဖြစ်စေ၊ လူတစ်ဦးတစ်ယောက် အတွက် ဖြစ်စေ ပါဝင် ဆောင်ရွက်ရန် အခွင့်ရှိသည်ဟု သော်လည်းကောင်း၊ ကိုယ်တိုင်ဆောင်ရွက်ရန် အခွင့်ရှိသည်ဟုသော်လည်းကောင်း အဓိပ္ပါယ် ပိုင်းခြားကောက်ယူခြင်း မရှိစေရ။

The Myanmar people call their country the Golden Land. As such, it will be professional as well as civilized if the Myanmar people were to use the Universal Declaration of Human Rights as the touchstone in the judgment of the politics.

4
Pure Gold

As a matter of fact, there was a time that Burma (now Myanmar) sat on the top of the world in her attempt in making her politics *pure gold*. The pure gold of Myanmar conscience is evidenced from the 1961 speech of Brigadier General Aung Gyi. In the morning of 1961 July 4th, Vice Chief of Staff (Army) Brig. General Aung Gyi addressed on the occasion of the surrender of the Mujahids. My English translation given here is based upon the article from the Journal of Today Affairs (Khit-ye Sa-saung), a weekly or monthly news magazine in the days of Myanmar parliamentary democracy. The images of the article posted by a blogger named Kyaw Kyaw Oo at

http://kyawkyawoo.wordpress.com/2012/07/13/historical-facts-caught-on-documents-who-are-the-rohingya-people/   and retrieved on December 02, 2012. The images of the article are also given at the end (Exhibit-R5 to R9).

The speech begins:

"At this "coming-to-light" (exchange of arms for democracy) ceremony, I would like to speak a few words with the comrades who, in the name of the revolution, have fought the government in Maungdaw region since the day of Myanmar's independence.

First, I would like to talk about the matter that is concerned for all people of Mayu District. Our Mayu[23] District is bordered in the West with Pakistan. Due to the border connection there are people of Muslim religion both at the East and West sides of the border. The people at the West [of the border] are called Pakistan[i] and those at the East [of the border] inside Myanmar are known as the Rohingya.

I would like to say this: This place [Mayu District], which is connected with Pakistan, is not the only place where the same "kind of people" (Lumyo) lives at both sides of the border. In the regions [of Myanmar] which are bordered with

---

[23] Pronounced May-u or May-yu. It is the Burmese version of Mount Meru.

China the same situation exists. For example, there is a "kind of people" (Lumyo) known as Lisu at Myanmar Kachin State. There are Lisu at Myanmar side and there are Lisu at China side. There are E-kaw at Myanmar side and there are E-kaw at China side. There are La-Wa at China Side and there are La-Wa at Myanmar side. There are Shan in Myanmar and there are Shan, known as "Tai" in China side. They all speak the same language; they also practice the same religion. Similarly, if we look at the Yodaya (Thai) border there are Tai inside Yodaya (Thai) as well as inside Myanmar. There are Mon inside Yodaya (Thai) as well as inside Myanmar. In the same pattern, there are Karen inside Myanmar and Yodaya (Thai) as well. The situation is the same at the Pakistan border; there are the people of same religion inside Pakistan and similarly there are the "kind of people" (Lumyo) known as the Rohingya inside Myanmar.

At this moment, before the audience, I would like to say openly and precisely. People in the bordering regions have relatives on either side. Despite having the relatives, those who live over there must be Pakistan[i] and those who live here must be citizens of the Myanmar Union. Like this the people living in the bordering region must have a clear and precise and decided mind. For example, when we look at the Kachin State [we find that] some people of Kachin State have their relatives in China. However, the Kachin people in China are "Chinese" and the Kachin people at this Myanmar side are the "Burmese". Some of them are daughters and in-laws; some of them are sons and nephews. In spite of being relatives and same "kind of people" (Lumyo) the country is now different. We must clearly and precisely understand and know this status. With regard to allegiance it must also be clear and precise. Similarly, the Rohingya people, within our jurisdiction, must have allegiance to the Union of Myanmar whereas those people at the western side must have allegiance to Pakistan; only then, it will be natural (meaning in accord with the law). What I would like to tell the "city-father', "city-mother", and the comrades is this. In the west, in Pakistan, you may have your relative, in-laws, sons, and daughters. The relatives are the relatives. Nevertheless, in terms of the nationality, you, comrades, are the Myanmar Union citizens and accordingly, you must have clear and resolute allegiance to the Union (of Myanmar). Your relatives who are in West Pakistan or East Pakistan, despite you are their relative living in Myanmar, must have allegiance to Pakistan only. Only then it will be natural. The honorable people who are in this audience must disseminate this concept clearly and precisely to all who are close to you. Please also make this resolute decision, I plead you.

In this connection, I would like to tell you a short history. Some time ago, as you may all know, the people of Myanmar Proper (Myanmar pyima) maintain the opinion that the Rohingya are the Mujahids, Muslims, and pro-Pakistan who want to join Pakistan. Some of the people who live in this region also have the opinion that "we are the Muslims, and so we must join Pakistan." On this ground the political movement was carried out with the objective of establishing a Pakistan's extension in the line of Germany's Sudetenland. In reality, it is not natural; it is also not feasible. What happened with Germany's Sudetenland was in the time of pre-war, and such expansionism disappeared in the days of post-war. Pakistan maintains right policy. For example, they do not claim the rights over the Kyi Island. In view of its lack of interest even in Kyi Island, Pakistan will not even dream of annexation of Mayu District to East Pakistan. No, Pakistan does not entertain such thoughts. Similarly, the Chinese people cannot move to annex the Kachin State to Yunan province with a concept that Myanmar Kachin are the same as the Chinese Kachin. These days, there exists no such behavior. Yes, there was in the old days. Some people of Burma Proper consider that the people here (in Mayu District) are not Tai-yin-thar (native). There is also certain truth in the fact that some people here (in Mayu District) also live with one leg in Pakistan. These are all wrong. Some people of Burma Proper are wrong and some people here (in Mayu District) are also wrong. Therefore, beginning at this time, today, I would say frankly. Mayu District [people] will be considered as an ethnic minority–*Lunesu Lumyosu*–of the Union (of Myanmar). I will tell you precisely. People from here (Mayu District) must also consider as an ethnic minority–*Lunesu Lumyosu*. Only then, there will be peace in this country.

So, if we have made mistakes in the past let us forget them. For example, when we conduct military operations in those days villages in this region might have been torched due to a necessity or simply out of anger. If there have been such mistakes, let us forget these now. From this time forward, you, the people of Mayu District, must live a life of "we-are-the-citizens-of-Burma-Union"; live with the oath that "the country we must bear allegiance is the Burma Union"; and live with a heart that "we are an ethnic group of the Union". Only then, there [will be] peace in the future of this region.

[The document ends here, with a note "continue to page 23 but I have no page 23. SLM(SK), the translator, December 02, 2012].

Exhibit-R4
U Nu (1907-1995)
One and the only legitimate Prime Minister
of Burma. This is the official photo
that hung in every government office
in Burma during his tenure.

"It is a sin to kill, but it is a greater sin to watch
the killing with folded arms,"
U Nu's words in 1970.

Lest we forget, I would like to remind the world that U Nu was the prime minister of Burma when the Burmese government embraced the Rohingya people into the fold of Myanmar multiculturalism and parliamentary democracy. Burma had a respectable parliamentary democracy under his leadership. He was vanished not only from the Myanmar politics but also from the history. The disappearance of the reasonable and thoughtful persons like U Nu and Brigadier Aung Gyi must not be forgotten. U Nu was disposed by the ultranationalist Burmese led by General Ne Win in 1962 because U Nu was in favor of an equitable federalism. Ne Win's action against U Nu was tacitly supported by the world powers in fear that U Nu was opting to end the civil war not only by transforming Burma into a federal union to satisfy the ethnic diversity but he was also considering to legalize the communist parties of Burma (both the Red Flag and White Flag parties) for a lasting peace in Burma. The thought of the Burmese communist legal existence sent a wave of fear to the SE Asia and the West.[24]

The fear of federalism and communism impersonalized U Nu and sent him to the realm of null and void. Ne Win and his ultranationalism crushed and dehumanized the federalists, the Rohingya, and the communists, with unfathomable brutality, which still thrives on in Burma.[25] The communists were wiped out to great happiness of the anti-communist powers. The federationists were charged with the crimes of secessionism and subjected to the genocidal ethnic cleansing wars; the on-going Kachin war is a good standing example.[26] The Rohingya were alienated and ethnic cleansing began as early as in 1978 when more than 200,000 Rohingya were driven out of the country. These are very sad events of history.

If General Ne Win was not encouraged (by the Burmese ultranationalists and the international non-communist powers) to seize power and if the Burmese parliamentary democracy was

---

[24] Also see Shwe Lu Maung, *The Price of Silence: Muslim-Buddhist War of Bangladesh and Myanmar – A Social Darwinist's Analysis*, DewDrop Arts & Technology, USA, 2005, Chapter 5.1 and 5.2.

[25] Also see Shwe Lu Maung, *Burma Nationalism and Ideology*, University Press Ltd., Dhaka, 1989 and Shwe Lu Maung, *The Price of Silence: Muslim-Buddhist War of Bangladesh and Myanmar – A Social Darwinist's Analysis*, DewDrop Arts & Technology, USA, 2005.

[26] For general information visit http://en.wikipedia.org/wiki/Kachin_conflict or google 'kachin war'.

allowed to progress and matured the probabilities are high that we would all have Burmese pure gold in our hands now.

Exhibit-R5
Aung Gyi's speech-image1 at the occasion of the surrender of the Mujahids on the 4th of July 1961

Exhibit-R6
Aung Gyi's speech-image2 at the occasion of the surrender of the Mujahids on the 4th of July 1961

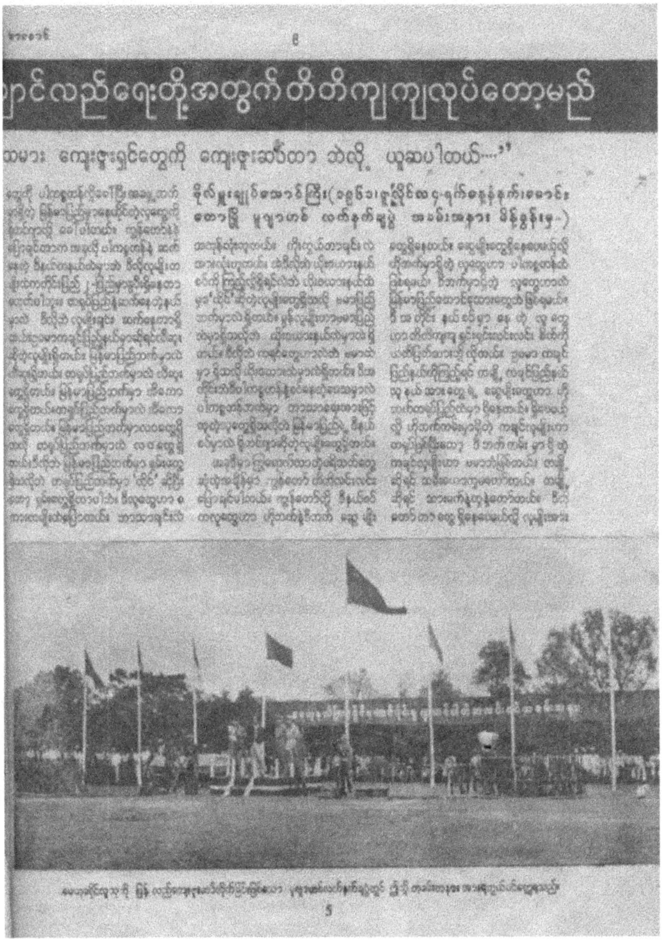

ျပင်လည်ရေးတို့အတွက်တိတိကျကျလုပ်တော့မည်

သမား ကျေးဇူးရှင်တွေကို ကျေးဇူးဆပ်တာ ဘဲလို့ ယူဆပါတယ်…”

Exhibit-R7
Aung Gyi's speech-image3 at the occasion of the surrender of the Mujahids on the 4th of July 1961

Exhibit-R8
Rohingya damsels welcome Aung Gyi
at the occasion of the surrender of the Mujahids
on the 4th of July 1961

The caption says:
These damsels are not used to coming out of
the house to meet the strangers. Today, in
view of peace in their region, and with great
joy, they come out overcoming shyness, and
in tireless effort, they welcome Brigadier
General Aung Gyi and the guests.

Exhibit-R9

News on Aung Gyi's speech at the occasion of the surrender of the Mujahids on the 4th of July 1961. Please note that they were soaked in monsoon rain.

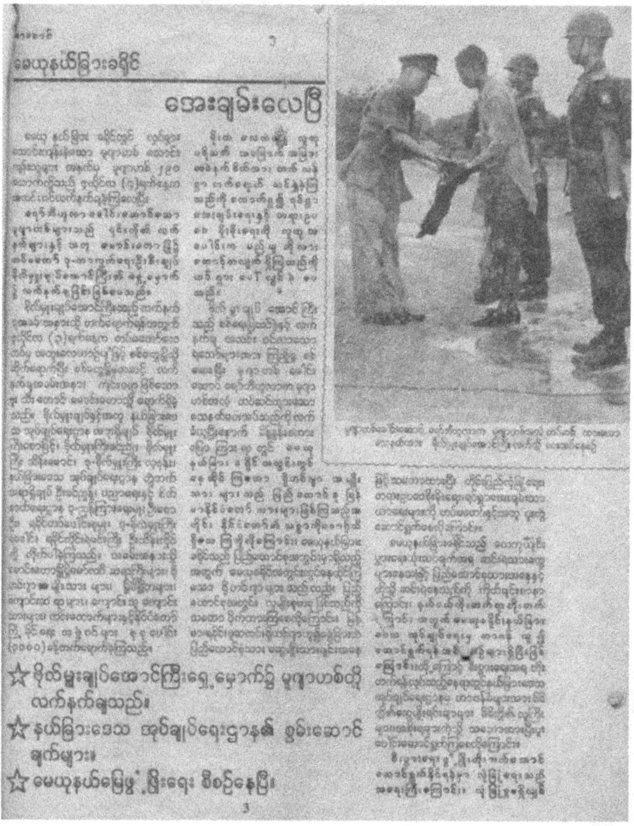
မေယုနယ်ခြားခရိုင်

အေးချမ်းလေပြီ

☆ ဗိုလ်မှူးချုပ်အောင်ကြီးရှေ့မှောက်၌ မူဂျာဟစ်တို့ လက်နက်ချသည်။

☆ နယ်ခြားဒေသ အုပ်ချုပ်ရေးဌာန၏ စွမ်းဆောင်ချက်များ။

☆ မေယုနယ်မြေဖွံ့ဖြိုးရေး စီစဉ်နေပြီ။

3

5
1982 Citizenship Act – Ne Win

The 1982 Citizenship Act is the most visible cruel operation of Myanmar ultranationalism under the patronage of General Ne Win and his Burmese Way to Socialism. I analyze that Myanmar ultranationalism bears the following characteristics, (1) pride in the residual feudal Myanmar imperialism, (2) a feeling of inferiority due to intrinsic weakness of culture, science, and technology, (3) a deep sense of xenophobia due to uncompetitiveness in a multicultural environment, (4) a refuge in self-esteem in the face of the repeated failures (e.g. lost of independence, civil wars, and absolute poverty *et cetera*), (5) lack of knowledge of the world cultures, (6) prejudice toward the non-Myanmar features and characters, and (7) the prioritization of traditionalism with a view that modem liberalism (e.g. democracy and open market economy) and science and technology are the threats to 'Burmese-ness'.[27] Myanmar ultranationalism is also a good subject to analyze in light of palingenetic ultranationalism of Roger Griffin.[28] The reader shall be the judge. Again, we should not forget that Nazism stands for *Nationalsozialismus* in German or National Socialism in English.[29]

Exhibit-R10

This is a classic photo of General Ne Win that hung in the government offices after he took over power in 1962

---

[27] Also see "Burmese-ness" in Shwe Lu Maung, *Burma Nationalism and Ideology*, University Press Ltd., Dhaka, 1989, p 102, and Wylma C. Samaranayake-Robinson, *Alternative Futures for Governance in Burma: 2040*, in The Asian Conference on Asian Studies 2011, Official Conference Proceedings 2011, The International Academic Forum (IAFOR), 2011, p 12.

[28] Roger Griffin *The Nature of Fascism*, Routledge, 1993

[29] http://en.wikipedia.org/wiki/Nazism

These ultranationalist characteristics are expressed in General Ne Win's address of the introduction of the 1982 Citizenship Act to the Central Committee of the Burmese Socialist Programme Party (BSPP), in the Central Meeting Hall, President House[30], Ahlone Road, on the 8th of October 1982. Therefore, I would like to take liberty of reproduction of his address. It is the official English version printed in the government newspapers *The Working People Daily* on the 9th instant.[31]

The address begins –

"Comrade Central Committee members:
What I am going to speak today is about an important law, the Burmese Citizenship Law. If this law must be explained, what has happened in the past must necessarily be recalled. I have no desire to hurt anybody in recounting this recent history. However, the truth might perhaps hurt somebody sometimes, but I do not wish to hurt anyone and I will try not to do so.

I would like first to explain about conditions that prevailed in Burma as a subject nation. After a part of Burma had been annexed by foreigners in 1824, one war after another was fought and the whole of our country subsequently became a subject nation. After becoming a subject country, we officially regained independence on 4 January 1948, as is known to all. During the period between 1824 and the time we regained independence in January 1948, foreigners, or aliens, entered our country un-hindered under various pretexts. They came to live in Burma and mainly for economic reasons. The first to come were the English who ruled our country. After them came many of their camp followers. Let us say only that much.

We, the natives or Burmese nationals, were unable to shape our own destiny. We were subjected to the manipulations of others from 1824 to 4 January 1948. Let

---

[30] This is the former British Governor Mansion, a colonial heritage that became the Presidential Mansion in the independent Myanmar.
[31] http://www.burmalibrary.org/docs6/Ne_Win's_speech_Oct-1982-Citizenship_Law.pdf . The text is downloaded from this web link on August 09, 2012. Myanmar uses the British English.

us now look back at the conditions that prevailed at the time we regained independence on 4 January 1948. We then find that the people in our country comprised true nationals, guests, issues from unions between nationals and guests or mixed bloods, and issues from unions between guests and guests. So at the time of independence there were not only true nationals, but also guests, issues of unions between nationals and guests, and issues from unions between guests and guests. This became a problem after independence. The problem was how to clarify the position of guests and mixed bloods. When the problem was tackled, two laws emerged.

The Union Citizenship Act, 1948. This Act was promulgated on 4 January 1948, as Act No. 66. The Second Act was the Union Citizenship (Election) Act, 1948. This Act was promulgated on 3 May 1948, as Act No. 26. The aim of the first Act was first to define citizens and their rights. The Aim of the Union Citizenship (Election) Act was to solve the problem of immigrants I had mentioned. These people were already in Burma when we regained independence and they were to elect for Burmese citizenship if they so desired. They were to apply for it. Not that citizenship was to be granted without limitation. Certain qualifications were to be fulfilled. For this purpose the Act was promulgated.

I would like to explain certain significant points of this Act. Section 5 of the Citizenship Act provides that persons born after the Constitution had come into force were to be citizens of Burma (a) if born in the Union of Burma of parents one of whom is a Union citizen: where the father is a citizen of a foreign country, that person is to make a declaration within one year after reaching the age of majority that he renounced the foreign citizenship and elected to remain as a Union citizen. If he or she did not make such a declaration he or she cease to be a Union citizen at the end of that year; (b) if born outside of the Union of Burma of a Union Citizen father but had registered his birth in the prescribed manner and within the prescribed period at a respective Consulate of the Union;

(c) born outside of the Union of Burma of a parent serving as a Government servant: where one of the parents is a foreigner he or she is to make a declaration within one year of having attained the age of majority renouncing foreign citizenship and electing to remain a Union citizen. If he or she failed to do so he or she is to cease to be a Union citizen at the end of that year.

I have singled out this matter because our blood is involved -our citizen, our national, is involved either as father or mother. He or she having married a foreigner had an issue. That issue has the duty within one year on attaining the age of majority, to make a declaration renouncing foreign citizenship and electing to remain a citizen of ours. It is as if even a person of our blood must do this. This Act was promulgated as a matter of course. Should a person of mixed blood forget to elect Burmese citizenship as required by law before authorities concerned he or she automatically loses citizenship on completion of 19 years of age. That is one point.

Section 7 of the same Act states: (i) A foreigner may apply for citizenship certificate giving the following reasons. If the reasons are acceptable to the Minister a citizenship certificate may be issued to him. (a) Has completed the age of 18 years; (b) has lived continuously for not less than five years within the Union under the authority of the Union prior to submitting the application... I will read out only the relevant portion. There are many more points. What is meant here is that a foreigner who (a) had completed the age of 18, (b) had lived continuously for at least five years in the Union under the authority of the Union can apply for citizenship.

You might not have noticed what I had read out just now. It is mentioned that if the Minister accepts the reason given a citizenship certificate may be granted to the applicant. This means that a citizenship certificate may be granted at the discretion of the Minister, appointed and empowered by the President for this purpose. That is, the Minister acting alone, has full power to decide as he wishes.

In this same Act there are other points relating to those who had entered our country that I did not go into details to avoid hurting others. However I feel one point should be brought out. Section 13 of the Act states that a person who had served for at least three years either continuously or not may apply for citizenship during his service or within six months after termination of his service and may be granted citizenship if he fulfils requirements of the law even if he had given (i) no prior intimation of his desire to do so (ii) or had not resided within the Union. Of foreigners who came into Burma there were many who served the English, but of them extra care has to be taken of armed forces personnel.

I will say only this much about this Act. The next Act is the Union Citizenship (Election) Act, 1948. I will read out section 3 of that Act. Any person who fulfils the following qualifications may apply to the District officer concerned for Union citizenship. The qualifications are: (a) being born in a territory under the suzerainty of the British monarch.

The British Empire at that time was very extensive and it was then said that "the sun never sets on the British Empire" in various parts of the world. People from within this Empire who wish to reside in our country as citizens were allowed to apply for such citizenship. This was a special privilege. Since we live in amity with the whole world, it is not right to give preference to one country only. We must be fair to all.

That same Section 3 has a sub-section (b) that states that those who have lived within the territory of the Union of Burma for eight years out of ten years prior to 1 January 1942 or 4 January 1948 are eligible to apply for Burmese citizenship. The qualifications therefore are that one must have lived within the territory of Burma for eight years out of ten years prior to 1 January 1942 or 4 January 1948. These, of course, are points of law.

There are actions to be taken under this law. For instance, those who are in Burma and who satisfy those conditions must declare that they would like to elect

Burmese citizenship and apply for Burmese citizenship.

On the part of the Burma Government, personnel from the department concerned must scrutinise the applications and issue citizenship certificates. In this respect, certain foreigners were illiterate or were unaware of the existence of this law. They therefore have not made the applications up to now and if legal action were to be taken against them there would be no end. A lot of bother and a lot of trouble for them as well as for us. What is worse and what should not have happened is as we had been saying all along since our Party was founded: the giving of full powers to a single person. Power was however entrusted to a single person under the conditions that prevailed at that time. Decision taken by the person in power was final. There were some irregularities with regard to grant citizenship to persons before Independence; and have not persons arriving in Burma after Independence in 1948, also been given citizenship?

We cannot look on with folded arms on cases of grants of citizenship to those who had arrived in Burma after Independence. As I have said earlier, those foreigners who had settled in Burma at the time of independence have become a problem. We made these two laws to solve this problem. But we were not able to apply these laws strictly with the result that the problem of these people exists up to this day. The problem not only remains: because of this problem, these people are now living in panic because most of them have no definite status.

If we could do something definite to define their rights, they would be happy. We on our part must also be magnanimous. These people, the foreigners, had settled down here since after 1824, 1830, 1835, 1840, and had been here for more than 100 years. Their descendants retained their own nationality and were not Burmese citizens before Independence. After Independence, some left. Those who remained behind did not know what nationality they were. If we choose not to be magnanimous to them, if we consider that we have nothing to do with them, and that they have come here of their own accord and if we are to

deal with them accordingly, they would be in great trouble
with nowhere to go because they have lost contact with
their native places. We are here talking about the remote
past, about foreign settlers who had come in the aftermath
of the first Anglo-Burmese war.

And then we have those persons who came before
1948 Independence or before 1942, the year the war broke
out. We therefore decided to make the latest Citizenship
Law to solve all these problems together.

We are, in reality, not in a position to drive away all
those people who had come at different times for different
reasons from different lands. We must have sympathy on
those who had been here for such a long time and give them
peace of mind. We have therefore designated them eh-
naingngan-tha (associate citizens) in this law. Why have we
given them this name? Because, we were all citizens in the
beginning; then these people came as guests and eventually
could not go back and have decided to go on living here for
the rest of their lives.

Such being their predicament, we accept them as
citizens, say. But leniency on humanitarian ground cannot
be such as to endanger ourselves. We can leniently give
them the right to live in this country and to carry on a
livelihood in the legitimate way. But we will have to leave
them out in matters involving the affairs of the country and
the destiny of the State. This is not because we hate them. If
we were to allow them to get into positions where they can
decide the destiny of the State and if they were to betray us
we would be in trouble.

I will tell you an instance. Now let us use the term
eh-naing-ngan-tha from now on. After the country gained
independence, some of these *eh-naing-ngan-tha* left this
country again, leaving behind some of their family
members. Some of them -*kalas* to be frank- did not go back
to their *kala-pyi* but went to Singapore, Hong-Kong or
America. Some *tayokes* did not return to *tayoke-pyi* but
went to Singapore, Hong-Kong, Australia, and America.
They left behind a relative, say a brother, here. This brother
would contact his brother in Hong-Kong and his brother in

England and would smuggle goods out of our country. We have actually seen such smugglings. We are aware of their penchant for making money by all means and knowing this, how could we trust them in our organizations that decide the destiny of our country? We will therefore not give them full citizenship and full rights. Nevertheless, we will extend them rights to a certain extent. We will give them the right to earn according to their work and live a decent life. No more.

I have recounted the past. Now I shall speak on the present Burmese Citizenship Law. Beginning now, up to a certain point in the future, there will be three classes of citizens. Racially, only pure-blooded nationals will be called citizens. As for those foreign settlers who came here before Independence and who could not go back and who have applied for citizenship under the two law mentioned before, we will scrutinise their applications and will grant them *eh-naing-ngan-tha* if all conditions are satisfied. For those who have not applied for citizenship out of ignorance, we will tell them to apply for citizenship and consider them as *naingngan-tha-pyu-khwint-ya-thu* (naturalized citizens) if all conditions are met. Citizenship will this be granted in three categories (i) citizens; (ii) *eh-naing-ngantha;* (iii) *naing-ngan-tha-pyu-khwint-ya-thu.* Who are the *eh-naing-ngan-tha*? They are those who arrived in Burma before Independence and satisfy all conditions laid down in those two laws and who already applied for citizenship. They are *eh-naing-ngan-tha.* What is the difference between *eh-naing-ngan-tha* and *naingngan-tha-pyu-khwint-ya-thu*? Both came here in similar circumstances –before Independence, January 1948. The difference lies in whether they applied for citizenship or not. Those who have not yet applied for citizenship are, let us say, a bigger problem. Therefore, we have made a distinction between *eh-naing-ngan-tha* and *naing-ngan-tha-pyu-khwint-ya-thu.*

According to the Union Citizenship (Election) Act, 1948, a person with Burmese blood who failed to make certain declarations and renouncements when he or she comes of age loses his or her citizenship. Under our present law, not only those persons both of whose parents are nationals but also those persons only one of whose parents is a national automatically becomes a citizen on coming of age, without having to make declarations or renouncements.

There are three types of citizens at present as said earlier. There will be only one type in our country at some time in the future; that is there will be only citizens. What is known *eh-naing-ngan-tha* and *naing-ngantha-pyu-khwint-ya-thu* will gradually disappear. How? A person classified as an *eh-naing-ngan-tha* at present if qualifications, I said earlier, are met. We cannot trust them fully. That is why one is called *eh-naing-ngan-tha.*

If the descendants of *eh-naing-ngan-tha* continue to be regarded as *eh-naing-ngantha,* they will never be in a position to enjoy the rights of citizens. I said earlier, that in view of what is happening at present, this *eh-naing-ngan-tha* is not trustworthy at present. As I said earlier one lives in Burma, one in Hong-Kong, and one lives in England and are engaged in bad business. However, this blood relation will more or less cease to exist at the time of his or her grandchildren. When the grandchild is given citizenship, he will, just like any other citizen, become a full citizen. Similarly, with the children, grandchildren and great-grandchildren of a *naing-ngan-tha-pyukhwint-ya-thu* continue to be a *naing-ngantha-pyu-khwint-ya-thu?* Will a *naing-ngantha-pyu-khwint-ya-thu* not be able to enjoy full rights? As I said earlier, his grandchildren will be given citizenship. Although there are three types of citizens at present -*eh-naing-ngan-tha, naingngan-tha-pyu-khwint-ya-thu* and pure citizens, the grand children of *eh-naingngan-tha* and *naing-ngan-tha-pyu-khwintya-thu* will become full citizens. Then there will be only one type of citizen.

If the grandchildren of *eh-naing-ngan-tha* or a *naing-ngan-tha-pyu-khwint-ya-thu* are to become full citizens, the *eh-naing-ngantha* or *naing-ngan-tha-pyu-khwint-ya-thu* himself or herself, and his or her children and their children must live in our country correctly and must not misbehave. Only then can his or her grandchildren become citizens. As to action to be taken against them for misbehaviour, time limits, etc., are to be prescribed in Rules.

This is the first time we are taking action to enable those who have been in our country since before Independence to escape from a life of uncertainty about their own nationality. If necessary qualifications are met, they can live in our country; if they live correctly and properly, their grandchildren will become full citizens. What I would like to tell such persons is that, in recognition of what we have done to enable them to be certain of their own nationalities, they should live correctly and properly. I would also like to tell our true citizens, the Burmese, that they should not treat such persons arrogantly, saying they came from abroad or they are guests, but should realise that one day they will become one with us and all will be traveling in the same boat.

As everybody knows, this law was drafted in consultation with the whole country and a lot of time has been taken in drafting it. I do not know how many drafts were drawn up at the lower level. After it came to me, six more revisions had to be made because some terms and facts had been left out.

Even now I found one fact missing. I discovered that when I re-read it while writing this speech this morning. A clause about pure citizens. Citizenship is a person's birthright. Excepting for treason during war, nobody can strip him of citizenship. This is what this clause is about. However, there is also another clause which gives him responsibilities. There is one point left unmentioned in this Section. If this is not put in, it may create disputes later on. That is why I am saying this. What is to be added is "A citizen shall have no right to renounce his or her citizenship in time of war in which the country is involved". This is what is to be included in the law. There is such a clause in the part concerning *eh-naing-ngan-tha* and *naing-ngan-tha-pyu-khwint-ya-thu.* It was inadvertently left unmentioned in the Sections on pure citizens. We must therefore put it under Section 13 as Section 14. Section 13 says: "A citizen shall have no right to be a citizen of another country".

Section 14 should read: "A citizen shall have no right to renounce his or her citizenship in time of war in which the country is involved". This must be put in because in time of war a citizen not wanting to go to war may say he no longer wants to be a citizen. "

(Applause)

The address ends.

General Ne Win honestly and frankly expressed the Myanmar mind and heart. The Rakhine State violence in July 2012 and subsequent brutality against the Rohingya have clearly revealed that Myanmar people at large share Ne Win's sentiment. The silence of the Myanmar political parties and the icon of Burmese democracy and human rights freely infuses the poison of hatred in the ailing situation.

Exhibit-R11

The World demands for the repeal or amendment of the 1982 Citizenship Act

Myanmar: Abuses against Rohingya erode human rights progress ...
www.amnesty.org/.../myanmar-rohingya-abuses-show-human-rights-...
Jul 19, 2012 – Amnesty International is calling on **Myanmar's** Parliament to amend or repeal the **1982 Citizenship Law** to ensure that Rohingyas are no longer ...

INGOs Call for **Repeal** of **Burma's Citizenship Law** | The Irrawaddy ...
www.irrawaddy.org/archives/8664
Jul 9, 2012 – The INGOs said the 1982 **law**, which was issued during the reign of ....
parties in **Burma** to support the **repeal** of the 1982 **Citizenship Law**, and ...

UNPO: Chin: A Call To **Repeal Burma's Citizenship Law**
www.unpo.org/article/14540
Jul 10, 2012 – Chin: A Call To **Repeal Burma's Citizenship Law**. A coalition of international NGOs stated that the current **Citizenship Law** issued in 1982 is not ...

Today, the world is all connected. Myanmar cannot be isolated. Injustice in a place means injustice everywhere. The demand for the repeal or amendment of the 1982 citizenship act is loud and clear on this planet (Exhibit-R11).

U Shwe Maung aka Abdur Razak, the Member of the Parliament, Lower Chamber (Pyithu Hluttaw) from the Buthidaung Constituency, submitted a proposal to amend the

1982 Citizenship Act with a good reason that it is not in harmony with the 21st century. He presented his proposal on the 25th day July 2012, at the First Pyithu Hkuttaw, 4th Regular Session, 14th day[32]. (Exhibit-R12 and -R12A).

Hluttaw Chair
Thura U Shwe Mann

Exhibit-R12

U Shwe Maung on 1982 citizenship act
July 25, 2012
First Pyithu Hkuttaw, 4th Regular
Session, 14th day.

http://www.youtube.com/watch?v=A6lgmc98TQg

U Shwe Maung

ဘူးသီးတောင်မဲဆန္ဒနယ်မှ ဦးရွှေမောင်(ခ)ဦးအဒူရော့ဇက်က ဆွေးနွေးရာတွင် ယနေ့အချိန်သည် နိုင်ငံတော်ဖွဲ့စည်းပုံအခြေခံဥပဒေ(၂၀၀၈)ခုနှစ်ဖြင့် ခေတ်မီဖွံ့ဖြိုး တိုးတက်သော ဒီမိုကရေစီနိုင်ငံတော်သစ်ကြီးဆီသို့ ချီတက်နေသောအချိန်ဖြစ်ပါ ကြောင်း၊ လွှတ်တော်၌ ခေတ်နှင့်လိုက်လျောညီထွေမဖြစ်တော့သည့် ဒီမိုကရေစီ နိုင်ငံတော်သစ်တည်ဆောက်ရေးတွင် အဟန့်အတားဖြစ်စေသည့် ဥပဒေများကို ပြည့်စွက်ခြင်း၊ ပြင်ဆင်ခြင်း၊ ဖျက်သိမ်းခြင်း၊ နိုင်ငံတော်နှင့် ပြည်သူများအတွက် အကျိုးရှိသော ဥပဒေသစ်များပြဋ္ဌာန်းခြင်းလုပ်ငန်းများကို အရှိန်အဟုန်ဖြင့်ပြုလုပ်နေပါ ကြောင်း၊ ဥပဒေများပြဋ္ဌာန်းရာတွင် နိုင်ငံတော်အာဏာ၏ မူလပိုင်ရှင်များဖြစ်သော

Myanma Alinn July 26, 2012, p6

---

[32] See Myanma Alinn July 26, 2012, p6 and listen to
http://www.youtube.com/watch?v=A6lgmc98TQg

Hluttaw Chair
Thura U Shwe Mann

Exhibit-R12A

U Shwe Maung on 1982 citizenship act
July 25, 2012
First Pyithu Hkuttaw, 4th Regular
Session, 14th day.

http://www.youtube.com/watch?v=J9lDcG2u7QA

8:21 / 8:41

MP U Shwe Maung Explained on Amendment 1982 Citizenship Law

Rohingya Blogger 56 videos   7,056

Subscribe 321   19   0

The following is the Myanmar transcript I noted down from the
video. See the text for the English transaltion.

သို့ဖြစ်ပါ၍ တိုင်းရင်းသားလူမျိုးများ၏ အခြေခံအခွင့်အရေး
မဆုံးရှုံးစေရန်အတွက်၊ ၁၉၈၂-ခုနှစ် မြန်မာနိုင်ငံသား ဥပဒေကို၊ ခေတ်သစ်–
စနစ်သစ်နှင့်လိုက်လျော ညီထွေဖြစ်အောင် ယုတ္တိရှိအောင်၊ လူ့အခွင့်အရေး
စံချိန်စံချက်များနှင့် ကိုက်ညီအောင် ပြင်ဆင်ပြီး၊ ကွတ်ကိုင် မဲဆန္ဒနယ်ပြည်သူ့
လွှတ်တော် ကိုယ်စားလှယ် ဦးတီခွန်မြတ် အဆိုတင်သွင်းခဲ့သည့်အတိုင်း၊
တိုင်းရင်းသားလူမျိုးများ၏ အခွင့်အရေးကာကွယ်စောင့်ရှောက်သည့်
ဥပဒေတရပ်ပြဋ္ဌာန်းပေးသင့်ပါကြောင်း၊ ဒီလွှတ်တော်သို့ အလေးအနက်ထား
အကြံပြုတင်ပြအပ်ပါသည်ခင်ဗျား။

On July 19, 2013, I noted down his words in Myanmar
transcript from the video at-
http://www.youtube.com/watch?v=J9lDcG2u7QA, - and
presented in the Exhibit-R12A. English translation of U Shwe
Maung's speech is given below.

"... in order to safeguard the rights of the national people, it
is clear that 1982 Myanmar Citizenship Act must be weighed with
new age and new system and amended to bring it in line with the

norms of human rights, and, accordingly, in support of Kutkai Pyithu Hluttaw Representative U Ti Khun Myat's proposal, I would like to sincerely urge this [Pyithu] Hluttaw to formulate and adopt a law that protects the rights of the national people."

U Shwe Maung was discussing in response to U Ti Khun Myat's proposal at the Pyithu Hluttaw that there must be laws to enforce and protect national people's rights. Also see the commentary report on this matter at http://karennews.org/2012/07/mp-proposes-laws-to-enforce-and-protect-ethnic-rights.html/. The armed groups the Karen National Union (KNU) and New Mon State Party (NMSP), which have entered ceasefire and peace accord, are in support of this proposal.

Also, on the day of 6th November, 2012, in the Amyotha Hluttaw (Upper House), Sagaing Region Constituency 7 Representative U Tin Mya moved a motion for the repeal of 1982 Burma Citizenship Law, known as the Pyithu Hluttaw Law No. 4 of 1982 (Exhibit-R13).[33]

The motion was discussed by –
1. U Mann Kan Nyunt (Kayin State Constituency 2),
2. U Khin Maung aka U Aung Kyaw U (Rakhine State Constituency 3),
3. U Maung Aye (Rakhine State Constituency 9),
4. U Kyaw Kyaw (Rakhine State Constituency 2),
5. Dr. Banya Aung (Mon State Constituency 7),
6. U Khin Maung Latt (Rakhine State Constituency 6),
7. U Tin Ohn (Rakhine State Constituency 10), and
8. U Sai Bao Nat (Shan State Constituency 12).

The discussion was concluded by the Union Minister U Khin Yi, the Ministry of Immigration and Manpower, who emphasized the need to pinpoint the weak points of the law in need of amendment or if a brand new law has to be formulated it will need time as it has to be done as per rules, regulations, and procedures of the parliament.[34]

---

[33] See Myanma Alinn November 7, 2012, p7 at http://www.myanmar.com.
[34] Myanma Alinn November 07, 2012, p7, www.myanmar.com

Exhibit-R13
A motion to repeal
the 1982 Burma Citizenship Law at the
Amyotha Hluttaw, November, 06, 2012

ဗုဒ္ဓဟူး၊ နိုဝင်ဘာ ၇၊ ၂၀၁၂

၁၉၈၂ ခုနှစ် မြန်မာနိုင်ငံသားဥပဒေ ပည့်သည့်အခန်း၊ ပည့်သည့်ပုဒ်မသည်
အားနည်းနေသောကြောင့် ပြင်ဆင်ရန် လိုအပ်ကြောင်းကို တိကျစွာအတည်ပြု ထောက်ပြပေးသင့်

နေပြည်တော် နိုဝင်ဘာ ၆

ပထမအကြိမ် အမျိုးသားလွှတ်တော်
ပဉ္စမပုံမှန်အစည်းအဝေး နဝမနေ့ကိုယနေ့
နံနက် ၁၀ နာရီတွင် နေပြည်တော်ရှိ
လွှတ်တော်အဆောက်အအုံ အမျိုးသား
လွှတ်တော်ခန်းမ၌ကျင်းပရာ အမျိုးသား
လွှတ်တော်ဥက္ကဋ္ဌ ဦးခင်အောင်မြင့် အပါ
အဝင် အမျိုးသားလွှတ်တော် ကိုယ်စား
လှယ် (၁၉၃) ဦးတို့ တက်ရောက်ကြသည်။

In the Amyotha Hluttaw (Upper House), Sagaing Region Constituency 7 Representative U Tin Mya moved the motion for the repeal of the 1982 Burma Citizenship Law, on November 06, 2012.

ဆက်လက်၍ စစ်ကိုင်းတိုင်းဒေသ
ကြီး မဲဆန္ဒနယ်အမှတ်(၇)မှ ဦးတင်မြ
တင်သွင်းထားသည့် မြန်မာနိုင်ငံသား
ဥပဒေကို အသစ်ရေးဆွဲပြဌာန်းပြီး လက်ရှိ
မြန်မာနိုင်ငံသားဥပဒေ (၁၉၈၂ ခုနှစ်၊
ပြည်သူ့လွှတ်တော် ဥပဒေအမှတ်-၄)အား
ပယ်ဖျက်သင့်ကြောင်း ပြည်ထောင်စု
အစိုးရအား တိုက်တွန်းကြောင်းအဆိုနှင့်
စပ်လျဉ်း၍ ကရင်ပြည်နယ်မဲဆန္ဒနယ်
အမှတ်(၂)မှ ဦးမန်းကံညွန့်၊ ရခိုင်ပြည်
နယ် မဲဆန္ဒနယ် အမှတ်(၃)မှ ဦးခင်မောင်
(ခ) ဦးအောင်ကျော်ဦး၊ ရခိုင်ပြည်နယ်
မဲဆန္ဒနယ် အမှတ်(၉)မှ ဦးမောင်အေး
ထွန်း၊ ရခိုင်ပြည်နယ် မဲဆန္ဒနယ်အမှတ်
(၂)မှ ဦးကျော်ကျော်၊ မွန်ပြည်နယ်
မဲဆန္ဒနယ် အမှတ်(၇)မှ ဒေါက်တာ
ဗညားအောင်မိုး၊ ရခိုင်ပြည်နယ် မဲဆန္ဒ
နယ် အမှတ်(၆)မှ ဦးခင်မောင်လတ်၊ရခိုင်
ပြည်နယ် မဲဆန္ဒနယ်အမှတ်(၁၀) မှ
ဦးအုန်းတင်နှင့် ရှမ်းပြည်နယ် မဲဆန္ဒနယ်
အမှတ်(၁၂)မှ ဦးဆိုင်ပေါင်းနပ်တို့က
ဆွေးနွေးကြသည်။

According to another piece of news at http://www.dvb.no/news/mp-hits-back-at-official-denial-of-rohingya/26571 U Shwe Maung firmly clarified that the Rohingya are the natives of Myanmar as follow.

"Shwe Maung cited historical research carried out prior to the British colonisation of Burma in 1824, which formally recognised some 30,000 "Rohingya" Muslims living in Arakan state. Both Burma's first president and prime minister, Sao Shwe Thaik and U Nu respectively, reportedly recognised the Rohingya as one of the country's "indigenous races". The group was later stripped of their citizenship by former military dictator Ne Win.

"During my recent visit to Sittwe I have seen a lot of families with birth certificates with the ethnic name Rohingya, but still [some are] denying [them]," he said, dismissing allegations that "Bengalis" are migrating into Arakan state."

I identify that the following facts constitute injustice.

(1) In long 66 years, from 1948 to 2014, those who are so-classified as the aliens have not been given a chance to challenge the alienation in a court, to apply for the citizenship, or to be represented by a lawyer.

(2) For long 66 years, those who are so-classified as the aliens are systematically deprived of education, healthcare, shelter, property ownership, rights to work, and rights to their culture.

(3) The provision that only the third generation of a so-classified alien has rights to apply for the full citizenship is very cruel and inhuman.[35]

(4) Those who are so-classified as the aliens are systematically dehumanized and brutally discriminated on account of their origin, skin color, race and faith.

(5) Those who are so-classified as the aliens are not allowed to present their case in the Hluttaw. In the case of Rohingya they have their representatives in Hluttaw. U Shwe Maung aka Abdur Razak, the Member of the Parliament, Lower Chamber (Pyithu Hluttaw) from the Buthidaung Constituency, is one of their representatives but he was and still is not allowed to present the case freely.

(6) Denial to recognize the identity of a person in the pretext of so-classified alien is a means of cultural genocide that

---

[35] I am deeply disgusted to see that the Myanmar Americans who became the "US Citizens" within 5 to 15 years of immigration support the Burma Citizenship Law 1982 and accompanied cruelty and human rights violations.

resulted in the 2012 Rakhine State pogrom.

(7) When the villages and homesteads of the so-called aliens are burnt down and they are forcefully concentrated in the regulated refugee camps, with restriction of healthcare and food supply, creating slow death, it becomes a crime against humanity.

(8) When terrorism is unleashed upon the so-classified aliens forcing them take perilous escape in small boats across the oceans to other countries it becomes an international concern but the international community fails to act on the principles of "Responsibility to Protect."[36] The international failure also constitutes injustice.

As long as the Citizenship Act of Burma 1982 is in place and the wrong is not righted Myanmar will be seen as a racist country.

PS. The Burmese as well as the people at large across the world put the blame on General Ne Win and the Burmese Armed Forces for all Burmese illness from the education, social security, and economy to politics. I disagree. The Burmese people and Burmese society are responsible for the action(s) of General Ne Win and the Burmese Armed Forces. Today, the responsibility of the people and the society is more demanding than pre-1988.

---

[36] See http://responsibilitytoprotect.org/Resolution%20RtoP(3).pdf (UNGA resolution no. A/RES/63/308) and
http://www.un.org/en/preventgenocide/adviser/responsibility.shtml

6
The Rohing-ya Linguistic Manifestation

It is a universal perception that the names and identities are not the factors that determine human rights and everybody has right to self-identification and self-determination. I cherish this universal perception. In light of this universal perception, it is not necessary to know the origin of a person's name or identity in order to determine the person's rights. Nevertheless, from knowing the origin of a name and identity we enrich the understanding of the culture and, hence, enhance   appreciation of our multicultural entwinement. In many cities and many countries, on the airplanes, trains, buses, launches, and in the social gatherings, I have told my stories–my culture, my life, my belief, my struggle, my failures, and my success. By doing so I gained understanding, friendship, and trust. By doing so I was able to change hostility to hospitality, and I was even allowed to proceed with my clandestine journey in a neighboring country during my guerrilla life in the late 1960s. In light of my own experience, this chapter is an attempt to enrich our multiculturalism and entwinement in view of building peace and harmony in the society.

There exists much information and confusion on the term and origin of the Rohingya as well as Rakkha (hence Rakhine). Many of the circulating interpretation and explanation of the term 'Rohingya' and 'Rakhine' are based on the religious and racial bias, on the top of the political manipulation. I, however, find that the Rakhine and the Rohingya are two sides of the same coin. It is as simple as that. Therefore, I have made this humble attempt to present the linguistic manifestation of the term 'Rohingya'.

I am confident that I have done adequate field research, meeting and talking the people in the ancient Rakkhapura, (Arakan or Myanmar Rakhine State), Chittagong Hill Tracts, Chittagong District, and also read the pros and cons of the Rohingya. I also visited Chittagong Ethnological Museum, Chittagong University Museum, Mainamati Museum, National Museum at Dhaka, and Varendra Museum at Rajshahi University. I have explored along such rivers as Karnaphuli (Nar-daung-ja-Mrite, the river where the ear ornament fell, in Rakhine language), Naaf (Nat-Mrite; river of heavenly person), Mayu (river of Mayu[37] mountain), Kissapanadi (river of trades), Laymro (river of four cities), Irrawaddy (Ravi, Raavi Iravati, Airavati),[38] Chindwin (river of Chin Hills). During my tenure at Magwe College (now Magway University), as a junior faculty (1968-71), I explored Vishnu (Beikthano), Taungdwingyi, Shinmadaung, Pagan, Natmauk (the birth place of Aung San), and many villages and towns in the rolling plains of Central Burma. I have been to Mizoram, Meghalaya, and West Bengal. I performed the 'walkabout' pretty good simply because I wanted be a 'naturalist'. There was no job for a 'naturalist' in Burma but my 'walkabout' with a curiosity of zoologist helped me get many friends in a large diversified area of India-Bangladesh-Myanmar region. I have lived with the people who simply call themselves 'Taung-tha', meaning people living on the mountain, or 'Chaung-tha', meaning people living along a creek in a mountain valley. They do not even know what tribe they belong to! Their villages are as small as 5 homesteads but never bigger than 30 homesteads, and the nearest village is *at least* a day walk (dawn to dusk) over a few mountain ridges. They do not use paper money but salt and dried fish are the major medium of exchange in their barter system. The salt and dried fish are the rare commodities and the value attached to them is considerably high. Please see the Exhibti-MR1 for area covered by my 'walkabout' and the homeland of the Rohingya. The Rohingya people live in the regions of the Karnaphuli, Naaf, and Mayu Rivers.

I have given good account of the Rohingya in my previous book – *The Price of Silence,*[39] and in an open letter to Dr. Dipu Moni, Bangladesh Foreign Minister[40] in 2009 (see Appendix-1). This presentation supplements to my earlier ones. Based on my own experience I will try to present the key points here.

---

[37] Also written Mayu, in literal terms. Mayu is the Rakhaing colloquial pronunciation. Mt. Mayu is Mt. Meru of Hindu cosmology.

[38] http://en.wikipedia.org/wiki/Ravi_River

[39] Shwe Lu Maung, *The Price of Silence Muslim-Buddhist War of Bangladesh and Myanmar, A Social Darwinist's Analysis*, DewDrop Arts & Technology, USA, 2005.

[40] Shwe Lu Maung, *When Dr. Dipu Moni goes to Myanmar on May 15: Responsibility to Protect,* http://newsfrombangladesh.net/view.php?hidRecord=263475. For the full text see the Appendix-1.

Exhibit-MR1
Rohingya Home Land

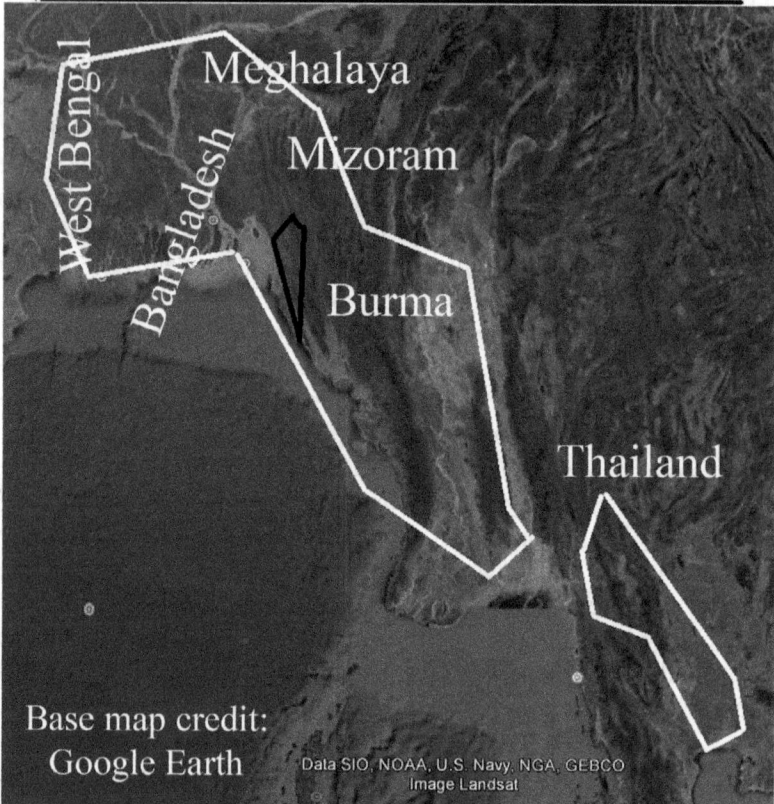

Base map credit:
Google Earth   Data SIO, NOAA, U.S. Navy, NGA, GEBCO
Image Landsat

1. The areas enclosed in the white borders indicate the areas of my 'walkabout'.
2. The area within the black borders is the area where the Rohingya people live.

How do people get their names?

Names are given by the parents and guardians.

Where do we get such names as Chinese, Indian, English, British, German, Zulu, Apache, Eskimo, Maori, American and etc.?

We, for sure, know that the Philipphines (or *Filipinas* in Spanish)) was named after the King Philip II of Spain in the 16th century.[41] But we do not know the origin of most names simply because history is too much controversial. For example, it is common teaching that America is named in honor of a 15th century explorer named Amerigo Vespucci. When I read an article of Johnathan Cohen[42] it appears that the name 'America' could be of Scandinavian origin but not Italian. It could also be originated from a native American tribe, Amerrique, of Nicaragua. It could also be of British origin "from the name of a Bristol-based Welshman, Richard Ameryk", as Johnathan Cohen described.

So?

Why bother to trace the origin of the names? It is simply waste of time! Not really, some people do earn doctoral degrees and become professors simply by studying the origin of the names. It is part of the human history.

What about Myanmar?

Some say it comes from Chinese "Mien" and some say it is a derivative of "Brahma". One school of scholars says it derives from the Bangladeshi Tribe called Mrama, which is pronounced ma-ra-ma. Nobody knows for sure.

What about the Rakhine who appear to be determined to wipe out the Rohingya in a Nazi-style? Where do they get their name "Rakhine" or "Rakhaing"?

We shall find out as we explore the nomenclature and geopolitics of the Rohingya.

The term Rohing-ya is a synonym of Rakhine-thar or Rakhaing-thar. The former is a Sanskrit derivative whereas the latter

---

[41] http://en.wikipedia.org/wiki/Name_of_the_Philippines

[42] Johnathan Cohen, *The naming of America: Fragments we've shored against ourselves*, http://www.uhmc.sunysb.edu/surgery/america.html, retrieved on 2/20/2013.

is Pali derivative. It is that simple. Why it is so complicated in reality then? It surely is all politics on the top of the linguistic glitch in the course of more than two thousand years. I shall deal with the politics later but let me deal first with the nomenclature. The nomenclature is complicated due to the local phonetic variation for the same word in the spoken languages in the course their long evolution from the ancient Sanskrit and Pali.

Let us begin with the description of Arakan[43] by Sir Arthur Purves Phayre (1812-1885). Captain Arthur Purves Phayre was made the Commissioner of Arakan and Tanessarim in 1826. The British became the master of these territories under the Rantabo[44] Treaty, which ended the First Anglo-Burman War (1824-1826). The sovereign Kingdom of Arakan was earlier annexed by the Burmese king in 1784. When the Second Anglo-Burma War (1852) ended, lower Burma also came under Phayre's administration. He, then a colonel, was appointed as the British Envoy to the Burmese court in 1855, when the diplomatic relationship was established between the crowns of Great Britain and Burma. With his office at Pegu Colonel Arthur P. Phayre was the first British Ambassador to Burma. In 1862, Arakan, Tanessarim, and Lower Burma were brought under a single administrative unit, known as the Burma Province of British India. In the same year, Arthur P. Phayre was knighted and appointed as the Chief Commissioner of Burma to rule the new province of British Empire. His tenure ended in 1867. He also served as the Governor of Mauritius from 1874-1879. In 1883, he published his book *History of Burma* in the name of Lieut.-General Sir Arthur P. Phayre, G.C.M.G., K.C.S.I., and C.B. In 1885, the year of the Third Anglo-Burma War, he died in Great Britain.

As the administrator of Arakan and Burma, Arthur Phayre utilized his offices very well learning much about the country. His book *History of Burma*, Trübner & Co., London, 1883, is the first history book of Burma in English. It is a 311-page hard cover book, 5 1/2 x 8 inch in size. He also gave a 12x15 inch map of the Burmese Empire. In his preface he mentioned that he used the Burmese

---

[43] Sir Arthur P. Phayre, *History of Burma*, London: Trübner & Co., 1883, p41.
[44] I believe Rantabo or Yandabo is Burmese version of French 'Rendezvous'. Now, it is village by Ayeyarwady river in Mandalay Region and famous for its pottery.

MahāRājāweng, a history of Arakan authored by a learned Arakanese Hsayā Maung Ni, and a history of Pegu in Mon Language by Hsayā dau Athwā. Arakan is described in the chapters V, IX, XVIII, and XX, making 54 pages. He described the Burmese conquest of Arakan in very detail. His writing is based on his long experience from 1826 to 1867 in Arakan and Burma as a soldier, diplomat and top administrator. Therefore, Sir Arthur P. Phayre's *History of Burma* will forever remain classic.

I notice that he is very much amused with the origin of Arakan; his pleasant and light description is given below.[45]

"The country known in Europe as Arakan extends for 350 miles along the eastern shore of the bay of Bengal. It is called by the natives Rakhaingpyi, or land of the Rakhaing. The same word in the Pali form, Yakkho, and also Raksha, is applied to beings, some good and some bad, who have their abode on Mount Meru, and are guards round the mansion of Sekra or Indra. It was given to the aborigines of Ceylon by their Buddhist conquerors.[1] The term appears to be applied by Indian Aryans to people of Dravidian and Mongolian race before conversion to Buddhism. Among the Arakanese of the present time, the word means a monster of the ogre sort, in the vernacular Bîlu, which, it has already been seen, is applied in the history of Pegu to the wild inhabitants of the country while still unconverted. The people of Arakan have not been ashamed to retain the name for themselves as dwellers in Rakhaing-land, but they claim to be by descent Mrâmmâ, and the elder branch of that family. They no doubt are descendants from ancestors belonging to Mongoloid tribes, closely akin to those from whom sprung- the Burmese of the Upper Irâwadi. Their language is the same, with a few dialectical differences, though the pronunciation . . ."

1. Emerson Tennent's Ceylon, vol. i. p. 331; Hardy's Manual of Buddhism, pp. 44, 47, 56.

[45] Sir Arthur P. Phayre, *History of Burma*, London: Trübner & Co., 1883, p41.

Please note the Phayre's description, "and also Raksha, . . . , who have their abode on Mount Meru . . ." It is a striking co-incidence that we have the Rohingya, which means the descendants of the Raksha, in the Mayu region, and Mayu is the Burmese corruption of Mount Meru. Let us see.

Exhibit-R14
Sanskrit derivative
Rakshak = defence or military
http://www.bharat-rakshak.com

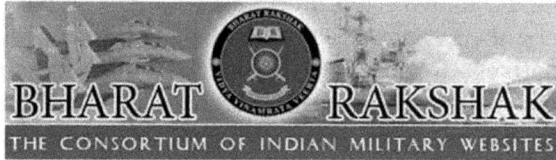

Exhibit-R15
Pali derivative
Rakkha = defence or military

Proti-Rakkha Montrinaloi

প্রতিরক্ষা মন্ত্রণালয়

গণপ্রজাতন্ত্রী বাংলাদেশ সরকার

Ministry of Defence

Government of the People's Republic of Bangladesh

http://www.mod.gov.bd/

Exhibit-R16
Pali derivative
Rakkhi = defense or military

considerably when Mujib formed the Jatiyo Rakkhi Bahini (National Defense Force), an elite parallel army intended to insulate the regime against military coups and other armed challenges to its authority. By 1975 the Jatiyo Rakkhi Bahini had swelled to an estimated 30,000 troops. Repatriates

http://www.photius.com/countries/bangladesh/national_security/bangladesh_national_security_postindependence_per~263.html

From Phayre's description I would like to pick up three words, (1) Yakkho, (2) Raksha, and (3) Bîlu. The three words are used to call the guards of Sekra or Indra who is the king of Seven Heavens in Buddhist belief. In other word, they mean soldiers. Now, please look at the Exhibits given in the coming pages. Alternatively, these words also refer to the cannibals, also see page 108 and Exhibit-R34A.

From the Exhibits 14, 15, and 16, it will be clear that Rakshak or Rakkha means defense or military. It can also be used to refer to a defense or military personal, or simply a soldier. Both words are of Indo-Aryan language having origin in Sanskrit and Pali. However, the words–Rakkhi, Rakkha, and Rakshak–are alien to Myanmar where the defence (defense) is called 'kar-kway-yay' (Exhibit-R17). In Myanmar literature and language these words are classified as "old usage" or "paurana". Myanmar literature has many words having lineage or direct descent from the Indo-Aryan languages like Sanskrit and Pali. Some examples that strike my mind without any thought-effort are given in the Exhibit-R18. Most of the 'paurana' words are used only in literature such as poems, songs, novels, and scientific and technical articles.

Exhibit-R17
In Myanmar 'defence' is called "karkwayyay

Constitution of the Republic of the Union of Myanmar (2008)	ြပည်ထာင်စုသမ္မတြမန်နိုင်ငံတော် ဖွဲ့.စည်းပုံအြခခံဥပဒေ (၂၀၀၈ ခုနှစ်)
Chapter V	အခန်း (၅)
Executive	အုပ်ချုပ်ေရး
The Union Government	ြပည်ထောင်စုအစိုးရအဖွဲ့.

Formation of the National Defence and Security Council

အမျိုးသားကာကွယ်ေရးနှင့်လုံြခုံေရးေကာင်စီ ဖွဲ့.စည်းြခင်း

National   → အမျိုးသား   → Amyothar
Defence   → ကာကွယ်ေရး → Kârkwáyyay
and   → နှင့်   → hnã
Security → လုံြခုံေရး → Lonchonyay
Council → ေကာင်စီ → Caúsi

Exhibit-R18
Myanmar words lineage
to such Indo-Aryan languages
as Bengali and Hindi

English	Myanmar	Bengali	Hindi
Old	ေပါရဏ (paurana)*	পুরাতন (puratan)	पुराने (purani:)
River	နဒီ (nadi)	নদী (nodi)	नदी (nodi)
Gold	ေရွ (shwe)	স্বর্ণ (sona)	सोना (sona)
Name	နာမည် (narmyin)	নাম (narm)	नाम (narm)
Life	ဇိဝ (ziwa)	জীবন (jibon)	जीवन (jibon)
Star	တာရာ (tara)	তারা (tara)	सितारा (shitara)
Moon	စန္ဒာ (sanda)	চাঁদ (chand)	चांद (chand)
Country/ Province	ေဒသ (deytha) Pegu Deytha	(desh) দেশ বাংলাদেশ Bangladesh	(desh) देश उत्तर प्रदेश Uttar Pradesh

*Paurana is used only in the literature.
In modern Myanmar it is 'ahaun' (အေဟာင်း)

It is also a common knowledge that "Dharmo Rakshati Rakshita" or "Dhammo Rakkhati Rakkhita" is the very ancient phrase dating back to the days of Vedic Religion[46] (1500 to 500 BCE). The phrase is well-presented in Mahabharata 3:311, Yudhishthira said it to Yaksha[47,48] (Exhibit-R19).

[46] http://en.wikipedia.org/wiki/Historical_Vedic_religion

[47] *The Mahabharata of Krishna-Dwaipayana Vyasa* translated into English prose from the Sanskrit by Pratap Chandra Roy, C.I.E., Vol. III, Vana Parva, Section CCCXI, p677. Oriental Publishing Co., Calcutta, 1886. Digital version downloaded on April 24, 2013 from http://www.archive.org/details/mahabharataofkri03roypuoft.

[48] Sanskrit version is from http://www.samvitsamvad.com/additional_materials_main_files/Books/Yaksha-Prasna-Sanskrit-English.pdf

---

Exhibit-R19
Dharmo Rakshati Rakshita
from Mahabharata
See the text for the references

Sanskrit in Devanagari script
धर्म एव हतो हन्ति धर्मो रक्षति रक्षितः ।
Dharmo Rakshati Rakshita

Common translation:
"Dharma protects
those who protect Dharma"

Translation by Pratap Chandra Roy
"virtue cherisheth the cherisher"

The same phrase "Dharmo Rakshati Rakshita" is also presented in the Chapter 8, section 15 of the Laws of Manu[49] (Manu-smriti, Mānava-Dharmaśāstra, Exhibit-R20). Please note Dharmo is translated 'virtue' by Pratap Chandra Roy[50] in Mahabharata whereas 'justice' by George Bühler in the Laws of Manu.

---

[49] Sanskrit-English version is posted by api_user_11797_singamani at http://www.scribd.com/doc/7189037/Manu-Smriti-Sanskrit-Text-With-English-Translation. English translation is by George Bühler, *The Laws of Manu*, Sacred Books of the East, Volume 25, http://www.sacred-texts.com/hin/manu.htm

[50] Kisari Mohan Ganguli also translated 'Dharmo' into 'virtue'. http://www.sacred-texts.com/hin/m03/m03311.htm

---

Exhibit-R20
Dharmo Rakshati Rakshita
from the Laws of Manu (8:15)
See the text for the references

Sanskrit in Devanagari script

धर्म एव हतो हन्ति धर्मो रक्षति रक्षितः ।
तस्माद् धर्मो न हन्तव्यो मा नो धर्मो हतो वधीत् ॥ ८-१५

George Bühler's translation
8:15. 'Justice, being violated, destroys;
justice, being preserved, preserves:
therefore justice must not be violated,
lest violated justice destroy us.'

Online translation[51] of Sanskrit Rakshak into English gives the following results.

Rakshaka: Protector , amulet.
rakshakari: saviour of Jivas from Samsara.
rakshakaH: guard, protector

Similarly, online translation[52] of Pali Rakkha into English gives the following.

rakkhā: Protection

In the same website referred above, a search for Yakkho returned the following result.

yakkho: Name of certain superhuman beings. Some of the yakkhas are attendants on Vessavaṇa, who is called Yakkhādhipo, lord of yakkhas.

---

[51] at http://dictionary.tamilcube.com/sanskrit-dictionary.aspx
[52] http://dictionary.tamilcube.com/pali-dictionary.aspx

In light of the above discussion both words, "Rakhaingthar and Rohingya", would literally mean a soldier. Furthermore, the meaning of these words tallies with the legend of the people of Arakan, which, as per Tibeto-Burman chronicles, in ancient days was known as Rakkhapura or Rakhaingpyi. On the basis of these information I constructed the following chart to trace the evolution of the today vocabularies–Rohingya and Rakhine (Exhibit-R21).

Exhibit-R21
Evolution of Rohingya and Rakhinethar*

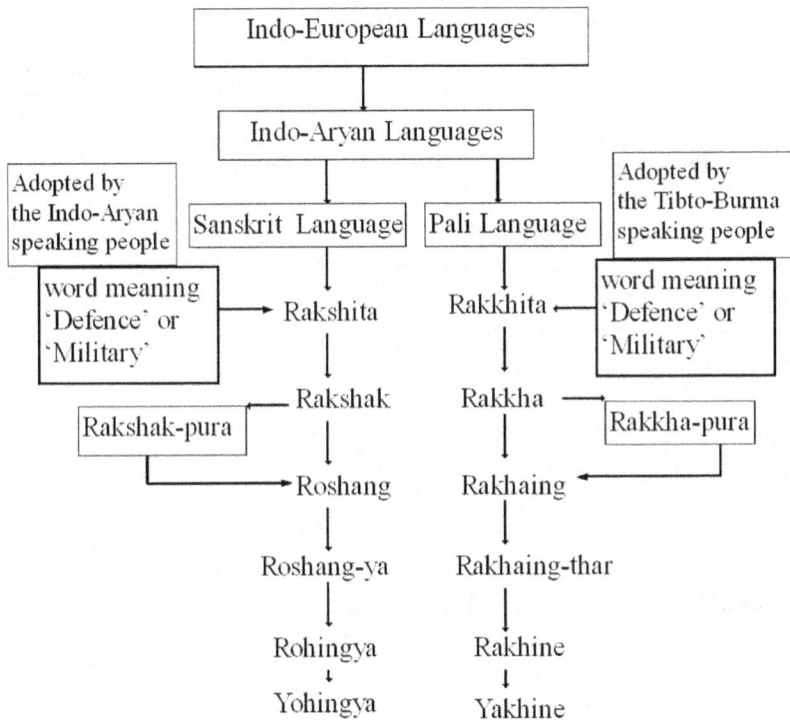

```
                    ┌─────────────────────────────┐
                    │   Indo-European Languages   │
                    └─────────────────────────────┘

                    ┌─────────────────────────────┐
                    │    Indo-Aryan Languages     │
                    └─────────────────────────────┘

┌──────────────┐                               ┌──────────────┐
│ Adopted by   │  ┌────────────┐ ┌───────────┐ │ Adopted by   │
│ the Indo-Aryan│ │  Sanskrit  │ │   Pali    │ │ the Tibto-Burma│
│ speaking people│ │  Language  │ │ Language  │ │ speaking people│
└──────────────┘  └────────────┘ └───────────┘ └──────────────┘

┌──────────────┐                               ┌──────────────┐
│ word meaning │                               │ word meaning │
│ 'Defence' or │ →  Rakshita    Rakkhita    ←  │ 'Defence' or │
│ 'Military'   │                               │ 'Military'   │
└──────────────┘                               └──────────────┘

                  ┌── Rakshak      Rakkha ──┐
┌──────────────┐  │                         │  ┌──────────────┐
│ Rakshak-pura │──┘                         └──│ Rakkha-pura  │
└──────────────┘ → Roshang      Rakhaing ←

                   Roshang-ya    Rakhaing-thar

                   Rohingya      Rakhine

                   Yohingya      Yakhine
```

Rohingya or Rakhinethar literally means a 'soldier'.

Rakkhapura probably was a military outpost of the Maurya Empire.

*Reference: Shwe Lu Maung. *The Price of Silence* (ISBN: 978-1-928840-03-9), 2005. p243-44.

We have to go back to the ancient days when the land now known as the Rakhine State was once called Rakkhapura. The Rakhine chronicles put the origin of Rakkhapura squarely at 2666 BCE;[53] that is 4680 BP[54] in 2014. Today, there exists no scientific archaeological evidence to accept this claim. The descendants of the Rakkhapura Kingdom are known as the Rakhine, Rakhaing, or Rakhaingthar. The terms 'Rohingya' and 'Rakhaingthar' are two sides of a coin; Rakhaing-thar or Rohing-ya refers to the people of Rakhaing in Tibeto-Burman version or Rohang in Indo-Aryan version. Again, Rohingya is the Burmese corruption of Rohang-ya[55].

The Myanmar word "thar" means "son". Therefore, Rakhine-thar is a son or child of a Rakhaing. Then, what does "ya" mean? Where does it come from?

The word "Ya" could have its origin at the Myanmar word "Yoya", which means tradition, culture, descendent, and family tree. If so, Rohing-ya refers to a person of having lineage to Rohang *aka* Rakhine. Let us start with a popular song, "Please come back to Silver Mountains" of Sai Saing Maw. There are three Shan people namely, Sai Khum Leik (composer), Sai Htee Sai (composer and singer), and Sai Saing Maw (composer and singer), who modernized Myanmar music in 1970s. In the Exhibit-R22, I present how the word "yoya" is used the lyric of Sai Saing Maw's song.[56]

(Note: The word Rakhine or Rakkhaing first appeared only in the 14th century literature. in an epic poem known as *Shin Nagainda Mawgwun.* In the Exhibit-R34, as described in the Chapter 7, p106).

---

[53] Before the Common Era.
[54] Before Present, that is present year 2014 plus 2666 equal to 4680.
[55] Please see the earlier topic "Rohingya Anthropology".
[56] http://www.youtube.com/watch?v=bc7jPJksJoI, last visited on March 17, 2013.

Exhibit-R22

"Come back to silver mountains",
a song by Sai Saing Maw,
explains the meaning of 'yoya'
http://www.youtube.com/watch?v=bc7jPJksJoI

With full of happiness

At our lovely Shan Hills

Things to love and to be loved

We have our traditions and culture

But why

you departed and left this land?

The meaning of "yoya" is explained in the Exhibit-R23.

Exhibit-R23: Yoya Meaning

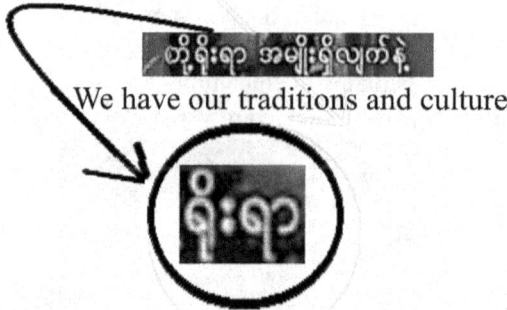

We have our traditions and culture

"Yoya" means tradition, customs, culture, descendent, and family tree.

"Yoya" means tradition, customs, culture, descendant, and family tree. It is written "Rora" but pronounced "Yoya", just like Rangoon is pronounced "Yangon". "Ya" in Rohing-ya might have a lineage to the word "Yoya". If so, Rohing-ya will mean a person having traditions and culture of (or descendants of the people of) Rohing, Roshang, Rohang, or Rakhaing, which are the linguistic variances of today official name Rakhine. (*cf*. Mârayo, explained by Sir Arthur Phayre, page 89 of this book).

As described above, *the land Rakkhapura means a defense or military village, camp or cantonment, and hence the Rakhaingthar means a soldier.* I believe that Rakkhapura or Military Village was first established as a military outpost of the Maurya Empire[57] (322 to 185 BCE, Exhibit-R24). It probably was upgraded to a Rajadom by a Maharaja for his son or a rebel prince made it into a kingdom at a later date.[58] *If I were to agree with the claim of the Rakhaing historians that Rakkhapura was*

---

[57] http://en.wikipedia.org/wiki/Maurya_Empire
[58] See Shwe Lu Maung, *The Price of Silence Muslim-Buddhist War of Bangladesh and Myanmar, A Social Darwinist's Analysis*, DewDrop Arts & Technology, USA, 2005, p 243.

founded in 3,000 BCE, some 5,000 years ago, then, Rakkhapura will mean a 'village of herders' because the people of Bengal still call the herders "Rakkha Chaylay." This will mean that we are referring to a Neolithic herding community.[59] Later, it is also possible that the Mauryan military outpost was established with the help of the herding and agricultural communities. If so, it is reasonable to believe that the word *Rakkha* evolves from its original meaning of *herding* or *guardian* to the modern meaning of *defense*. Please also see the Mauryan tributaries (the gray region, now within Myanmar) in the map of Exhibit-R24.

Exhibit-R24
Maurya Empire at its peak
Credit: Vastu at http://en.wikipedia. org/wiki/Maurya_Empire

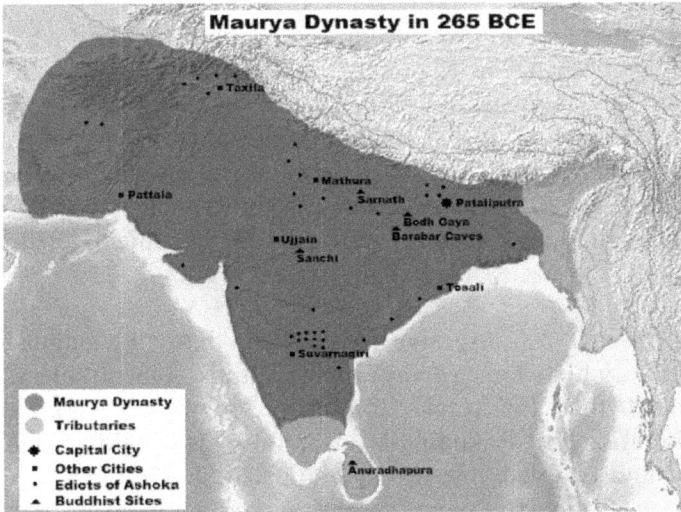

The Rakhaing chronicles claim that the first king of Rakkhapura Dhannyawady Dynasty was a Maghada descent named Marayu.[60] It is probable that Marayu is the corruption of

---

[59] For Neolithic Era general information please see http://en.wikipedia.org/wiki/Neolithic.
[60] Also see Sir Arthur P. Phayre, *History of Burma*, London: Trübner & Co., 1883,

Maurya. As I grew up in the Kyain Province, which is believed to be the power house of the ancient Rakkhapura, my parents and the local historians showed me a water reservoir and cave-pagoda, which were believed to have built by the Asoka The Great.[61] They also showed me the Crown Prince Palace, believed to have existed in the days of the LayMro as well as Mrauk U Dynasties. On the other hand it is also probable that there was a Neolithic settlement, which came to be known as Rakkhapura by the Indo-Aryan speaking people in the days of Vedic Culture.

One thing is sure and clear. The words, Rakkha, Rakshak, Rakshati, Rakshita, Rakkhapura, Rakshak, and Rakshakpura, are the vocabularies of Indo-Aryan languages, well documented in the epics of millennia-old Mahabharata, Ramayana, and in the Laws of Manu. In light of this linguistic history, it is affirmative that the ancient Rakkhapura was established by the Indo-Aryan speaking people.

There are only two groups of people, namely the Chakma, known as Thet inside Myanmar, and the Rohingya, who speak Indo-Aryan languages in the eastern territory of the ancient Rakkhapura, which is the Rakhine state of today Myanmar, and even in all Myanmar. Therefore, it is affirmative that the Rohingya, like the Chakmas, are the most ancient people of the Rakkapurean Land, which now is an occupied territory of Myanmar.

It may be obsessive to go deep into the language and phonetics, which are not my area of study. Nevertheless, I am convinced that the term 'Rohingya' simply is a product of transliteration of Rakhaingtha as illustrated below, and they existed and evolved side by side since the Neolithic Age, in the region of Ganga-Brahmaputra Basin and Himalayan Belt. The researchers[62] have concluded that "The technological and typological similarities and distribution of fossil wood

---

[61] Also see Shwe Lu Maung, *The Price of Silence: Muslim-Buddhist War of Bangladesh and Myanmar – A Social Darwinist's Analysis*, DewDrop Arts & Technology, USA, 2005, p 248
[62] See Manjurul Hassan and Syed Mohammad Kamrul Ahsan at
http://archive.today/3FMSh#selection-379.1-633.981

assemblages in considerable high frequency throughout the eastern and southeastern part of Bangladesh, Haora, and Khowai valley of Tripura, and Irrawaddy valley of Burma suggest a regional prehistoric cultural tradition in this region."

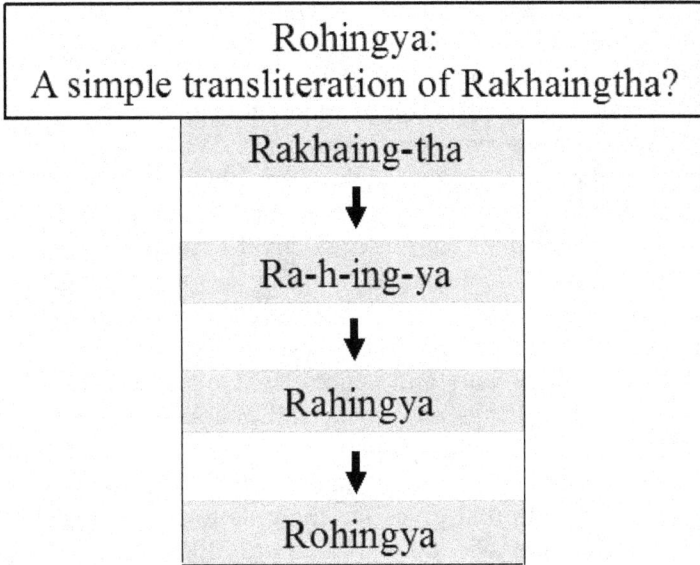

**Rohingya:
A simple transliteration of Rakhaingtha?**

Rakhaing-tha

↓

Ra-h-ing-ya

↓

Rahingya

↓

Rohingya

7
The Aborigines

Can we travel say 10,000 years back from the present? The time travel is more than philosophical and fiction. In light of the theories of *special relativity, general relativity,* and *quantum mechanics* time travel is scientifically possible.[63] Recently, a group of physicists at the University of Queensland, Australia, published a research paper that gives strong support to the theory of quantum time travel.[64] If we can get hold of Dr. Who's time traveling machine[65] and make a journey back to say 10,000 BCE we will able to confirm I am right or wrong when I say the Rohingya are among the aboriginal peoples of the present Bengal-Myanmar region. I will in this chapter try to demonstrate that they are the aborigines; their land was conquered and they were enslaved again and again by the various groups of invaders in the last two thousand years. The history is filled with wars and genocides. One very visible factor, among many, that brings about war and genocide is what we call 'racism'. The Rohingya people are in the final stage of termination under the Myanmar racism. Very unexpectedly, it is the Myanmar racism that gives me the clue to the aboriginality of the Rohingya people who are 'dark and ugly like ogre.'

Racism is a very powerful belief and it has been practiced by every nation, and is still being practiced by some nations. Accordingly, 'racism' is a hot subject of study by numerous scholars. Some definitions of racism are given below prior to my time travel into the past.

Racism definition

     1. **racism,** *also called racialism, any action,*

---

[63] See for general information at
http://en.wikipedia.org/wiki/Quantum_mechanics_of_time_travel.

[64] Martin Ringbauer, Matthew A. Broome, Casey R. Myers, Andrew G. White, and Timothy C. Ralph, Experimental simulation of closed timelike curves,
http://www.nature.com/ncomms/2014/140619/ncomms5145/full/ncomms5145.html. Also see
http://www.science.uq.edu.au/index.html?page=212544

[65] See http://en.wikipedia.org/wiki/Doctor_Who for some general information.

*practice, or belief that reflects the racial worldview—the
ideology that humans are divided into separate and exclusive
biological entities called "races," that there is a causal link
between inherited physical traits and traits of personality,
intellect, morality, and other cultural behavioral features, and
that some races are innately superior to others.*
Source: http://www.britannica.com/EBchecked/topic/488187/racism

*2. A belief that race is the primary determinant of
human traits and capacities and that racial differences
produce an inherent superiority of a particular race.*
Source:
> http://www.merriam-webster.com/dictionary/racism?
> show=0&t=1369149510

A distinguished professor of clinical psychology, Jefferson
M. Fish, Ph.D. (http://jeffersonfish.com/) explained racism as follow.
"The word racism is now used in a variety of ways,
but substituting other words for each meaning and employing
it in a particular anthropological sense can clarify matters and
make for greater precision--like distinguishing lasagna from
spaghetti or macaroni... The German "Nuremberg Laws"
(1935) established a pseudo-scientific basis for racial
discrimination.

I would argue for a particular anthropological
definition, even though it may seem strange on first
view–racism is the belief that culture is inherited. That is, it is
a belief that groups of people behave in distinctive ways not
because they have learned to do so, but because their members
share some inherited essence (called "blood"; or sometimes
"genes"--but without reference to specific DNA sequences)."
Source: http://www.psychologytoday.com/blog/looking-in-the-
cultural-mirror/201101/how-should-racism-be-defined

Racism is a very big subject. Numerous scholars have
contributed for better understanding and overcoming of racism. The
article 'racism' at https://en.wikipedia.org/wiki/Racism is a good
starting point for the study. "The Myth of Race" (Argo-Navis, 2012,

ISBN-13: 978-0786754366) by Jefferson M. Fish, and "Encyclopedia of Race, Ethnicity and Society" (SAGE Publications, Inc, 2008, ISBN: 9781412926942) by Richard T Schaefer, Ph.D., a distinguished sociologist, http://www.schaefersociology.net/, are good books to read.

In our days we have seen severe racism in Germany (Nazism), the United States of America (Slavery and Segregation), and in South Africa (Apartheid). Today, the world is witnessing the rise of Myanmar Racism which is characterized by alienation, segregation, subordination, and negation, accompanied by destruction of the home and villages, establishment of concentration camps, planned deprivation of food and water, targeted birth control,[66] and above all organized killing.[67] I have warned the world with my book *The Price of Silence*, published in 2005.[68]

The world has responded racism with the Universal Declaration of Human Rights[69] but to no effect in real life.

Myanmar racism, which is a strong component of Myanmarism,[70] is not new. It has roots in its history. Here I will attempt to trace the Myanmar historical racism with the hope that we will find a way to overcome it. My discussion will be maneuvered around the Rohingya Muslims who are facing the danger of extermination with the pretext that they are Bengali Kala, illegal infiltrators. Bengali is an anthropological cultural and ethnic identity, which can be used in a racial context. Kala[71] is a corruption of *Kula*, which literal means 'international' or 'foreign', for example *Kula Thamaga* is Burmese for the United Nations.

---

[66] Paul Vrieze and Zarni Mann, Govt sets two-child limit for Rohingya in Northern Arakan, The Irrawaddy, Monday, May 20, 2013. http://www.irrawaddy.org/archives/35017. Accessed on May 24, 2013.

[67] For a comprehensive report see 'All you can do is pray', Human Rights Watch, ISBN: 978-1-62313-0053., 2013. http://www.hrw.org/.

[68] Shwe Lu Maung, *The Price of Silence: Muslim-Buddhist War of Bangladesh and Myanmar – A Social Darwinist's Analysis*, DewDrop Arts & Technology,USA, 2005.

[69] https://www.un.org/en/documents/udhr/

[70] For more information see Shwe Lu Maung, *The Price of Silence: Muslim-Buddhist War of Bangladesh and Myanmar – A Social Darwinist's Analysis*, DewDrop Arts & Technology,USA, 2005, Chapter 4 and 5.

[71] For more information see Shwe Lu Maung, *The Price of Silence: Muslim-Buddhist War of Bangladesh and Myanmar – A Social Darwinist's Analysis*, DewDrop Arts & Technology,USA, 2005, p 248

Myanmar people insist that the Rohingya does not exist in the history. It is true that the Rakhine (Arakanese) Muslims had never bothered to come up with their identity 'Rohingya' because Rohingya is nothing but a synonym of Rakhine-thar (as described in the previous section) and they had lived together for thousands of years, establishing kingdoms and empires;[72] there was no reason or necessity to identify separately. However, Myanmar racism revived at the independence of Myanmar in 1948 and they were discriminated and alienated in the context that they were *Kala*. Their assertion of their dormant Rohingya identity in independent post-1948 Myanmar is their struggle to escape from the modern slavery known as the *Kala*.[73] The word 'Kala' is a term equivalent to 'nigger' in America.

Discrimination against Kala was recorded in the Burmese chronicles from the days of Pagan King Kyansittha (r.1067-1085).[74] Sir Arhtur P. Phayre[75] described it as follow.

"The mother of Kyansittha was said to have been a daughter of the king of Vaisali in Tirhût. Not long after Kyansitthâ, came to the throne, there appeared at Pugân an Indian prince, who is styled in the Mahâ Râjâweng the son of the king of Palikkarâ.[76] The prince desired to marry the daughter of Kyansitthâ, but by the advice of the nobles this alliance was publicly disallowed, lest the country should become kulâ or foreign. But a strange story is told as the sequel of this adventure. The Indian prince from chagrin committed suicide. The daughter of Kyansitthâ, whom he had desired to marry, gave birth to a son, and notwithstanding the refusal to celebrate the proposed marriage, the king caused the child to be consecrated by the ceremony of *bithêka*, as if he were to be

---

[72] The Arakan Empire is a good example Rohingya-Rakhine unity.

[73] For more information see Shwe Lu Maung, *The Price of Silence: Muslim-Buddhist War of Bangladesh and Myanmar – A Social Darwinist's Analysis*, DewDrop Arts & Technology,USA, 2005., p250.

[74] Chronological time is from Sir Arthur P. Phayre, *History of Burma*, London: Trübner & Co., 1883,

[75] Sir Arthur P. Phayre, *History of Burma*, London: Trübner & Co., 1883, p38

[76] That is Pattikera.

forthwith acknowledged as king."

First some clarifications; Dr. Htin Aung[77] believes that Kyansittha was a son of Burmese Noble and a Patikkera princess; and *Palikkera* must be a typo of *Pattikera*[78] in the process of digitalization.

From the above description it appears that Kyansittha's daughter (Shwe Einthi) was married to a Pattikera Prince but could not be solemnized due to objection of the nobles. The Pattikera Prince was Kala in the eyes of the nobles. Neverthelss, Kyansittha crowned their son, Alaungsithu, with due coronation, making him *The King* right at his birth in order to overcome the oppositions and obstacles posed by the nobles. Kyansittha ruled the kingdom in the capacity of a 'regent.' This was also the reason why his son Raza Kumar, whose mother was Sambul, did not become a king. Kyansittha did not know that he had a son with his wife Sambul (Thambula) of Mrama tribe. When Sambul brought his son, Raza Kumar, to him it was too late. We were taught that Kyansittha upon

Exhibit-R25
Kyansittha's words that become a proverb

သား:ကား:အချစ်

မြေး:ကား:အနှစ်

The son is the beloved but the grandson is the essence

seeing his son, Raza Kumar, who was then 7-year old, uttered, "The son is the beloved but the grandson is the essence." He then showered Raza Kumar with all love and honor in order to overcome his guilty conscience of being unjust to his son. I will come back to this story in the later part of this chapter again. Kyansittha's words became a popular Burmese proverb that highlights people's favoritism given to their grandchild (Exhibit-R25).

Let us note this. As per Burmese chronicles the first

---

[77] Maung Htin Aung, *A History of Burma*, Columbia University Press, 1967, page 40. I believe that it was a Pattikera Princess. Pattikera is a pre-Bengal Kingdom, now near Comilla of Bangladesh.
[78] Pattikera is a pre-Bengal Kingdom, now near Comilla of Bangladesh.

opposition to Kala in Burmese palace was recorded with King Kyansittha in 1085.[79] Let us remember. King Anawrahta and Kyansittha each had a queen who was a Pattikera Princess. Also King Alaungsithu had a Pattikera Princess as one of his queens. Burmese kings were allowed to have four queens because it follows the tradition of Thikyamin[80] (the *alias* are Magha and Indra), King of Six Heavens, who keeps four wives. Buddhist history says that Buddha destined his religion to last only 2,500 years. Upon that Thikyamin (which literally means king of all-knowing-all-seeing) requested Buddha to make it 5,000 years and he would look after the second 2,500 years. The first 2,500[th] year was observed and celebrated in 1956 in Myanmar.[81] In the interest of the Buddhist's view of other religions it is worthwhile to mention here that many Buddhists consider the post-Buddha religions like Christianity and Islam are of Thikya Religion,[82] meaning these religions are sponsored by Thikyamin (King of Heaven).

Another Burmese-Kala tragedy occurred in the days of Alaungsithu's son Narathu (r.1160-64). Narathu killed his father, Alaungsithu, and his elder *half* brother Meng Shengsao, the rightful heir, and took the throne. He also killed many of followers of his father and brother, according to Phayre.[83] Phayre also wrote, "the most notorious of this king's crimes was the murder of his father's widow, the daughter of the king of Palikkara (Pattikera), whom he slew with his own hand." But other records[84] say that Narathu killed his own queen who was a Pattikera Princess. It is possible that he killed both. The vengeful king of Pattikera sent eight assassins who came in disguise as Brahmins to bless King Narathu. One after another, each of them blessed him and, at the same time, stabbed him to death with the hidden dagger; then they all committed suicide. Narathu was dubbed *Kala-kya-min* or *Kala-dethroned-king* by the historians.

---

[79] Chronological time is from Sir Arthur P. Phayre, *History of Burma*, London: Trübner & Co., 1883.

[80] သိကြားမင်း

[81] In City of Minbya where I grew up the city built a 2500Y Pagoda at Kyain Hill in 1956. My father was a member of Gaupaga (Governing) Committee of the Pagoda.

[82] Thikya-thathana (သိကြား သာသနာ) in Burmese.

[83] Sir Arthur P. Phayre, *History of Burma*, London: Trübner & Co., 1883, p40 and p49.

[84] For example http://en.wikipedia.org/wiki/Narathu

If we read the Burmese chronicles we can easily sense the Burmese hatred growing toward the Kala in that time frame. It is possible that the Burmese of Pagan had the feeling of Kala infiltration into their kingdom just like the way today Burmese are feeling with the presence of the Rohingya and Muslims. This tragedy occurred in 1164. Since then the Kala has been in Burmese psyche as an undesirable element. I, however, believe that pre-Bengal Buddhist Pattikera alliance with Burmese kings was a strategic move to face the advancing Muslims from Northern India but the Burmese did not understand it.

Burmese hatred toward Kala was again compounded when Sultan Jalaluddin Muhammad Shah of Gaur, then the capital of independent Bengal, helped the dethroned Rakhine King Mun Saw Mwan, with an army of 30,000 soldiers,[85] to restore his throne from the Burmese occupation.[86] Again, Burmese hatred toward Rakhine and kala possibly sky-rocketed in 1599 when the Rakhine King Raza Gri (r.1593-1612), who proudly adorned the Muslim title 'Salim Shah', invaded and destroyed the Second Myanmar Empire built by Bayinnaung. The army of Raza Gri's was manned by many Muslims in addition to Rakhines and Portuguese.[87] Then there was the Burmese genocide of Rakhine in 1784. Burmese occupied the Rakhine kingdom from 1784 until 1823. In 1824 the First Anglo-Burma War broke out and the Rakhine Land came under the British rule. The Rakhine oral traditions say that two third of Rakhine population was wiped out[88] during the 40-year (1784-1823) Burmese rule.[89] The Rakhine oral tradition is supported by the British records. The officers of East India Company, including Captain Arthur P. Phayre who later became Governor of British Arakan and Burma,

---

[85] Some scholars believe that the number was 50,000.

[86] For more information see Shwe Lu Maung, *The Price of Silence: Muslim-Buddhist War of Bangladesh and Myanmar – A Social Darwinist's Analysis*, DewDrop Arts & Technology,USA, 2005, p 208-209

[87] See Shwe Lu Maung, *The Price of Silence: Muslim-Buddhist War of Bangladesh and Myanmar – A Social Darwinist's Analysis*, DewDrop Arts & Technology,USA, 2005., p 137,139,209.

[88] For more information see Shwe Lu Maung, *The Price of Silence: Muslim-Buddhist War of Bangladesh and Myanmar – A Social Darwinist's Analysis*, DewDrop Arts & Technology, USA, 2005.

[89] Shwe Lu Maung, The Prisoner of Mandalay and Democracy-Part1, The Arakanese Student and Youth Movements, Arakanpost, Issue 8, May 2005, http://shwelumaung.org/publications/series7.pdf

witnessed the Burmese occupation in 1784.[90] The reports of the British officers render strong support to the Rakhine oral history. I learned the 1784 event from my grandparents whose ancestors played major roles in the war.[91]

I am giving here two excerpts from Bertie Reginald Pearn's article *King-Bering*. These two pieces of excerpt give vital information of the events from 1784 onwards during the Burmese occupation of Arakan. The article was from the Google book site, I accessed the article on May 23, 2013.

Excerpt-1 from B.R. Pearn's King-Bering[92]

"By the year 1798, two-thirds of the inhabitants of Arakan were said to have deserted their native land. In one year, 1798, a body of not less than ten thousand entered Chittagong, followed soon after many more; and while their compatriots who had been longer settled there endeavoured to assist them, they were nevertheless reduced to a condition of direst poverty, many having nothing to eat but reptiles and leaves."[12] (12. Malcolm, I. p. 550-1)

Excerpt-2 from B.R. Pearn's King-Bering[92]

"Cox, who arrived in Chittagong in July, 1799, reported that twenty or thirty thousand Arakanese had entered Chittagong in previous twelve months, and that including those who had previously settled there were all told forty or fifty thousand. The distress among the recent arrivals was appalling, and he estimated the mortality among the children alone at twenty a day. The fugitives are described as "flying through wilds and deserts without any preconcerted plan numbers perishing from

---

[90] Please also note that Arakan was an independent kingdom in 1776 when the United States of America declared independence.

[91] See Shwe Lu Maung, *The Price of Silence: Muslim-Buddhist War of Bangladesh and Myanmar – A Social Darwinist's Analysis*, DewDrop Arts & Technology, USA, 2005, p 173-75.

[92] B.R. Pearn. *King-Bering*, Jour. Burma Research Soc., Vol. XXIII (II), 1933, p445. Online source, Google book site, is given in the text.

want, sickness and fatigue. The road to the Naaf river (which forms the boundary between Arracan and Chittagong) was strewed .... With the bodies of the aged and decrepit, and of mothers with infants at the breast."[13] Cox settled about ten thousand in the large areas of waste land in Chittagong, but many had already dispersed more widely among the hills and jungles. The chief settlement was made at the place which derived from its founder the name of Cox's Bazaar."
(13. Malcolm, I. p. 550-1)

The reader may compare present Rohingya refugee crisis with that of 1784 horrific episode. The racial strife in Myanmar became hidden as the Burmese king faced the threat of the British occupation, which finalized in 1885. The First Anglo-Burma War, 1824-1826, brought Arakan and Tanessarim (Tanintharyi) under the British rule; the Second Anglo-Burman War in 1852 put Lower Burma (Irrawaddy Delta up to Pegu) into the hands of British; and the British made the final blow in 1885 seizing Burmese King Thibaw and entire Burma. The British occupation brought about the unity of the Burmese people, regardless of race or religion for the first time in the history.[93] As soon as the British left and the Burmese got an upper hand with the advent of Japanese occupation in 1941, the Burmese rose under the leadership of Burma Independence Army (BIA). The Burman massacred the Karens in Irrawaddy delta that played a major role in the birth of Karen rebellion in 1948. Similarly, Burman-Muslim riot took place in delta. The Muslims retreated into Arakan where severe Rakhine-Muslim riot broke out, pushing the Muslims to Buthitaung and Maungdaw area at Burma-India border. The riot contributed hatred in the emergence of Mujahid rebellion in 1955 in the border area.

Myanmar oppression against the Muslims and Rohingya with the hate-accusation of foreign origin has been going on nonstop. The expulsions of the Rohingya in 1978 and 1991-92 into Bangladesh, and the Burma Citizenship Act 1982 are well designed campaigns of extermination. Now, beginning in 2012, there again explodes the Rakhine-Muslim and Burma-Muslim bloodshed. This prompted me to dig Myanmar history again in search of the origin of

---

[93] See Shwe Lu Maung, *Burma Nationalism and Ideology*, University Press Ltd., Dhaka, 1989, Chapter 2.

hatred based on skin color.

One of the astounding evidences of the Myanmar (Narathurian)[94] hatred of Kala based on skin color and religion came very unexpectedly from a Myanmar diplomat,[95] Consulate-General Ye Myint Aung, at Hong Kong in 2009. According to a piece of news by Greg Torode published in the South China Morning Post[96] the diplomat Ye Myint Aung sent a letter to the heads of the foreign missions in Hong Kong telling them that the Rohingya are 'dark in color' and 'ugly as ogres'.[97] What Ye Myint Aung said is not much of academic value but it carries a common racial value that the Myanmar people cherish. His expressions, 'dark in color' and 'ugly as ogres', are reference made by the Indo-Aryan and Myanmar Tibeto-Burman people to those they consider barbarians or savages, especially to the dark skinned people. Therefore, it is a racial slur.

I pick up the word 'ogres' because it carries a value of historical vintage. The ogres are known as Yakkha in Old Myanmar language.[98] Lt. General Sir Arthur P. Phayre, the Governor of Arakan and Burma, recorded in his famous book[99] that the Myanmar Rakhine are the descendants of Rakkha or Yakkha or Ogres. When Ye Myint Aung's words and Sir Arthur P. Phayre's description are linked together it creates virtual evidence that the Rohingya or Ogres (also see Exhibit-R26) of the Indo-Aryan linguistic group[100] are the original inhabitants of Arakan and Burma. In light of this the Indo-Aryan speaking Rohingya are the aboriginals and Tibeto-Burman speaking people are the later settlers or conquering invaders.

---

[94] I have mentioned above that King Narathu was the first person to kill his own queen with his own hands for account of her foreign origin, in 1164 CE.

[95] Myanmar diplomats are specially selected and reserved for those who have Mongolian skin color.

[96] http://www.scmp.com/article/669529/myanmese-envoy-says-rohingya-ugly-ogres

[97] Also see Alan Morison and Chutima Sidasathian, *More Rohingya Will Flee the New Apartheid*, Phuket Wan, 28/05/2012, http://www.unhcr.org/cgi-bin/texis/vtx/refdaily? pass=463ef21123&id=4fc45f135

[98] 'Old Myanmar language' known as Paurana or old language is mostly of Pali origin. Paurana is 'Puron' in Bengali language, meaning old.

[99] Sir Arthur P. Phayre, *History of Burma*, London: Trübner & Co., 1883, p41.

[100] There could also be the Dravidian and Austro-Asian language speakers.

Exhibit-R26
Myanmar Ogre is now
all over the world

http://phuketwan.com/tourism/burmas-unwanted-
rohingya-ogres-aiming-australia-18007/

PHUKET WAN Tourism News

PROPERTY ENTERTAINMENT JOBS PREMIUM ADS ABOUT US

Unwanted Burma 'Ogres' Now Aim for Australia

By Chutima Sidasathian and Alan Morison

Sunday, May 5, 2013

News Analysis

PHUKET: Australia is the new destination of choice for some captive boatpeople in Thailand after the surprise appearance this week of an adventurous young Rohingya refugee from Adelaide.

Mohammed Salim, who carries international travel documents and a UNHCR card, has flown from Australia to be reunited with his mother and three brothers at a Thai government family care centre north of Phuket.

| 58 |
| Tweet |

Why am I wasting time with the legends? The legends are considered 'alternative anthropology and history', for example Homer's *Iliad* and *Odyssey* as well as Indian *Mahabharata* and *Ramayana* serve as the counter references to the ancient history. I am dealing with these legends in Myanmar history in order to understand pre-history and ancient history of Myanmar civilizations. Many tribes and many people have disappeared not only in Myanmar but all over the world. The land known as Myanmar today was inhabited by a totally different population of different cultures and languages at different times. Around and after the 12th century there were drastic and dramatic changes in demography, culture, language and people, not only in Myanmar but also in South and Southeast Asia. Today Myanmar is a representative of post-12th century scenario. Officially, Myanmar began with the ascendance of King Anawrahta to the throne in 1010 CE. In a comparative study it is worthwhile to note that there was Anuradhapura in Sri Lanka from 3rd century BCE to 11th century CE.[101] The existing Myanmar chronicles were written only after King Anawrahta of Pagan, now called Bagan. Such standard historical records Maharazawingyi was written by U Kala in 1724,[102] the Glass Palace Chronicle was compiled only in 1829–1832,[103] and the Rakhine Maha Razawin by Saya Me was written on palm leaves in 1840.[104] How much can we depend on these relatively recent and ultra-nationalistic chronicles for accurate and comprehensive account of early and ancient Myanmar history? For example, according to my high school history teacher U Nga Aung,[105] Pagan (now Bagan) was known as Pākārama, meaning 'Fort of Rama', an Indian establishment, and it existed long before Anawrahta. Myanmar chronicles fail to clarify this important point.

My exploration deep into early legends and history turn out to be amusing because there is a Burmese proverb that says "In digging the Banyan roots Lizard eggs are revealed." (Please see the Exhibit-R27). Banyan tree is considered holy but Lizard eggs are unholy. Therefore, the proverb is a mockery meaning that there is something unholy hidden under the holiness. Now, when I dig Myanmar history the Myanmar historical racism is revealed.

Exhibit-R27
A Burmese proverb

ညောင်မြစ်တူး ပုသင်ဥပေါ် ။

Nyaung myittu puthin ô paw

In digging the Banyan roots
Lizard eggs are revealed.

Myanmar history is revered in the same way as the Banyan or Bodhi tree (*Ficus benghalensis*)[106] is revered in Buddhism and racism is a

---

[101] Now, it is a UNESCO world Heritage site, http://whc.unesco.org/en/list/200.

[102] http://en.wikipedia.org/wiki/Maha_Yazawin

[103] http://en.wikipedia.org/wiki/Burmese_chronicles

[104] http://en.wikipedia.org/wiki/Maha_Razawin_%28Saya_Me%29

[105] Only when I was at Rangoon University I came to realize that U Nga Aung was a very knowledgeable historian.

[106] https://en.wikipedia.org/wiki/Banyan

Lizard egg.

Now, please read the following excerpt from an article of well-known Myanmar scholar U Thaw Kaung.[107]

"The legend begins in Tagaung which is supposed to be the capital of the earliest kings of Myanmar. At one time it was ruled by a powerful Queen whose lover was a fire-breathing Naga serpent who could assume human form. After hero Maung Pauk Kyaing slew the Naga lover and became king, twin sons were born to the Queen. They were both blind, so they were put on a raft and floated down the Ayeyawady River. After an ogre nymph cured their blindness, the younger prince married Baydayi at Pyay and had a son Duttabaung who became a powerful king at Thayekhitaya.

Duttabaung's father also had a daughter named Panhwar who became a great Queen at Beikthano. Her mother was the ogre-nymph and so she was the half-sister of Duttabaung".

Please see the map in the Exhibit-R28 to get the picture of the journey mentioned in the legend. The legend is brought up here to draw the attention of the terms "Naga", "Ogre-nymph", and "Panhwar". Please also note that Myanmar version 'Thayekhitaya' is 'Srikhetra' and 'Beikthano' is 'Vishnu'.

The terms 'Naga' and 'Hsatma'

In contrast to the Myanmar historical belief, it is logical to accept that "Naga" was a person of Naga tribe but not a 'serpent'. According to the Naga historians they migrated from Myanmar into India.[108] The Myanmar historians have the art of transforming people into animals. They also transform a Chakma woman into a doe. Sir Arthur Phayre wrote in his book *History of Burma*[109] as follow.

---

[107] Beikthano, Vishnu City: An Ancient Pyu Center By Thaw Kaung, Myanmar Perspectives, Vol:II 6/97, http://www.seasite.niu.edu/burmese/Culture/beikthano.htm.

[108] R.B. Thohe Pou. The Myths of Naga Origin at http://e-pao.net/epSubPageExtractor.asp?src=manipur.Ethnic_Races_Manipur.The_Myths_of_Naga_Origin

[109] Sir Arthur P. Phayre, *History of Burma*, London: Trübner & Co., 1883, p43.

Exhibit-R28: A sketch map showing the journey
of two Tagaung Princes.
The cities are the geographical references but in
different timeline. See the text for detail.

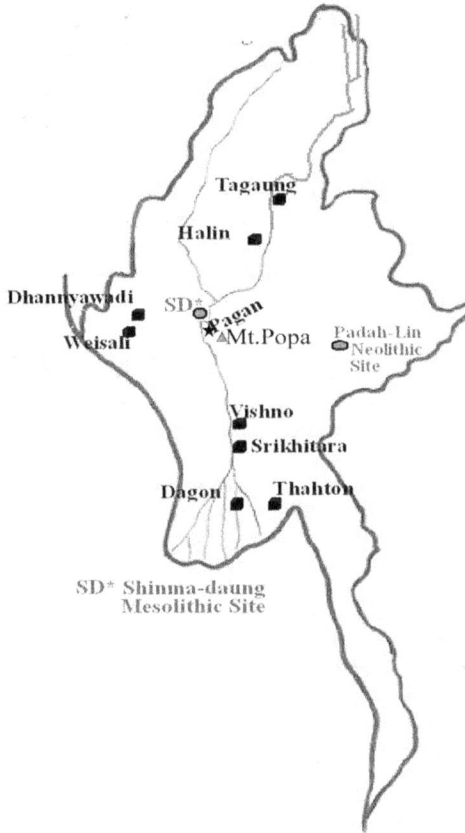

"A strange legend tells how a wild doe in the forest brought forth a human child in the country of the upper Kuladân, the principal river of northern Arakan. A chief of the Mro or Mru tribe, a remnant of which still exists, was out hunting; he found the new-born boy, and carried him home. The boy was brought up among the Mrútribe, and is called Mârayo, a name which has probably been formed by the chroniclers from Mâramâ, the Arakanese form of Mrâmma, and yo or aro—race."

Chakma or Changhma is called and written 'Thet' or 'Thek' (သက်) in Burmese. Burmese historian did not and still do not think that 'ဆတ်မ' (chatma or hsatma) mentioned in the ancient Rakhine tradition must be a Chakma woman but not a doe (Exhibit-R29). Her son, Marayu, was fathered by a Maurya-Magadha prince. Marayu founded the First Dhannyawadi dynasty, probably in the days of Mauryan Empire, 4th to 2nd Century BCE. I believed that 'Marayu' simply is a corruption of the Maurya. Thus the ancient Rakhine kingdom originated from Chakma (a Tibeto-Burman tribe) and Magadha people (an Indo-Aryan tribe), and promoted by the Mro people.

Exhibit-R29
Chakma aka Changhma

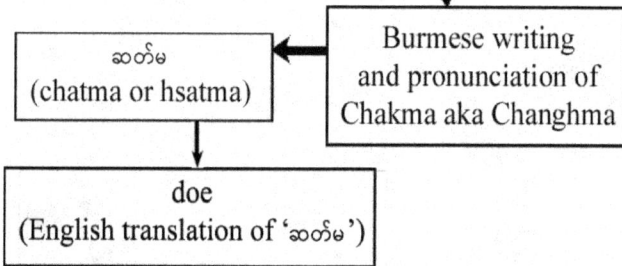

ဆတ်မ
(chatma or hsatma)

Burmese writing and pronunciation of Chakma aka Changhma

doe
(English translation of 'ဆတ်မ')

Please note here that there is no mentioning of Rakkhapura and Rakhine in the legend of Dhannyawadi.

The legend of the Chakma and doe is presented here as the parallel example of the Burmese distortion of Naga into a serpent. In overview, it is a wishful transformation of a human into an animal or dehumanization (human rights violation) in modern concept.

The term "ogre-nymph"

Here, it is important to note the similarity of the term 'ogre' used for a native woman, just like in the history of Prince Vijaya and Kuveni in Sri Lanka. A brief visit to the history of Sri Lanka will help here. Its geology, anthropology and history are most fascinating in the world, with the settlement of *Homo erectus* and *Homo sapiens*, dating back far deep into the pre-historic period.[110] Fascinating is also the story of Prince Vijaya, believed to be an Indo-Aryan, of Bengal and a Yakkha woman named Kuveni, an aborigines.[111] A wikipedia article on Sri Lanka history described about them as follow (http://en.wikipedia.org/wiki/Vedda_people).

> "According to the genesis chronicle of the majority Sinhala people, the Mahavamsa (*"Great Chronicle"*), written in the 5th century CE, the Pulindas believed to refer to Veddas are descended from Prince Vijaya (6th–5th century BCE), the founding father of the Sinhalese nation, through Kuveni, a woman of the indigenous *Yakkha* he married. The *Mahavansa* relates that following the repudiation of Kuveni by Vijaya, in favour of a Kshatriya-caste princess from Pandya, their two children, a boy and a girl, departed to the region of *Sumanakuta* (Adam's Peak in the Ratnapura District), where they multiplied, giving rise to the Veddas. Anthropologists such as the Seligmanns (*The Veddhas* 1911) believed the Veddas to be identical with the *Yakkha*".

In Myanmar, Vijaya is known as Wizaya and he is worshipped as a conqueror of universe, and propagator and defender of Buddhism. General Ne Win, a profound Burmese national socialist,[112] following the footsteps of the Myanmar Buddhist kings, built Maha Wizaya Pagoda at Rangoon (Yangon), near Shwedagon Pagoda, in 1980. Kuveni is known as May Kuwan, a Yakkha princess. Let us keep in our mind that 'Yakkha' is an 'ogre' in English. The same story of Vijaya and Kuveni is cherished in Myanmar and popularly depicted in movies, plays, ballets and dramas. The impact of the conquest of Sri Lanka by Vijaya of Bengal was so great that even an emperor in the name of Sri Vijaya[113] rose in Sumatra and his thalassocratic empire prospered,

---

[110] Pre- and protohistoric settlement in Sri Lanka by S. U. Deraniyagala, Director-General of Archaeology, Sri Lanka, in International Union of Prehistoric and Protohistoric Sciences, Procedings of the XIII Congress, Forli', Italia -8-14 September 1996. Retrieved on March 30, 2013 from http://www.lankalibrary.com/geo/dera1.html.

[111] Probably the oldest settlement, validated to be as earlier as 16,000 BP. Please see the reference at footnote#16.

[112] Burmese Way to Socialism and Burmese Socialist Programme Party (BSPP) together constitute Myanmar Nazism. See the Chapter 5, p 41 of this book.

[113] http://en.wikipedia.org/wiki/Srivijaya

occupied the ancient Thai, Myanmar, Cambodia, Vietnam, and dominated the South China Sea for four centuries from 8th to 12th century CE.

In light of the striking same inference of 'ogre' or 'Yakkha' to a native woman in Sri Lanka and Myanmar it is reasonable to consider that there must have as well been a very ancient human settlement in Myanmar–a population similar to that of Sri Lanka.

Myanmar archaeologists have reported the Mesolithic (~20,000 to 10,000 BP) culture in Shinma-daung, west of Ayeyarwaddy, Magway District, Central Burma, and Neolithic (~10,000 to 5,000 BP) culture in Padah-Lin near Taungyi, Southern Shan State. These findings are in line with the 'out-of-Africa' human migration evidence, which is discussed in the earlier chapters.

It is also mind-throbbing to note in the legend that the Tagaung princes met the 'Ogre-nymph' somewhere between Shinma-daung and Mt. Popa along the Ayeyarwady River (see the map in Exhibit-R28). Ayeyarwady is post-1995 Myanmar version of Irrawaddy, which is believed to have named after *Ravi (modern Urdu)* or *Iravati,*[114] which is "a trans-boundary river flowing through Northwestern India and eastern Pakistan."[115] Again, Mt. Popa is Myanmar corruption of Mt. Puppa,[116] which means Mt. Flower in Pali.[117] It now makes sense of what I learned in my high school history that the Tagaung princes met a 'flower-eating ogre-nymph' who cured their blindness. The historians are referring to an earliest native woman from the "Mountain of Flowers," who probably was a Dravidian. It is also highly possible that the woman and her people were knowledgeable herbalists who could restore the eyesight of the Tagaung princes. All these names and metaphors indicate to an Indian origin of people and culture in pre-Pagan Myanmar. More can be evidenced from the term "Panhwar" of U Thaw Kaung,[118] as discussed below.

The term "Panthwar"

I believe U Thaw Kaung's 'Panhwar' is a misnomer of Panthwa described by other historians.[119] It may also be just a 'typo'.

---

[114] See http://en.wikipedia.org/wiki/Irrawaddy_River

[115] http://en.wikipedia.org/wiki/Ravi_River

[116] http://en.wikipedia.org/wiki/Mount_Popa

[117] Also see the translation at http://dictionary.tamilcube.com/pali-dictionary.aspx

[118] Beikthano, Vishnu City: An Ancient Pyu Center By Thaw Kaung, Myanmar Perspectives, Vol:II 6/97, http://www.seasite.niu.edu/burmese/Culture/beikthano.htm.

[119] See Elizabeth Moore, Interpreting Pyu material culture: Royal chronologies and finger-

Therefore, I use the word 'Panthwar.' The historical records say that City of Vishnu (Beikthano) was also known as "City of Panthwa"[120] or "City of Prayer" in modern Burmese literature. On the other hand, according to a Chinese scholar, Chen Yi-Sein (cited by Elizabeth Moore),[119] Panthwa was a name of the Dravidian tribe. In other words the people of Vishnu aka Beikthano aka Panthwa were the Dravidians. Again, the term *"Panthwar," which represents the Dravidian speakers,* points to the people having South Indian origin, in line with the scientific evidence of 'out-of-Africa' human settlement.

Myanmar chronicles mentioned the power struggle between Dwuttabaung of Srikhetra and Queen of Panthwa (Vishnu aka Beikthano). Dwuttabaung was a descendent of Tagaung Kings who were the children of King Abi Raja of Sâkya clan[121] from Kapilavastu. Abi Raja came to Tagaung of Myanmar and established his kingdom long, long before Buddha was born. As such the story of Dwuttabaung and Queen of Panthwa (Vishnu aka Beikthano) depicts the struggle between the Indo-Aryan and Dravidian tribes, and eventual politico-cultural melting of the people. This again is in line with what have been observed in entire Indian Subcontinent and Bengal area.[122]

There is more evidence of Indian origin of Myanmar people. It is common knowledge that Myanmar came into existence only in the 12th century with the ascent of Anawrahta, r.1010-1052[123] (Myanmar version of Anurudha)[124] to the throne at Pagan. Myanmar kingdom was preceded by the Pyu kingdoms and city states. In parallel with Pyu there were Mon of Mon-Khmer people. Who were Pyu and Mon? Who lived there alongside with Pyu and Mon?

At this point, the famous words of King Kyansittha, the "unifier of the Myanmar cultures" deserve attention in this matter.

Kyansittha was a hero of Pagan Kingdom in the days of

---

marked bricks, Myanmar Historical Research Journal, No(13) June 2004, pp1-57.

[120] See "History of Taungdwingyi."cited by Elizabeth Moore above.

[121] Gautama Buddha was born to Sâkya clan in 563 BCE (google search), as per traditional Buddhist records but in 623 BCE as per UNESCO, http://whc.unesco.org/en/list/666.

[122] Dilip K. Chakrabarti, Ancient settlements of the Ganga Plans: West Bengal and Bihar. http://www.indologica.com/volumes/vol23-24/vol23-24_art08_CHAKRABARTI.pdf. Retrieved in May 11, 2013.

[123] Sir Arthur P. Phayre, *History of Burma*, London: Trübner & Co., 1883, p294.

[124] Also see Sri Lankan 'Sacred City of Anuradhapura', 3rd century BCE to 999 CE, UNESCO World Heritage at Sacred City of Anuradhapura.

King Anawratha who entrusted him to escort his bride, Princess Manisanda (Monichanda) of Ussa Pegu, from Pegu Kingdom to his Pagan. Usaa is Burmese corruption of Orissa or Odhisa.[125] But, the soldier-playboy Kyansittha fell in love with the princess. (According to Dr. Htin Aung,[126] Kyansittha was a son of Indian Princess and a Burmese Noble). Angered, Anawratha got hold of Kyansittha, tied him around a tree and then Anawratha threw his powerful Arindama Lance (which was a gift from King Indra of Heaven) at Kyansittha. Unfortunately for Anawrahta but fortunately for Kyansittha, it was a miss; the lance hit the rope and Kyansittha escaped with Arindama Lance. (I can imagine how mad Anawrahta would be!) Kyansittha ran and ran until he reached the land of Mrama Tribe at India-Burma border. He was sheltered by a Mrama mountain farmer and he got married with the farmer's daughter named Sambul[127] (Thanbula in Burmese). They lived happily. Meanwhile King Anawratha died and his son Sawlu succeeded him. King Sawlu had a milk-brother, Nga Raman Kam. Milk-brothers or sisters are boys or girls who suckle milk side by side from the same woman. In this case, the woman is the biological mother of Nga Raman Kam and milk-mother of Sawlu. It is a standard practice of the Burmese queens to keep a 'milk-mother' for their babies. It is believed the practice was to maintain the queen's bust line and beauty. It was a common practice of the Burmese royals and nobles.

The Muslims of Burma believe that the actual name of Nga Raman Kam is Rahman Khan but Burmese record says that Nga Raman Kam is a nick name. When he was young and while fishing one of his eyes was hit by the dorsal fins a fish called Nga-ranh {a species of Ophiocephalus} and he became blind. As such he was known as Nga Raman Kam or 'Nga Ranh Blind'.

King Sawlu was a pleasure lover and gambler. One day he lost a bet to Nga Raman Kam on a dice game. Upon winning the bet, Nga Raman Kam jumped up and danced beating his arms loud. King Sawlu got much upset and angry and challenged Nga Raman Kam for a duel. Nga Raman Kam, believing that Sawlu would kill him

---

[125] Also see The Rakhine State Violence, Vol. 1: The Rakhaing Revolution, p 22.

[126] Maung Htin Aung, *A History of Burma*, Columbia University Press, 1967, page 40. I believe that it was a Pattikera Princess. Pattikera is a pre-Bengal Kingdom, now near Comilla of Bangladesh.

[127] It was their son, Raza Kumar, who masterminded famous Myazedi Stone Inscription in 1113 CE, with four languages namely Pali, Pyu, Mon, and Myanmar. http://en.wikipedia.org/wiki/Myazedi_inscription

one way or another, ran away and joined the Talaing rebels. There was no mentioning that Nga Raman Kam and his mother were Talaings. Sawlu went after Nga Raman Kam but was caught and imprisoned by Nga Raman Kam, with the help of the Talaings. Sadly, Pagan became kingless. Thereupon, the palace ministers sent a message to Kyansittha, requesting to come back and take the throne. Kyansittha came but refused to take the throne as long as Sawlu was alive. He set out on a rescue mission, sneaked into Nga Raman Kam's camp, freed Sawlu, and escaped carrying Sawlu on his shoulder. Sawlu did not trust Kyansittha who was almost killed by his father. "Kyansittha would take revenge on me but Nga Raman Kam is my milk-brother and unlikely to kill me," he thought. With this thought he yelled, "Kyansittha kidnaps me, Kyansittha kidnaps me." The Talaing rebels woke up and chased Kyansittha. At that point Kyansittha threw down Sawlu with cynical words, "Bad King, Dirty King, in the hands of Talaing, you choose to die." See the Exhibit-R30. Sawlu was killed by Nga Raman Kam and Kyansittha eventually ascended the throne.

Exhibit-R30

Famous words

of King Kyansittha on Talaing

မင်း ဆိုး မင်း ညစ်	Bad King, Dirty King
တလိုင်း တို့ လက်တွင်	In the hands of Talaing
သေ ရစ် တော.॥	You choose to die.

This was the story. In Burmese history the Talaings were the bad guys. The historians believe that Talaings are the people of Telingâna[128] of South India. Sir Arthur P. Phayre wrote as follow.[129]

"At the time—the first century of the Christian era—when the fall of the monarchy is placed, and for some centuries later, the kingdom, of which Thahtun was the capital, was existing in prosperity. Though the chief city was outside the basin of the Irâwadi, the territory included the whole of the delta of that river. The kings were of Indian race from Telingâna, and

---

[128] Present day Telangana, http://en.wikipedia.org/wiki/Telangana
[129] Sir Arthur P. Phayre, *History of Burma*, London: Trübner & Co., 1883, p19.

their country was known as Suvarna Bhûmi, of Buddhist fame. But as the country, known better from the later capital as Pegu, was conquered in the eleventh century by the king of Pugân, and all records were destroyed or carried away, no account remains of the early history and the extension northward of the Talaing kingdom. That can only be now gathered from tradition and a few fragmentary notices."

Burmese used to refer the Mon people as the Mon-Talaing. It was intolerable for the Mons who disliked the term 'Talaing'. In the history I learned in my school days, Kyansittha made peace with the Mon and Talaings, and consequently Pagan and its allies, the Mon Kingdoms, flourished and prospered. It appeared that the Talaings were absorbed into the mainstream of Myanmar society. Kyansittha was credited as the 'peace-making-unifier' who solidified Anawrahta's First Myanmar Empire, not by force or might but by friendship, mutual respect and acceptance of cultural diversity. The Kyansittha tradition of 'unification through peace' would be beneficial for the Myanmar people if appreciated.

Based on Sir Arthur P. Phayre's writing cited above it is probable that the Talaing or the people of Telingâna[130] were also in Burma along with Pyu and Mon people. It is of great fascination to note that even in Vietnam there is an ancient Sanskrit inscription written in South Indian Grantha alphabet of the Pallava dynasty (Exhibit-R31).[131] It is believed that the stone inscription was erected in 5th century CE by a Prince Gunavarman of the Kaundinya lineage of Kingdom of Funan (Exhibit-R32), to record his generous donation in honor of Vishnu.

---

[130] Also see Telingana at http://en.wikipedia.org/wiki/Telangana
[131] See http://en.wikipedia.org/wiki/Funan_Kingdom

Exhibit-R31

The Sanskrit Stone inscription in Pallava scripts found at
Thap Muoi, Dong Thap Province, Vietnam, is the indisputable
evidence of the Austronesian and Austroasian people
establishments and dominance in South and Southeast Asia
from the most ancient to 9th century CE.
http://en.wikipedia.org/wiki/Kingdom_of_Funan (last visit on
December 31, 2014).

Photo by Binh Giang 2009. He has released the copyright.
The photo is in public domain.

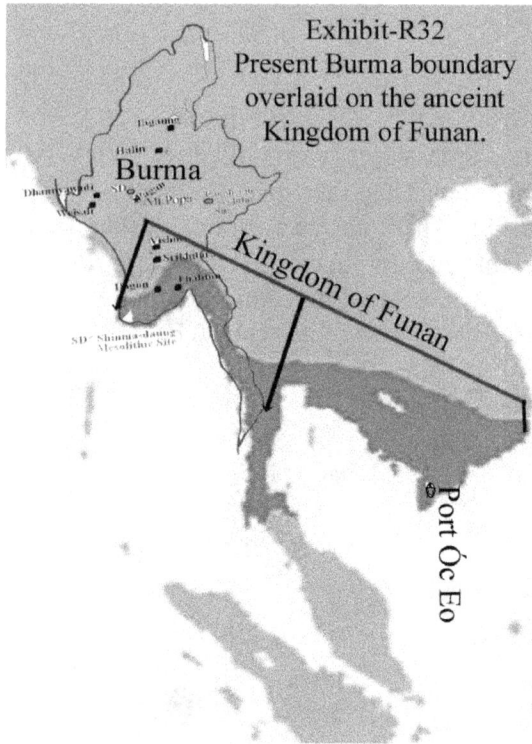

Exhibit-R32
Present Burma boundary
overlaid on the anceint
Kingdom of Funan.

Kingdom of Funan,[132] also known as Phù Nam or Nokor Phnom, is believed to have flourished from 1st to 7th century CE.[133] According the Vietnamese historian Ha Van Tan[134] the Kingdom of Funan "may have been a collection of city-states that sometimes warred with one another and at other times constituted a political unity." As to the question of the people of Funan the archaeological and linguistic evidence indicate that they were Austronesians, Austroasians, and settlers from South India (Dravidian and Indo-Aryan speakers). Archaeological artifacts "found in the kingdom's main port, Oc Eo (now part of Vietnam), contain Roman as well as Persian, Indian, and Greek artifacts". The name of the capital of the

---

[132] http://en.wikipedia.org/wiki/Funan_Kingdom

[133] http://countrystudies.us/cambodia/5.htm

[134] Cited in the article Kingdom of Funan at http://en.wikipedia.org/wiki/Funan_Kingdom

kingdom was Vyadhapura. Please note that the KnightxxArrow,[135] creator of the Funan Map used in the Exhibit-R32, includes the lower Burma within the boundary of the Kingdom of Funan.

Geographically, Myanmar is the bridge between South Asia and Southeast Asia. Therfore, Myanmar ethnological and linguistic bridge must have existed from time immorial throughout the days we refer as 'palaeolithic', 'mesolithic', 'neolithic', 'ancient', 'pre-history', and 'early history'. City-kingdoms of early Myanmar history is the evidence of such ethnological and linguistic bridge.

When the ancient culture and history of South Asia (eg. Pakistan, India, Sri Lanka), Myanmar (which is a transit point between South India and Southeast Asia), and Southeast Asia arc brought together into the picture it is clear that ethnic, cultural, linguistic diversities are common features since time immemorial. Despite having such diversities they all belong to human family. This factual reality of 'human family' or 'common humanity', found in the legends and historical records, has been substantiated and fortified by the most advanced molecular genetic science. Various researchers across the world have published astonishing and intriguing authentic and genuine original research articles strongly demonstrating the genetic basis of 'common humanity' and 'one human family'. I shall discuss 'genetic common humanity' with special reference to Myanmar in the next session.

Myanmar is not the sole domain of the Tibeto-Burman speakers. A prominent scholar of linguistics, Randy J. LaPolla,[136] (http://tibeto-burman.net/rjlapolla/), traced the Sino-Tibetan speaking people to be "originated in the central plains of what is now north China, in the valley of the Yellow River." They started moving out of the Yellow River valley at least 6,500 years ago.[137] He wrote as follow.[138] Tibeto-Burman is a sub-family of Sino-Tibetan language family.

---

[135] http://commons.wikimedia.org/wiki/File:Funan_Kingdom.png

[136] Randy J. LaPolla, *The role of migration and language contact in the development of the Sino-Tibetan language family*, in *Areal Diffusion and Genetic Inheritance: Case Studies in Language Change*, ed. by R. M. W. Dixon & A. Y. Aikhenvald, 225-254. Oxford: Oxford University Press, November 2001, p225-254,

[137] Ibid. p227

[138] Ibid. p237

"The people we have come to think of as the Burmese had been in Yunnan, under the control of the Nanzhao kingdom, and moved down into Burma beginning in the middle of the ninth century. They came down from the Northern Shan states into the Kyanksè area south of Mandalay, splitting the Mon in the north and south, and pushed the Karens east of the Irrawaddy. About 1000 AD the Burmese conquered the Mon to the south, and the first Burmese kingdom, the Pagan kingdom, was founded in 1044. The court adopted much of Mon culture (it became the official court culture, and the Mon language (or Pali) was used for inscriptions; the Mon script also became the basis of the Burmese writing system). This was the early period of major contact and influence of the Mon on the Burmese, which lasted until the late twelfth century. Indian influence on the Burmese was mainly indirect through the Mon, or from Ceylon."

It makes sense to read Professor LaPolla's assertion that Burmese moved into Burma only in the middle of the 9th century because the Pyu kingdoms disappeared around that time and Anawratha emerged as the first Burmese king in 1010 CE. The written Myanmar language first appeared in Raza Kumar's Myazedi Stone Inscription[139] along with Pali, Pyu, and Mon languages only in 1113 CE. The historians differ in fixing the dates in Myanmar history. According to some scholars[140] and also Professor LaPolla, Anawrahta reigned from 1044 – 1078 CE. I have followed the dates given by Sir Arthur P. Phayre[141] and Myazedi Stone Inscription[142] could have been made in 1085 CE, the year Kyansittha died.

It also makes sense in the context of the Rakhine State in the western Myanmar, I have presented with strong evidence that Rakkhapura and Dhannyawadi (Dhaññavati) were the establishments of the Indo-Aryan speaking people. In addition Vesali (Weithali), an independent city-kingdom that disappeared at the end of 8th century

---

[139] Visit http://en.wikipedia.org/wiki/Myazedi_inscription. It was Raza Kumar, the son of Kyansitta and Sambul, who masterminded famous Myazedi Stone Inscription in 1113 CE.

[140] http://en.wikipedia.org/wiki/Anawrahta

[141] Sir Arthur P. Phayre, *History of Burma*, London: Trübner & Co., 1883, Appendix, p 275-304.

[142] http://en.wikipedia.org/wiki/Myazedi_inscription

CE, deserves attention here. According to the renowned and well-respected historian Daniel George Edward Hall it was an Indian kingdom. He wrote as follow in his book *A history of Southeast Asia.*[143]

"The Burmese do not seem to have settled in Arakan until possibly as late as the tenth century A.D. Hence earlier dynasties are thought to have been Indian, ruling over a population similar to that of Bengal."

Hall's analysis is in conformity with LaPolla's assertion of Burmese arrival in Burma only in the middle of the 9th century. Anawratha's conquest of Northern Arakan in the 11th century and Kyansittha consolidation of the First (Anawrahta) Myanmar Empire brought in the Burmese who we now know as the Rakhine. The Rakhine still speak an archaic Burmese dialect but they learned from the native Indo-Aryan speakers to pronounce strong 'r' sound whereas the Burmese still cannot say 'r'. That is why, for example, Rangoon becomes Yangon; Irrawaddy becomes Ayeyarwaddy; and Pray (Prome) becomes Pyay. Also, the Rakhine dialect is still mixed with Burmanized Sanskrit and Pali words.

The above historical findings are also supported by the Ānandachandra Stone Inscription of Vesālī (Vaisali, Weithali) city-kingdom, which probably was later either conquered or subordinated by the Burmese. The Sanskrit inscription of Ānandachandra (Exhibit-R33) was deciphered by Professor E.H. Johnston.[144] When I carefully read Johnston's article it is clear that Vesālī was part of the Brahmaputra Civilization. It was ruled by a Chandra Dynasty. Brahmanism and Mahayana Buddhism were practiced. The Indo-European language, Sanskrit, the kingdom's official language, was used to inscribe the sacred record (Praśasti) of King Ānandachandra. Verse 61 of the inscription says that the king sent gifts "to the noble congregation of friars in the land of King Śilāmegha." Sri Lankan chronicle Culavamsa mentioned that Anuradhapura King Mahinda II

---

[143] DGE Hall, *A history of Southeast Asia*, McMillan, 1964, p367

[144] E. H. Johnston (1944). Some Sanskrit Inscriptions of Arakan. Bulletin of the School of Oriental and African Studies, 11, pp 357-385. doi:10.1017/S0041977X00072529. I downloaded it from http://journals.cambridge.org/action/displayAbstract?fromPage=online&aid=3805020 in 2010.

(r.787 to 807 CE) was popularly known as Śilāmegha. King Śilāmegha (Mahinda II) did organize "a great festival, the discerning (prince) had the Abhidhamma recited by the Grand Thera dwelling in the Hemasāli (-vihāra) and built a bathing tank there for his use."[145] Therefore, it can be sure that Ānandachandra was contemporary with Sri Lanka King Śilāmegha (Mahinda II, r.787 to 807 CE).

Most significant of all, there was no mentioning of Rakkhapura, Rakhine, or Myanmar in the inscription.[146]

Exhibit-R33
Sanskrit inscription of Anandachandra, King of Vesālī

PRAŚASTI OF ĀNANDACANDRA ON PILLAR AT SHITTHAUNG PAGODA, MROHAUNG (WEST FACE), LINES 57-72.

Reference:E. H. Johnston (1944). Some Sanskrit Inscriptions of Arakan. Bulletin of the School of Oriental and African Studies, 11, pp 357-385 doi:10. 1017/S0041977X00072529
http://journals.cambridge.org/action/displayAbstract? fromPage=online&aid=3805020

---

[145] Wilhelm Geiger, Culavamsa being the more recent part of the Mahavamsa, Asian Educational Services, Second AES Reprint, New Delhi, 1998, p 124 (48.141-143).
[146] Also see R.C. Majumder, *Hindu colonies in the Far East,* First Edition, General Printers and Publishers Ltd., Calcutta, 1944, p 189-220.

Again, Maurice Collis (1889-1973),[147] in his famous book *The Land of the Great Image*,[148] described that Arakan was conquered by the "Mongolian barbarians" in 957 CE, and, as a result, the inhabitants are "a mixture of Mongolian and Indian races" (Exhibit-R33A and R33B). Maurice Collis served as a District Commissioner in Arakan for many years.

Exhibit-R33A
Vesālī was conquered by the Burmese in 957 CE

The Image on the Pass

particularly sacred sculpture was sufficient to identify the Arakan area more with Buddhism than with Hinduism.
➤ In 957 the country was overrun by Mongolian barbarians, who must have been early Burmese, for the Arakanese language to-day is an early form of Burmese. Meanwhile, both

---

See: Maurice Collis, The Land of the Great Image (1943), New Directions Publishing; Reprint edition (November 17, 1985), p136

More, U Kyaw Min, ICS (Indian Civil Service), who was a native son of most educated and aristocratic family of Arakan,[149] and big bureaucrat in the days of British Burma, and member of parliament (1950-1962) in the independent Burma, asserted that "the Arakanese people are of Aryan stock mixed with the indigenous people who have inhabited Arakan from time immemorial" (Exhibit-R33C). He insisted that the Arakanese are not the Burmese stock.[150] In light of ICS U Kyaw Min's assertion, it is logical to assume that the Rakhaing (Arakanese) will speak a dialect of Indo-Aryan language. But, today, the Rakhaing speaks a Burmese dialect. *This*

---

[147] http://en.wikipedia.org/wiki/Maurice_Collis
[148] Maurice Collis, *The Land of the Great Image* (1943), New Directions Publishing; Reprint edition (November 17, 1985), p 136-137
[149] Also see The Rakhine State Violence Volume 1: The Rakhaing Revolution, p 124.
[150] U Kyaw Min, M.P., ICS (Retd.), Barrister-at-law, The Arakan State, the Pye Daw Tha Press, 1958(?). This is from the digital version from the Cornell University Library, DS 485.B892K77, https://archive.org/details/cu31924022999126.

is very disturbing because it indicates that the present Rakhaing (Rakhine, officially) and the past Rakhaing are two different populations.

Exhibit-R33B
A mixture of Mongolian and Indian races!

reconstruction of the Apostolic age. In about the year 1060 the Pagan dynasty extended its authority over Arakan, become, as we have seen, a state inhabited by a mixture of ➡ Mongolian and Indian races. As a result, Arakan was brought into the orbit of the Hinayana as practised in Pagan. The Mahamuni, though it had been overgrown by the jungle, was still in its place, and was now cleared and repaired. It was

See: p 136 and 137,
Maurice Collis, The Land of the Great Image (1943),
New Directions Publishing; Reprint edition, 1985

form of Buddhism. He was also making acquaintance for the first time with a Mongolian state, the inhabitants of which spoke Burmese or a dialect of it but who had a certain admixture of ➡ Indian blood in their veins. The state as such went back to the year 957, somewhat in the way that England goes back to the year 1066, and the hundred years between Min Bin (1531–53) and the reigning king, Thiri-thu-dhamma, had been the most progressive in its history. These are all very relevant facts for

The scenario of the demographic change in the Rakhaing Land in post 957 CE can be well imagined when we consider how the native American populations were totally replaced with the Spanish and Portuguese in the Latin American countries in the 15th and 16th centuries. For example, we know that in Venezuela almost all the male members of the native tribes were killed and the Spanish Y-chromosome haplotypes were forcefully introduced.

Exhibit-R33C

U Kyaw Min, ICS, Member of Parliament (1950-1962)

A mixture of Aryan and Indigenous races!

Mistaken Belief

Racially it is believed that the Arakanese people are of Aryan stock mixed with the indigenous people who have inhabited Arakan from time immemorial.

The Burmese however view the Arakanese from a different viewpoint. The Burmese consider the Arakanese to be the same as the Burmese but living in a localised spot and thus having acquired localised characteristics. The Burmese think that the Burmese and the Arakanese come of the same stock and are practically the same.

The Burmese viewpoint is completely mistaken. But if an Arakanese begins opening his mouth to say that the Arakanese are not the same as the Burmese, the Burmese will shut him up by saying that he is "dividing the blood"

Source:

THE PYE DAW THA PRESS.
No. 31, Dogonthiri Street,
KYAUKMYAUNG.

http://www.archive.org/details/cu31924022999126

The colonial effect on the population genetics is scientifically proven and the authors, Guerra et. al. (2011),[151] in their

---

[151] Guerra DC, Pérez CF, Izaguirre MH, Barahona EA, Larralde AR, Lugo MV. Gender differences in ancestral contribution and admixture in Venezuelan populations, Hum Biol. 2011 Jun;83(3):345-61. doi: 10.3378/027.083.0302, http://www.ncbi.nlm.nih.gov/pubmed/21740152

paper they conclude that "The results show a predominantly indigenous genetic contribution through the female. ... With regard to admixture through males, it is almost exclusively of European origin." In the case of Rakhaing, there had been three occasions of such forced change in the gene pool, the first in 957, the second in the period of 1403-1430, and the third in the period of 1784-1824.

This leads to another important fact that the word Rakkhaing first appeared only in the 14th century literature. The meaning of the term Rakkhaing or Rakkhine is explained in an epic poem known as *Shin Nagainda Mawgwun.* In the Exhibit-R34, I give what I learned since my childhood from my parents.[152] The verse is a mix of Pali and Burmese.

Exhibit-R34
The term Rakkhaing was first mentioned
in a 14th century epic poem known as
Shin Nagainda Mawgwan

အမျိုးသီလ နှစ်ဌါနကို
ပြည့်ဝမဏ္ဍိုင် စောင့်ရှောက်နိုင်၍၊
ရက္ခိုင်နာမ ဘွဲ့မည်လှဖြင့်
အနွတ္တ သဉ္ညာ ခေါ်အပ်စွတည်း။

Race and Religion, two institutions,
Are guarded fully and strongly;
Therefore, the beautiful name Rakkhaing
Is adorned and called.

Note: It is ရက္ခိုင် (Rak-khaing)
but not ရခိုင် (Ra-khaing)

Now:

Who are "the indigenous people who have inhabited Arakan

---

[152] Also see Professor Aye Kyaw, *A Position Paper of the Arakanese Perspective*, Presented at the Oslo Burma Seminar on January 15-17, 2004. It was also published in Arakanpost, Issue 5, 2004, Dhaka, Bangladesh. For the Neo-Nazism content of his article see my book *The Price of Silence*, pp 232-271.

from the time immemorial" that U Kyaw Min (ICS) talked about? (Please do not confuse U Kyaw Min (ICS) of the pre-1962 era with U Kyaw Min of Democracy and Human Rights Party ((DHRP) of the post-1988 era. They are two different persons at two different times; the former was a Rakhaing and the latter a Rohingya).

The answer came from another famous Rakhaing scholar named U San Tha Aung, who was a Professor of Physics at Rangoon University and became the Director General of the Higher Education in the days of Ne Win's military Socialist Government. Along with Dr. Maung Maung Kha (Professor of Physics and Rector of Rangoon University), he co-authored a physics textbook in English, which was one of the prescribed textbooks that I studied in my intermediate physics classes in the early 1960s. U San Tha Aung and Professor Aye Kyaw (a Rakhaing Professor of History at Rangoon University) were the two persons whom the Ne Win's military socialist government consulted in formulating the Citizenship Act of Burma 1982. It was strange that the Ne Win's government consulted the Rakhaing intellectuals only while the government maintained that there were (*and still are*) 135 national races in Myanmar. The cutoff time line year 1823 in defining the Myanmar *Tai-yin-thar* or *native ethnicity* was the proposal of Professor Aye Kyaw, based on the time line of the Burmese King Bodaw occupation of Arakan and the First Anglo-Burma War (1824-1826).[153] U San Tha Aung was a very senior person and also the patron and mentor of Professor Aye Kyaw, Sara San Kyaw Tun (who was the founding Secretary of the Arakan Independence Organization–AIO), and Kyaw Hlaing, who became the Chairman of AIO after the demise of San Kyaw Tun.[154] As a matter of fact, science is a stranger in the Land of Myanmar and U San Tha Aung was known only for his work on "The Buddhist Art of Ancient Arakan"[155] that he studied and wrote as his pass time while he was the Director General of the Higher Education.[156] The

---

[153] Also See Professor Aye Kyaw, *A Position Paper of the Arakanese Perspective*, Presented at the Oslo Burma Seminar on January 15-17, 2004. It was also published in Arakanpost, Issue 5, 2004, Dhaka, Bangladesh. For the Neo-Nazism content of his article see my book *The Price of Silence*, pp 232-271..

[154] San Kyaw Tun and Kyaw Hlaing are my friends. For more information on them please see The Rakhaing State Violence Vol. 1: The Rakhaing Revolution.

[155] San Tha Aung, *The Buddhist Art of Ancient Arakan*, 1979.

[156] Another scientist Dr. Nyi Nyi, an eminent micropaleontologist, Professor of Geology, Director General of the Higher Education (preceding U San Tha Aung) and Deputy Minister of the Education Ministry, was also known for his book on the "History of Rangoon University"

good point is that his work answered the question of who the indigenous people of Arakan are.

He wrote in his famous book Chapter 1: Geographical Description, Subheading: The Peoples of Arakan:

"The earliest people who lived in Arakan were Negritos who are mentioned in the chronicles as "Bilus" (cannibals). They appear to have been the direct neolithic descendents of the Arakanese soil. Later, waves of peoples of different races came into this land from the north,"[157] (Exhibit-R34A).

Exhibit-R34A
U San Tha Aung recorded that the earliest people of Arakan are Negritos.

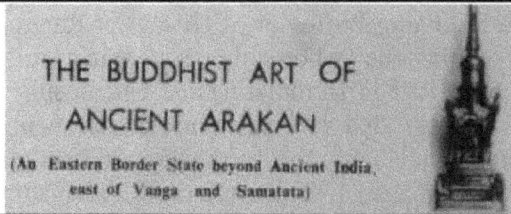

THE BUDDHIST ART OF
ANCIENT ARAKAN

(An Eastern Border State beyond Ancient India,
east of Vanga and Samatata)

By San Tha Aung, Director-General, Department of Higher Education, Rangoon, Burma, 1979.

The Peoples of Arakan (Chapter 1, page 2)

The earliest people who lived in Arakan were Negritos who are mentioned in the chronicles as "Bilus" (cannibals). They appear to have been the direct neolithic descendents of the Arakanese soil. Later, waves of peoples of different races came into this land from the north.

The Bilus or Cannibals or Raksha[158] are common characters in Vedic and Buddhist literature[159] and hence in the folk tales of Sri Lanka and Bengal as well.[160]

---

but not for his science. Myanmar people do nor care about science. Now I ended up writing the history of the Rakhaing politics, but I have authored or co-authored more than 60 scientific publications—a relatively small but decent number for a person caught up in the political turmoil.

[157] San Tha Aung, *The Buddhist Art of Ancient Arakan*, 1979, p 2.

[158] Rakshasa is male Raksha and Rakshasi is a female.

[159] http://en.wikipedia.org/wiki/Rakshasa

[160] for example, see Lal Behari Nay, *The Story of the Rakshasas*, in *The Folk Tales of Bengal*, ebook, Gutenberg Project. http://www.gutenberg.org/files/38488/38488-h/38488-h.htm, H. Parker, *The four Rakshasas*, in *Village Folk-Tales of Sri Lanka*, University of Michigan Library (January 1, 1910).

Now, below is the summary (Table C6-1) of what I elaborately described above.

Table C6-1

Summary of "Bilus", "Ogres", "Rakkha", "Yakka", and "indigenous'		
Author	Description	Page (Footnote)
Ye Myint Aung	"the Rohingya are 'dark in color' and 'ugly as ogres'"	85(96&97)
Arthur P. Phayre	"Rakhine are the descendants of Rakkha or Yakkha or Ogres"	63(45) & 85(99)
Randy J. LaPolla	"The people we have come to think of as the Burmese had been in Yunnan, under the control of the Nanzhao kingdom, and moved down into Burma beginning in the middle of the ninth century."	99-100 (136-138)
Daniel George Edward Hall	"The Burmese do not seem to have settled in Arakan until possibly as late as the tenth century A.D. Hence earlier dynasties are thought to have been Indian, ruling over a population similar to that of Bengal."	101(143)
Maurice Collis	"Arakan was conquered by the "Mongolian barbarians" in 957 CE, and, as a result, the inhabitants are a mixture of Mongolian and Indian races."**	103(148)
Kyaw Min (ICS)	"the Arakanese people are of Aryan stock mixed with the indigenous people who have inhabited Arakan from time immemorial."	103(150)
San Tha Aung	"The earliest people who lived in Arakan were Negritos who are mentioned in the chronicles as "Bilus" (cannibals). They appear to have been the direct neolithic descendents of the Arakanese soil."	107(155) & 108(157)

**I came to realize this fact when I learned the Mendelian Laws of Inheritance and the Punnett square in the genetic courses at Rangoon University. Except for the Shan and the Karen peoples, all other Myanmar peoples show the phenotypes of multicultural diversities.

It is now clear that there were people who spoke Austro-Asian, Dravidian, Indo-Aryan languages long before the Burmese (also known as Burman or Bama) who spoke Tibeto-Burman came into the land now known as Myanmar. A tradition in Myanmar says that "Everyone speaks Magadha in the old days." Today, only the birds speak Magadha, which is the sweetest language in the whole wide world. Poems and songs[161] are filled with the expressions that the birds sing in their sweet Magadha language. One example is given here (Exhibit-R34B).

Exhibit-R34B

Today only the birds speak Magadha
https://www.youtube.com/watch?v=kw1eqoMLZRs

You Tube — poe ei san songs

ချစ်ခွန်းဖွဲ့သံမြူငယ်ဆီ — Love songs in the woods

စတားရာ – စော်ဝင်းနိုင်
စတားဆို – ပိုးအိဲစံ
သရုပ်ဆောင် – စော်မိုင်ဆောင်၊
ဗေဟုဌ်ခေါင်

composer-Zaw Win Naing

Singer- Poe Ei San

Actors- Zaw Maing Aung
May Htut Khaung

သာရကာ ဝုက်ဖျေးလေးတွေ — birds of many colors

သံစုံညီညီ in chorus

မာဂထာ ချစ်ခွန်းဖွဲ့ထော — Magadha love songs

ပင်ယံဝေဆီ high up the trees

[161] For example see https://www.youtube.com/watch?v=kw1eqoMLZRs

Therefore, the Burmese (the Bama and its sibling the Rakhine) are not the aborigines in Myanmar but the Rohingya (dark and ugly like ogre!) are. *But, is it anything new? The world history is filled with human migrations, quests and conquests, colonialism and slavery, wars and genocides.* The most important question is– Shall we be the prisoners of the past? Shall we be the prisoners of the history? Or, shall we start a new age in light of common humanity for the advancement of humankind as a whole? The advancement of the modern science and technology and the environmental challenges of the planet Earth demand our united action on the platform of 'common humanity'.

8
Myanmar mtDNA

Hopefully, Myanmar mtDNA (mitochondrial Deoxyribonucleic Acid) will add support to the aboriginality of the Rohingya. Studies of the human mtDNA (mitochondrial Deoxyribonucleic Acid) have shed clear and strong scientific evidence of 'common humanity'. Therefore, a discussion of 'common humanity' will not be complete without a presentation of the commonness of human mtDNA, in addition to philosophical, political, social, and cultural aspects. Scientific papers on the mtDNA of Myanmar people are, however, very rare due to the lack of advancement of science in the country. Nevertheless, based on the a few research publications it is clear that Myanmar people belong to one big human family regardless of their diversities in cultural or biological appearances.

A multinational and multi-disciplinary research group presented a paper on the mitochondrial DNA in Myanmar, with first author J. Horst,[162] in the 2012 annual conference of the American Society of Human Genetics.[163] Their research team is composed of nine scientists from Universität Münster (Germany), Ludwig-Maximilians-Universität (Münster, Germany), Innsbruck Medical University (Austria), Columbia University, (New York, N.Y., USA), and Chiang Mai University (Thailand). Below, I give a short excerpt from the abstract of their presentation.

"In general, the Myanmar sample exhibited pronounced mtDNA diversity, with the ethnic group of the Bamar being the most diverse. The 44 complete mitochondrial genome sequences revealed 10 new so far un-described mtDNA lineages, represented by 15 haplotypes, all lying within macro-haplogroup M. One lineage, comprising 3 haplotypes, clustered within HG G2, two lineages represented

---

[162] Horst J., et. al. *Mitochondrial DNA in Myanmar*: Complete mitochondrial genome sequencing revealed several new lineages within macro-haplogroup M. Abstract, 2012X. The abstract was downloaded on May 28, 2013 from http://www.ashg.org/2012meeting/abstracts/fulltext/f120121871.htm.
[163] American Society of Human Genetics, http://www.ashg.org/

subgroups of HG M49 and two lineages with in total 4 haplotypes clustered within the M13'46'61 group. In addition, we found 5 yet undefined basal M lineages. Their exact phylogenetic position can only be defined with deeper knowledge of macro-haplogroup M. Conclusions: The multi-ethnic population and the complex history of Myanmar are well reflected in its distinct mtDNA heterogeneity. In this region with its long history of human settlement, plenty of mitochondrial haplogroups, especially in the complex haplogroup M, await to be newly described."

[Full text of the abstract can be read at http://www.ashg.org/2012meeting/abstracts/fulltext/f120121871.htm]

Without going deep into the scientific aspects I would like to draw the attention to their finding of the "mtDNA lineages ... all lying within macro-haplogroup M" in spite of the "mtDNA heterogeneity" reflecting "its long history of human settlement."

The scientists found the molecular genetics evidence of ethnic diversity from the earliest days of human settlement in Myanmar, just like in every other place on this rocky planet. Therefore, it is imperative that we should know some account of the mtDNA and its haplotypes, and their significance in relation to human evolution and eventual dispersion across the planet in order to understand the weight of this scientific finding. I will try to give a simplified presentation of the subject here.

Eukarya or eukaryote is an organism, made up of the membrane-enveloped cells, like the cell and nuclear membranes illustrated in the Exhibit-R35. Human is an Eukaryote and advanced multicellular organism, composing many cells, in a range of 100 trillions.[164] In the plant and animal kingdoms of multicellular organisms a cell (Exhibit-R35) is the basic unit of the body and our interest here is the nucleus and mitochondria. Singular form is mitochondrion but normally its plural form 'mitochondria' is used. The nucleus hosts the nuclear DNA and the mitochondria house the mitochondrial DNA.

---

[164] Page 21 Inside the human body: using scientific and exponential notation. Author: Greg Roza. Edition: Illustrated. Publisher: The Rosen Publishing Group, 2007. ISBN 1-4042-3362-8, ISBN 978-1-4042-3362-1. Length: 32pages. This is a citation from http://en.wikipedia.org/wiki/Human_body.

Exhibit-R35
A Diagram of Eukaryotic Cell

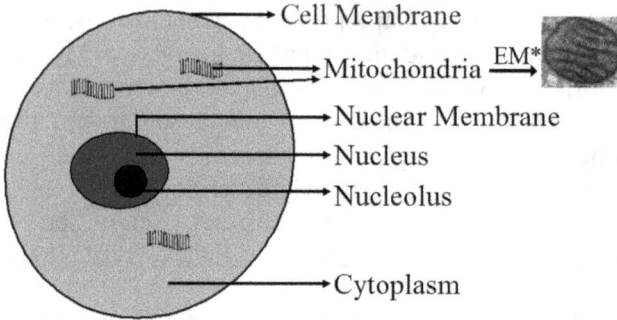

Cell Membrane

Mitochondria — EM*

Nuclear Membrane

Nucleus

Nucleolus

Cytoplasm

EM*:Electron micrograph of lung mitochondria in public domain
http://en.wikipedia.org/wiki/Mitochondrion
Credit: Louisa Howard
Dartmouth College Electron Microscope Facility
http://www.dartmouth.edu/~emlab/
http://remf.dartmouth.edu/images/mammalianLungTEM/source/8.html

DNA is a hereditary biochemical strand made up of four unique nucleotides, namely adenine (A), thymine (T), guanine (G), and cytosine (C), which are attached to the sugar phosphate backbone. Two (double) DNA strands, which are complimentary to each other, join together by pairing A and T, and G and C, and exist in a double helix conformation[165] (Exhibit-R36). Pairing is possible only between the A and T and G and C; no other pairing is possible, with the exception that T (thymine) is replaced with U (uracil) in the case of the messenger ribonucleic acid (mRNA).

"A Structure for Deoxyribose Nucleic Acid" was reported by Watson J.D. and Crick F.H.C. in *Nature* 171, 737-738 (1953) and can be read at-

http://www.nature.com/nature/dna50/watsoncrick.pdf,
and http://www.nature.com/nature/dna50/archive.html.

---

[165] http://ghr.nlm.nih.gov/handbook/basics/dna. The figure is a U.S. government information and is in the public domain.

Exhibit-R36
DNA double helix conformation

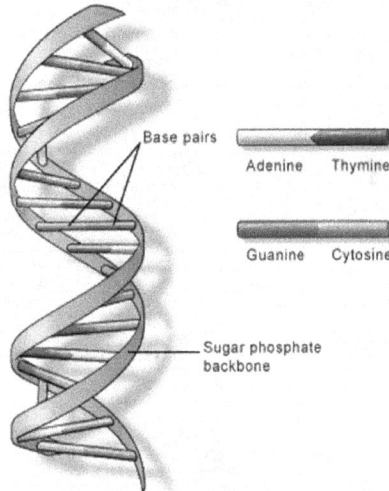

Base pairs

Adenine   Thymine

Guanine   Cytosine

Sugar phosphate
backbone

U.S. National Library of Medicine Source:
http://ghr.nlm.nih.gov/handbook/basics/dna
Government information at US National
Library of Medicine web sites
is in the public domain.
http://www.nlm.nih.gov/copyright.html

Some clips from the original paper are presented in the Exhibit-R37. The authors - Watson and Crick, along with Maurice Hugh Frederick Wilkins, were jointly awarded the Nobel Prize in Physiology or Medicine 1962 "for their discoveries concerning the molecular structure of nucleic acids and its significance for information transfer in living material".[166] Watson and Crick acknowledged the unpublished data and observation of Dr. Maurice Hugh Frederick Wilkins and Rosalind Elsie Franklin. According to the history of the double helix discovery many people give most credit to Dr. Rosalind Elsie Franklin for her outstanding work on X-Ray crystallographic diffraction images of DNA revealing the double helix and her determination that the sugar- phosphate backbone lies

---

[166] http://www.nobelprize.org/nobel_prizes/medicine/laureates/1962/

outside the nucleotide chains.[167]

Exhibit-R37
A Structure for Deoxyribose Nucleic Acid
Watson J.D. and Crick F.H.C. Nature 171, 737-738 (1953)
Clips from their original paper
http://www.nature.com/nature/dna50/watsoncrick.pdf
http://www.nature.com/nature/dna50/archive.html

No. 4356   **April 25, 1953**   N A T U R E   737

equipment, and to Dr. G. E. R. Deacon and the captain and officers of R.R.S. *Discovery II* for their part in making the observations.

[1] Young, F. B., Gerrard, H., and Jevons, W., *Phil. Mag.*, 40, 149 (1920).
[2] Longuet-Higgins, M. S., *Mon. Not. Roy. Astro. Soc., Geophys. Supp.*, 5, 285 (1949).
[3] Von Arx, W. S., *Woods Hole Papers in Phys. Oceanog. Meteor.*, 11 (3) (1950).
[4] Ekman, V. W., *Arkiv. Mat. Astron. Fysik. (Stockholm)*, 2 (11) (1905).

MOLECULAR STRUCTURE OF NUCLEIC ACIDS

A Structure for Deoxyribose Nucleic Acid

WE wish to suggest a structure for the salt of deoxyribose nucleic acid (D.N.A.). This structure has novel features which are of considerable biological interest.

A structure for nucleic acid has already been proposed by Pauling and Corey[1]. They kindly made

We are much indebted to Dr. Jerry Donohue for constant advice and criticism, especially on inter-atomic distances. We have also been stimulated by a knowledge of the general nature of the unpublished experimental results and ideas of Dr. M. H. F. Wilkins, Dr. R. E. Franklin and their co-workers at

738   N A T U R E

King's College, London. One of us (J. D. W.) has been aided by a fellowship from the National Foundation for Infantile Paralysis.

J. D. WATSON
F. H. C. CRICK

Medical Research Council Unit for the Study of the Molecular Structure of Biological Systems,
Cavendish Laboratory, Cambridge.
April 2.

is a residue on each chain every 3·4 A. in the z-direction. We have assumed an angle of 36° between adjacent residues in the same chain, so that the structure repeats after 10 residues on each chain, that is, after 34 A. The distance of a phosphorus atom from the fibre axis is 10 A. As the phosphates are on the outside, cations have easy access to them.

The structure is an open one, and its water content is rather high. At lower water contents we should expect the bases to tilt so that the structure could become more compact.

The novel feature of the structure is the manner in which the two chains are held together by the purine and pyrimidine bases. The planes of the bases are perpendicular to the fibre axis. They are joined together in pairs, a single base from one chain being hydrogen-bonded to a single base from the other chain, so that the two lie side by side with identical z-co-ordinates. One of the pair must be a purine and the other a pyrimidine for bonding to occur. The hydrogen bonds are made as follows : purine position 1 to pyrimidine position 1 ; purine position 6 to pyrimidine position 6.

DNA is a polymer as it is made up of many nucleotides and a nucleotide is known as a DNA base. The length of a DNA strand is commonly expressed in terms of how many base pairs (bp) it contains. The bases only exist in pairs of A-T or G-C (Exhibit-R36 and R38). The base A is the complimentary to the base T and vice versa. The same is true for G and C. They are known as the complimentary bases. A DNA sequence refers to the structure how the nucleotides are sequentially arranged in the DNA. An example of a DNA sequence[168], in FASTA format[169], is given in the Exhibit-R38.

---

[167] http://en.wikipedia.org/wiki/Rosalind_Franklin and http://www.lankanewspapers.com/news/2007/3/12829_space.html
[168] From http://www.mitomap.org/MITOMAP/HumanMitoSeq.
[169] It is a text-based format. http://en.wikipedia.org/wiki/FASTA_format.

Exhibit-R38
Example of DNA sequence
single and double strands
These are the first 120 sequences form human mtDNA

---

single strand

1 gatcacaggt ctatcaccct attaaccact cacgggagct ctccatgcat ttggtatttt
61 cgtctggggg gtatgcacgc gatagcattg cgagacgctg gagccggagc accctatgtc

double strand. Please note the pairing of
G-C, A-T, C-G, and T-A

10	20	30	40	50	60

GATCACAGGT CTATCACCCT ATTAACCACT CACGGGAGCT CTCCATGCAT TTGGTATTTT
CTAGTGTCCA GATAGTGGGA TAATTGGTGA GTGCCCTCGA GAGGTACGTA AACCATAAAA

70	80	90	100	110	120

CGTCTGGGGG GTATGCACGC GATAGCATTG CGAGACGCTG GAGCCGGAGC ACCCTATGTC
GCAGACCCCC CATACGTGCG CTATCGTAAC GCTCTGCGAC CTCGGCCTCG TGGGATACAG

Source:
http://www.mitomap.org/MITOMAP/HumanMitoSeq

All DNA (nuclear and mitochondrial DNA) present in a cell is known as genome. Human genome consists of more than three billion base pairs and more than 21,000 genes have been identified[170]. A gene is an organization of specific DNA sequences for the function of genetic transcription and subsequent protein synthesis. Each gene synthesizes one specific protein. The genes are organized in 23 chromosomes (22 autosomes and one sex, X or Y, chromosome, Exhibit-R39), which are bundled and packed inside the nucleus. These are known as the nuclear DNA and nuclear genes. The 22 autosomes are the same in both man and woman but a woman has two copies of sex chromosome (XX) and a man has a copy of Y and X each (XY). Autosomes, in contrast to the sex chromosomes, contain the genes that code for all somatic (or non-sex) cell function.

---

[170] http://jul2012.archive.ensembl.org/Homo_sapiens/Info/StatsTable?db=core

Exhibit-R39
Human Chromosomes
22 autosome, 2 sex (X or Y) chromosome and mitochondrail DNA

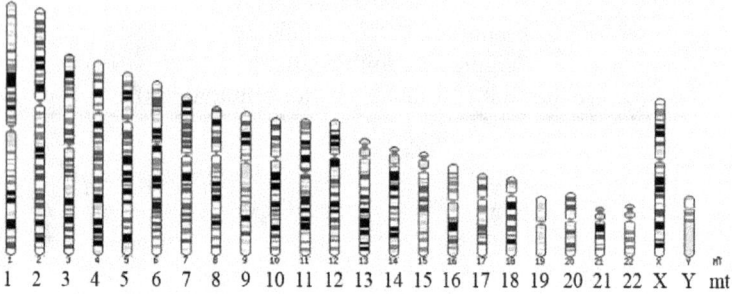

1 2 3 4 5 6 7 8 9 10 11 12 13 14 15 16 17 18 19 20 21 22 X Y mt

Source:
http://jul2012.archive.ensembl.org/Homo_sapiens/Location/Genome?r=6:133017695-133161157

Exhibit-R40
mtDNA circular structure with genes and regulatory regions labeled

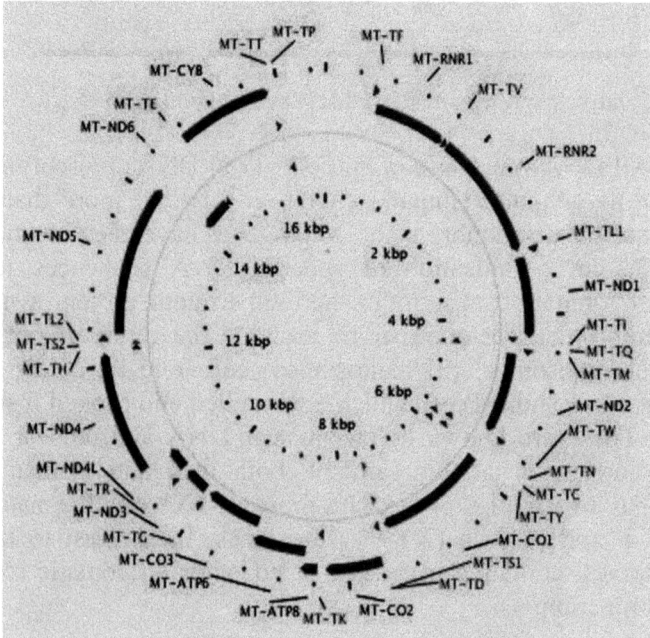

Credit:
http://ghr.nlm.nih.gov/mitochondrial-dna
This is a source of US government information and is in the public domain.

The human mtDNA, in contrast to the nuclear DNA, is very short, consisting of 16569 bp (base pairs) and 37 genes.[171] There is scientific evidence indicating that mitochondria actually are the alpha-bacteria (α-bacteria), which became fused and symbiotic with the eukaryotic cells some two billion years ago during the evolution of the multicellular organisms.[172] The bacterial origin is evidenced from its circular structure (Exhibit-R40),[173] contrasting from the linear strand of the nuclear DNA.

From visiting and studying about forty hours at the web sites of the National Institutes of Health, US government, one can become adequately educated in genetics and DNA science. A few links are given here.

- ❖ http://ghr.nlm.nih.gov/
- ❖ http://www.ncbi.nlm.nih.gov/
- ❖ http://hapmap.ncbi.nlm.nih.gov/
- ❖ http://www.nih.gov/
- ❖ http://blast.ncbi.nlm.nih.gov/Blast.cgi

The most significant fact is that mitochondria are maternally inherited and this biological phenomenon is almost universal[174] in the sexually[175] reproducing living organisms. That is why the maternal origin can be traced through the study of mtDNA whereas the paternal heritage can be traced through the Y-chromosome DNA. This is true for all multicellular (e.g., plants, animals, and fungi) organisms due the presence of the mitochondria in the cell. For example, the scientists have traced that Asian rice, *Oryza sativa*, was domesticated at around 8,200–13,500 years ago[176] and that all

---

[171] http://ghr.nlm.nih.gov/mitochondrial-dna

[172] Doolittle, W.F. Fun with genealogy, commentary, PNAS, 94, 1997, pp. 12751-53. http://www.pnas.org/content/94/24/12751.full#ref-1

[173] http://ghr.nlm.nih.gov/mitochondrial-dna
This is a source of US government information and is in the public domain.

[174] Thyagarajan, D. and Byrne, E. *Mitochondrial disorders of the nervous system: clinical, biochemical, and molecular genetics features*, in Mitochondrial function and dysfunction, ed. Anthony H.V. Schapira, International Review of Neurobiology Vol. 53, Academic Press, 2002, p131.

[175] Yes, 'asexual' reproduction also exists.

[176] Molinaa, J. et al. Molecular evidence for a single evolutionary origin of domesticated rice. *Proc. Natl Acad. Sci.* USA 108, 2011, pp 8351-8356.

varieties of rice was developed from a specific wild population of *Oryza rufipogon* "around the middle area the Pearl River in southern China."[177] As evidenced from the timing 8,200-13,500 years ago it is true that molecular dating cannot pinpoint to *the* year; just like the radiometric dating it gives a window of the time. Nevertheless, tracing of molecular marker(s) can accurately pinpoint *the* specific source of origin and place it in a time frame.

Humans have insatiable appetite for the knowledge of their ancestry. There are a number of commercial companies giving services for the genetic ancestry research, based on the paternal Y-chromosomal DNA and maternal mtDNA. The commercial companies also cooperate with the academics because of the complexity and sophistication of the DNA technology. National Geographic Magazine also has a big global Genographic project of human ancestry.[178] Recently, a group of eleven scientists and researchers from the United States of America, the United Kingdom and Cameroon, placed "the time to the most recent common ancestor (TMRCA)" of human paternity as far back as 338,000 years and traced to the Mbo people of Cameroon, west Central Africa, in their research article published in the American Journal of Human Genetics, volume 92, March 2013.[179] Their finding was based upon the research of the genetic markers of Y-chromosome, which is solely inherited from the father. It all started with an African American who wanted to know his ancestry and participated in the National Geographic Genographic project.[180] In this book my focus is on the maternal heritage mtDNA.

In the genetic studies, may it be in the field of evolution, hereditary, clinical medicine, or physiology, the molecular genetic markers are the key.

---

[177] Huang, X., et al. A map of rice genome variation reveals the origin of cultivated rice. *Nature* 490, 2012, pp 497-501. doi: 10.1038/nature11532. Epub 2012 Oct 3.

[178] https://genographic.nationalgeographic.com/about/

[179] Mendez, F.L., An African American Paternal Lineage Adds an Extremely Ancient Root to the Human Y Chromosome Phylogenetic Tree, *Am. J. Hum. Gen.* 92, 2013, pp 454-59 http://www.sciencedirect.com/science/article/pii/S0002929713000736

[180] http://www.science20.com/news_articles/human_y_chromosome_divergence_placed_least_300000_years_ago-105518

Exhibit-R41

Examples of DNA polymorphism (marker) that help to
identify the variant forms (haplotypes) of a DNA or gene

SNP (G to A mutation at position 8709 of M haplotype *Homo sapiens* mtDNA)

ACGATCAAAAGGGACAAGCATCAAG   M haplotype
| | | | | | | | | | | | | | | | | | | | | | | | |
ACGATCAAAAGGAACAAGCATCAAG   L3 haplotype

Insertion of a nucleotide T at the position 8278 of M
haplotype *Homo sapiens* mtDNA

CACCCCCTCTTACCCCCTCT   M haplotype
| | | | | | | | | | | | | | | | | | | |
CACCCCCTC-TACCCCCTCT   L3 haplotype

Note: the deletion is missing of nucleotide(s) but the
insertion is presence of extra nucleotie(s).

Short Tanden Repeat (STR) or microsatellites at the position
513 to 523 at M and L3 haplotype Homo sapiens mtDNA.
Short tandem CA repeats five times in this case.

CCCAGCACACACACACCGCT   M haplotype
| | | | | | | | | | | | | | | | | | | |
CCCAGCACACACACACCGCT   L3 haplotype

The molecular genetic markers are the *single nucleotide
polymorphism* (SNP, pronounced snip), *deletion or insertion* of one
or more nucleotide in the original (known as the wild type, *cf.* the
mutant) DNA sequence, and *tandem repeat polymorphism*. The
haplotypes are the variant forms of a DNA or gene. The examples of
the DNA polymorphism given in the Exhibit-R41 are from the
"blastn" result of KC896622.1 (Homo sapiens haplogroup M
mitochondrion) as query and (*Homo sapiens* isolate L3
mitochondrion, complete genome) as the reference subject at the
http://blast.ncbi.nlm.nih.gov/Blast.cgi with the option to "align two
or more sequences".

If you have interest please try out the following 'blast'. In
order to analyze the DNA sequences the researchers use
sophisticated software that are commercially available. Nevertheless,

it is not the software that makes the decision; it is the researchers who make the final scientific judgment based on their knowledge and experience. The genomic database at the NCBI (National Center for Biotechnology Information) is huge, consisting of all species of living things. A simple blast can help the scientist determine the place of a new DNA sequence in the world of living things. The following 'blast' worked on July 01, 2014 and it will work in future unless the NCBI modifies or alters it web site.

1. go to
http://blast.ncbi.nlm.nih.gov/Blast.cgi

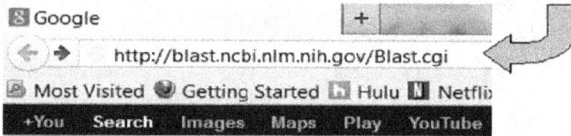

2. It will take you to the site of
http://blast.ncbi.nlm.nih.gov/Blast.cgi

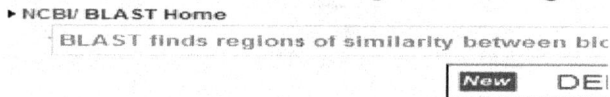

▸ NCBI/ BLAST Home

BLAST finds regions of similarity between bio

New   DEI

BLAST Assembled RefSeq Genomes

Choose a species genome to search. or list all ge

- Human
- Mouse
- Rat
- *Arabidopsis thaliana*

Basic BLAST

Choose a BLAST program to run.

nucleotide blast | Search a **nucleotide** databa
Algorithms: blastn, meg

3. Click at the "nucleotide blast"

Basic BLAST

Choose a BLAST program to run.

nucleotide blast | Search a **nucle**
Algorithms:

protein blast | Search **protein**
Algorithms:

4. It will take you the blast page

5. Enter the KC896622.1 at 'Query Sequence Check 'Align two or more sequences Enter JN580305.1 at 'Subject Sequence'

6. Scroll down the page and hit at 'BLAST'

Enter accession number, gi, or FASTA sequence ☺   Clear

JN580305.1

Or, upload file   Browse.. ☺

Program Selection

Optimize for   ◉ Highly similar sequences (megablast)

○ More dissimilar sequences (discontiguous megablast)

○ Somewhat similar sequences (blastn)

Choose a BLAST algorithm ☺

BLAST | Search nucleotide sequence using Megablast (Optimiz

☐ Show results in a new window

7. Results
Job title window will pop up for
a short time

▶ NCBI BLAST/ Format Request

Job Title: gb|KC896622.1| (16571 letters)

Request ID	U71THM7B114
Status	Searching
Time since submission	00:00:00

This page will be automatically updated in 1 seconds until search is done

8. Results

Alignment results will display provided that the correct information were entered. Scroll down the page, study, and analyze.
Take your time

9. Formatting options. If you do not see the sequence alignment displayed please check the formatting option and make sure to check the 'old view', 'Linkout', and 'Sequence Retrieval' and hit at 'Reformat'. The sequence alignment will show up with this format; if not, assume that the alignment server is too busy and try again sometime later.

9. formatting options. If you do not see the sequence alignment displayed please check the formatting option and make sure to check the 'old view', 'Linkout', and 'Sequence Retrieval' and hit at 'Reformat'.

▸ NCBI/ BLAST/ blastn suite-2sequences/ **Formatting Results - UZDNE1YV114**

| Edit and Resubmit | Save Search Strategies | ▽ Formatting options | ▷ Download |

Formatting options — Reformat

Show — Alignment as HTML — ☐ Old View — Reset form to defaults
Alignment View — Pairwise
Display — ☑ Graphical Overview — ☐ NCBI-gi — ☐ CDS feature
Masking — Character: Lower Case — Color: Grey
Limit results — Descriptions: 100 — Graphical overview: 100
Expect Min: — Expect Max:
Percent Identity Min: — Percent Identity Max:

Formatting options — Reformat

Show — Alignment as HTML — ☑ Old View — Reset form to defaults
Alignment View — Pairwise
Display — ☑ Graphical Overview — ☑ Linkout — ☑ Sequence Retrieval — ☐ NCBI-gi — ☐ CDS feature
Masking — Character: Lower Case — Color: Grey
Limit results — Descriptions: 100 — Graphical overview: 100 — Alignments: 100
Expect Min: — Expect Max:
Percent Identity Min: — Percent Identity Max:

Determination of a haplogroup and a haplotype are complicated and their nomenclature and classification is a scientific discipline established by various scientists across the world.[181] My presentation here is based upon the published papers in the peer-reviewed journals (print as well as online) and abstracts from the international conferences. Here, I give a list of bibliography so that the reader may explore for more information.

---

[181] Examples are http://www.hmtdb.uniba.it:8080/hmdb/ and http://www.mitotool.org/; http://hapmap.ncbi.nlm.nih.gov/

1. Baer AS (1995) Human Genes and Biocultural History in Southeast Asia, *Asian Perspectives*. 34: 21-35. http://scholarspace.manoa.hawaii.edu/bitstream/handle/10125/17 057/AP-v34n1-21-35.pdf?sequence=1

2. Basu A, Mukerjee N, Roy S, Sengupta S, Banerjee S, Chakraborty M, Dey B, Roy M, Roy B, Bhattacharyya NP, Roychoudhury S, and Majumder PP. (2003*) Ethnic India: A Genomic View, With Special Reference to Peopling and Structure,* Genome Res. 13:2277-90. http://www.ncbi.nlm.nih.gov/pmc/articles/PMC403703/

3. Bradley B (2008) Reconstructing phylogenies and phenotypes: a molecular view of human evolution *J. Anat.* 212: 337–353 doi: 10.1111/j.1469-7580.2007.00840.x http://onlinelibrary.wiley.com/doi/10.1111/j.1469-7580.2007.00840.x/full

4. Cordaux R, Saha N, Bentley G, Aunger R, Sirajuddin SM, and Stoneking M (2003) Mitochondrial DNA analysis reveals diverse histories of tribal populations from India *Eur J Hum Genet.* 11: 253–264 http://www.readcube.com/articles/10.1038/sj.ejhg.5200949

5. Derenko M, Malyarchuk B, Denisova G, Perkova M, Rogalla U, Grzybowski T, Khusnutdinova E, and Dambueva I. (2012) Complete Mitochondrial DNA Analysis of Eastern Eurasian Haplogroups Rarely Found in Populations of Northern Asia and Eastern Europe. PLoS ONE 7(2): e32179. doi:10.1371/journal.pone.0032179 http://www.plosone.org/article/info%3Adoi %2F10.1371%2Fjournal.pone.0032179

6. Gonder MK, Mortensen HM, Reed FA, de Sousa A, and Tishkoff SA. (2007) Whole-mtDNA Genome Sequence Analysis of Ancient African Lineages, *Mol. Biol. Evol.* 24:757–768. http://mbe.oxfordjournals.org/content/24/3/757.full.pdf+html

7. The HUGO Pan-Asian SNP Consortium (2009) Mapping Human Genetic Diversity in Asia, *Science* 326: 1541-45, *DOI:* 10.1126/science.1177074.
http://humpopgenfudan.cn/p/A/A1.pdf

8. Knight MT. (no date of web posting) An Introduction to Haplogroups: An Interactive Activity, Activity developed by Meredith T. Knight at Tufts University as part of David R. Walt's HHMI Professor's Award. Last accessed on June 07, 2013.
http://ase.tufts.edu/chemistry/hhmi/documents/Detailed_Haplogroup_Activity.pdf

9. Kong Q-P, Sun C, Wang H-W, Zhao M, Wang W-Z, Zhong L, Hao X-D, Pan Hui, Wang S-Y, Cheng Y-T, Zhu C-L, Wu S-F, Liu L-N, Jin J-Q, Yao Y-G, and Zhang Y-P (2010) Large-Scale mtDNA Screening Reveals a Surprising Matrilineal Complexity in East Asia and Its Implications to the Peopling of the Region, *Mol. Biol. Evol.* 28(1):513–522. 2011 doi:10.1093/molbev/msq219.
http://mbe.oxfordjournals.org/content/28/1/513.full

10. Kumar V, Langsiteh BT, Biswas S, Babu JP, Rao TN, Thangaraj K, Reddy AG, Singh L, and Reddy BM. (2006) Asian and Non-Asian Origins of Mon-Khmer- and Mundari-Speaking Austro-Asiatic Populations of India, Am J Hum Biol 18:461–469. http://wysinger.homestead.com/india.pdf

11. Kumar V and Reddy B M (2003) Status of Austro-Asiatic groups in the peopling of India: An exploratory study based on the available prehistoric, linguistic and biological evidences, *J. Biosci.* **28** 507–22. http://www.ias.ac.in/jbiosci/jun2003/507.pdf

12. Maji S., Krithika S. and Vasulu T. S. 2009 Phylogeographic distribution of mitochondiral DNA macrohaplogroup M in India. *J. Genet.* 88, 127–139
http://www.ias.ac.in/jgenet/Vol88No1/127.pdf

13. Metspalu M, Kivisild T, Metspalu E, Parik J, Hudjashov G, Kaldma K, Serk P, Karmin M, Behar DM, Gilbert MTP, Endicott P, Mastana S, Papiha SS, Skorecki K, Torroni A, and Villems R. (2004) Most of the extant mtDNA boundaries in South and Southwest Asia were likely shaped during the initial settlement of Eurasia by anatomically modern humans, *BMC Genetics* 2004, 5:26 doi:10.1186/1471-2156-5-26
http://www.biomedcentral.com/1471-2156/5/26/

14. Oppenheimer S (2012) Out-of-Africa, the peopling of continents and islands: tracing uniparental gene trees across the map, (a review), *Phil. Trans. R. Soc.* B 367: 770–784 doi:10.1098/rstb.2011.0306.
http://www.bradshawfoundation.com/journey/

15. Oven MV (2010) Revision of the mtDNA tree and corresponding haplogroup nomenclature, Proc Natl Acad Sci U S A 107: E38–E39.
http://www.pnas.org/content/107/11/E38.full

16. Pierson, MJ, Martinez-Arias R, Holland BR, Gemmell NJ, Hurles ME, and Penny D. (2006) Deciphering Past Human Population Movements in Oceania: Provably Optimal Trees of 127 mtDNA Genomes, *Mol. Biol. Evol.* 231966–1975 doi:10.1093/molbev/msl063.
http://mbe.oxfordjournals.org/content/23/10/1966.full.pdf

17. Quintana-Murci L, Chaix R, Wells RS, Behar DM, Sayar H, Scozzari R, Rengo C, Al-Zahery N, Semino O, Santachiara-Benerecetti AS, Coppa A, Ayub Q, 18. Mohyuddin A. Where West Meets East: The Complex mtDNA Landscape of the Southwest and Central Asian Corridor (2004) *Am. J. Hum. Genet.* 74: 827–845.
http://www.ncbi.nlm.nih.gov/pmc/articles/PMC1181978/

18. Rajkumar R, Banerjee J, Guntur HB, Trivedi R, and Kashyap VK (2005) Phylogeny and antiquity of M macrohaplogroup inferred from complete mt DNA sequence of Indian specific

lineages, *BMC Evolutionary Biology* **5**:26 doi:10.1186/1471-2148-5-26
http://www.biomedcentral.com/1471-2148/5/26

19. Reddy BM, Langstieh BT, Kumar V, Nagaraja T, Reddy ANS, Meki A, Reddy AG, Thangaraj K, and Singh L. (2007) Austro-Asiatic Tribes of Northeast India Provide Hitherto Missing Genetic Link between South and Southeast Asia. *PLoS ONE* 2(11): e1141. doi:10.1371/journal.pone.0001141
http://www.readcube.com/articles/10.1371/journal.pone.0001141

20. Rubino F, Piredda R, Calabrese FM, Simone D, Lang M, Calabrese C, Petruzzella V, Tommaseo-Ponzetta M, Gasparre G, and Attimonelli M. (2012) HmtDB, a genomic resource for mitochondrion-based human variability studies, *Nucleic Acids Research* 40:
doi:10.1093/nar/gkr1086.
http://www.ncbi.nlm.nih.gov/pmc/articles/PMC3245114/

21. Summerer M, Horst J, Erhart G, Weißensteiner H, Schönherr S, Pacher D, Forer L, Horst D, Manhart A, Horst B, Sanguansermsri T and Kloss-Brandstätter A (2014), Large-scale mitochondrial DNA analysis in Southeast Asia reveals evolutionary effects of cultural isolation in the multi-ethnic population of Myanmar, BMC Evolutionary Biology, 14:17
doi:10.1186/1471-2148-14-17
http://www.biomedcentral.com/1471-2148/14/17

22. Sun C, Kong Q-P, Palanichamy MG, Agrawal S, Bandelt H-J, Yao Y-G, Khan F, Zhu C-L, Chaudhuri TK, and Zhang Y-P. (2006) The Dazzling Array of Basal Branches in the mtDNA Macrohaplogroup M from India as Inferred from Complete Genomes, Mol. Biol. Evol. 23:683–690.
http://www.ymf.ynu.edu.cn/SCI/2006SCI/2006/SunC%20MBE%202006.pdf

23. Thangaraj K, Chaubey G, Singh VK, Vanniarajan A, Thanseem I, Reddy AG, and Singh L. (2006) In situ origin of deep rooting lineages of mitochondrial Macrohaplogroup 'M' in

India, BMC Genomics, 7:151. doi:10.1186/1471-2164-7-151
http://www.biomedcentral.com/1471-2164/7/151

24. Thangaraj K, Singh L, Reddy AG, Rao R, Sehgal SC, Underhill PA, Pierson M, Frame IG, Hagelberg E. (2003) Genetic Affinities of the Andaman Islanders, a Vanishing Human Population, Curr Biol. 13, 86–93. PII S0960-9822(02)01336-2
http://www.sciencedirect.com/science/article/pii/S096098220201 3362

Exhibit-R42
Homo sapiens mtDNA haplogroup family tree simplified, based on Gonder et al. (2007), bibliography list#6 in the text.

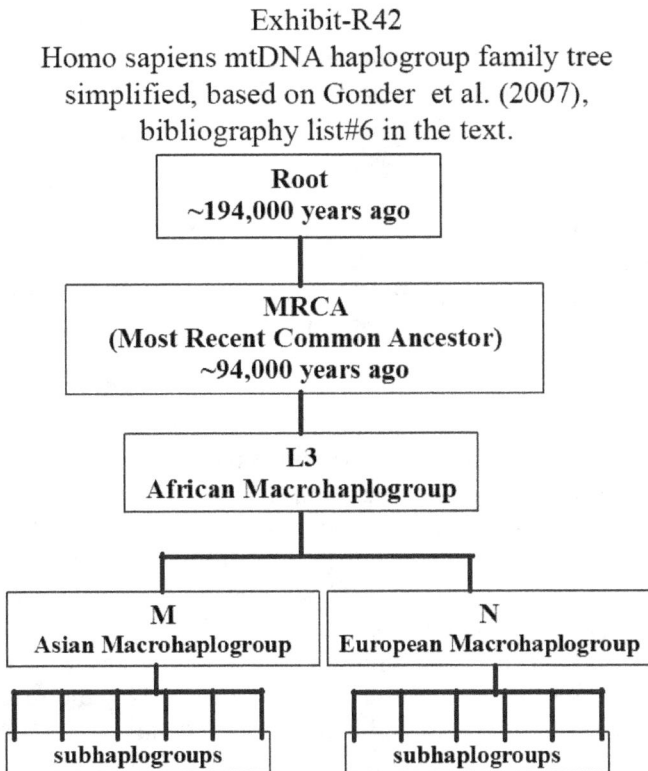

As cited and described at the beginning of this chapter the *Mitochondrial DNA in Myanmar*[182] as reported by J. Horst and his

---

[182] Horst J., et. al. *Mitochondrial DNA in Myanmar*: Complete mitochondrial genome sequencing revealed several new lineages within macro-haplogroup M. Abstract, 2012. The abstract was downloaded on May 28, 2013 from

colleagues (also see the footnote#162) reflects historical, cultural and people diversity in Myanmar, a paramount feature of common humanity. Above all, despite having *subhaplogroup* diversities (also known as subclades), Myanmar mtDNA belongs to the M *macrohaplogroup*, demonstrating the evidence of their common origin, as can be seen in the illustrated genetic mtDNA haplogroup tree (Exhibit-R42). This conclusion is in good agreement with that of the *Mapping Human Genetic Diversity in Asia* by the HUGO Pan-Asian SNP Consortium (see the bibliography list #7). The paper was authored by 92 scientists of the HUGO Pan-Asian SNP Consortium plus Indian Genome Variation Consortium, representing 31 institutes and universities of 10 countries, namely China, India, Indonesia, Japan, Korea, Malaysia, Philippines, Singapore, Taiwan, Thailand, and USA[183]. Therefore, the strength and significance of their research finding is formidable.

The authors concluded their research report as follows:
"Although this study does not disprove a two-wave model of migration, the evidence from our autosomal data and the accompanying simulation studies (figs. S29 and S30) point toward a history that unites the Negrito and non-Negrito populations of Southeast and East Asia via a single primary wave of entry of humans into the continent."[184]

The Hugo SNP Consortium finding "single primary wave" of modern human entry into Europe and Asian from Africa (popularly known as the *out-of-Africa* migration) is consistent with the evidence that is well researched and examined by another international research group, Metspalu *et al.* 2004 (bibliography list #13), with eighteen scientists from seven institutes and universities of five countries (Estonia, Israel, Italy, United Kingdom, USA). They explained the out-of-Africa migration in the Figure 5 of their article. Here, I am presenting the figure as the Exhibit-R43; the reader may consult the original paper cited here for more details.

No matter what–single, double or multiple migration(s)–all

---

http://www.ashg.org/2012meeting/abstracts/fulltext/f120121871.htm.,
American Society of Human Genetics, http://www.ashg.org/
[183] http://www4a.biotec.or.th/PASNP/front-page/pan-asian-snp-participants
[184] The HUGO Pan-Asian SNP Consortium (2009) Mapping Human Genetic Diversity in Asia, *Science* 326: 1541-45, *DOI:* 10.1126/science.1177074.
http://humpopgenfudan.cn/p/A/A1.pdf

scientific evidences vividly show that human is one kind and one family.

Exhibit-R43
'Out-of-Africa' modern human migration from 'Figure 5 Peopling of Eurasia' by Metspalu et al. 2004 (bibliography list #13)

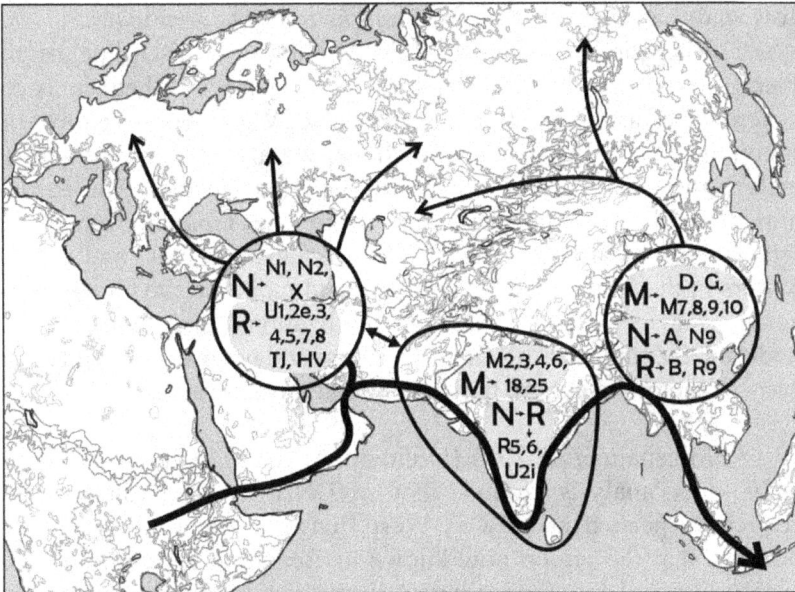

Metspalu et al. 2004 concluded that the out-of-Africa migration took place between 60,000 to 80,000 years before present (ybp) and the 'local haplogroups arose' around 40,000 to 60,000 ybp.

Now is the time and space to indulge in rhetoric.

Myanmar government and people are undertaking a process to 'clean up' the Rohingya with the racial excuse that they are the Bengalis.

"Are the Rohingya Bengali?"

This is not a scientific question. The question originated in Myanmar in a complex milieu of race, religion, culture, discrimination, hatred, jealousy, and politics, on the top of the struggle for existence. The Myanmar people have been biting hard at the Rohingya with the racial slur that they are the Illegal Bengali. Every living organism struggles for existence; it is the process of nature. A human, how great his or her esteem may be, is not above the natural law of the struggle for existence. I am not here to politicize science, but science can be used to solve the problems generated by the practice of non-science, quasi-science, pseudo-science, or quack-science. The question–"Are the Rohingya Bengali?"– is in the realm of non-science or unscientific culture. How shall I answer it? *Rhetoric could be a way to deal with it!*

Rhetoric is not quack-science, but is a discipline of the liberal arts. According to Dr. L. Kip Wheeler[185] "Rhetoric is the ancient art of argumentation and discourse. When we write or speak to convince others of what we believe, we are 'rhetors.' When we analyze the way rhetoric works, we are 'rhetoricians.' The earliest known studies of rhetoric come from the Golden Age, when philosophers of ancient Greece discussed logos, ethos, and pathos. Writers in the Roman Empire adapted and modified the Greek ideas. Across the centuries, medieval civilizations also adapted and modified the theories of rhetoric. Even today, many consider the study of rhetoric a central part of a liberal arts education."[186]

Metspalu *et al.* 2004 (bibliography list #13), in their in-depth study and analysis found that mtDNA M macrohaplogroup frequency "peaked at 86% in West Bengal." The finding strongly indicates that the region now known as Bengal at the confluence of mighty *Ganga* and *Brahmaputra* rivers was (and still is) a hub of human settlement and migration from South to Southeast and East Asia. In other words Bengal *is the Grand Central[187]* of human transit from the days of first modern human settlement in Asia. This conclusion finds its support in the statement, "the evidence from our autosomal data and the accompanying simulation studies (figs. S29 and S30) point toward a history that unites the Negrito and non-Negrito populations of Southeast and East Asia via a single primary wave of entry of humans into the continent,"[188] presented by the study of the HUGO SNP Consortium. It means that the dark-and-ugly-like-ogre Rohingya and fair-and-beautiful Consulate-General

---

[185] http://web.cn.edu/kwheeler/introduction_to_teacher.html

[186] http://web.cn.edu/kwheeler/resource_rhet.html

[187] A metaphor after the New York City Grand Central Terminal.

[188]The HUGO Pan-Asian SNP Consortium (2009) Mapping Human Genetic Diversity in Asia, *Science* 326: 1541-45, *DOI:* 10.1126/science.1177074. http://humpopgenfudan.cn/p/A/A1.pdf

Ye Myint Aung[189] both came from a single common ancestry. This in turn would mean that their most recent common ancestor (MRCA)[190] came from the Bengal region. *Therefore, the dark-and-ugly and the fair-and-beautiful are both Bengalis.*

The findings of the anthropological (population) molecular genetics are always checked and validated with the archaeological findings, and vice versa. Therefore, it is needed to know what the archaeologists find in the given region(s). As an example, I present here a piece of archaeological review by Syed Mohammad Kamrul Ahsan, Professor of Archaeology, Jahangirnagar University, Bangladesh, that I downloaded on June 30, 2014 from Banglapedia (http://www.banglapedia.org/HT/P_0276.htm). Professor Ahsan is a leading researcher in the Indian Subcontinent. The review is under the category of 'prehistory'. The interested reader may visit Banglapedia at http://www.banglapedia.org/ and also read the articles under the category 'archaeology'.

"The prehistoric site of Chaklapunji tea garden, near Chandirmazar of Chunarughat, has also revealed a significant number of prehistoric tools from the bed of a small ephemeral stream ... known as *Balu nadi*... Typologically, technologically, and morphometrically, the artefacts are more or less the same as those found in the Lalmai area. // ... similar pre-historic finds were reported from the Haora and Khoai valleys of Tripura State, India. The Anyathian and Neolithic tools from Irrawaddy Valley of Burma bear close resemblance to the finds of Lalmai hills and Chaklapunji of Bangladesh. The technological and typological similarities and distribution of fossil wood assemblages in considerable high frequency throughout the eastern and southeastern part of Bangladesh, Haora, and Khowai valley of Tripura, and Irrawaddy valley of Burma suggest a regional prehistoric cultural tradition in this region."

---

[189] Please recall from the previous chapter "The Aborigines."
[190] For more information on MRCA, see
http://en.wikipedia.org/wiki/Most_recent_common_ancestor

Therefore, my answer shall be "not only the Rohingya but also all Burmese and beyond are Bengalis."

Indeed, the answer may sound rhetorical and would upset some people. However, rhetoric is a means of communication that hammers a hard *nail* of idea, thought, or philosophy into a dogmatic, stubborn, and hard-to-crack mind, with the hope of making it re-think. Though rhetoric, it is based on the anthropological (population) molecular genetics and archaeological evidence. Therefore, please consider it as an incentive to Myanmar people to rethink and reanalyze *everything* of Myanmar in light of *common humanity*, culturally as well as scientifically, in order to build a healthier and happier Myanmar society.

In conclusion, no matter what, the scientific studies of the mtDNA of Asian people strongly support the aboriginality of the Rohingya found in the historical records and oral traditions of the region, which are discussed in the previous chapter.

Special Note.

I am aware of the fact that this piece of presentation will not solve the complicated questions of race or religion. The main objective of this chapter is to lay the foundation of 'common humanity'. 'Race and human genomic diversity' is a very big subject of study and research. All humans share more than 99.9 percent of the 3.3 billion DNA bases of the entire genome (see the Human Genome Project at http://www.genome.gov/). This means, roughly, 3,296,700,000 DNA bases are the same in everyone on this planet. This means, roughly, 3,300,000 (3.3 million) DNA bases are different between any two individuals. These differences make an individual. To a biologist, the differences are the individual variations or individualization in the given environment of habitat. There is no scientific evidence indicating that the 'individual variations' constitute the 'adaptive radiation' that may lead to cladogenesis or speciation in the process of human evolution, because the human distribution and adaptation is global in contrast to the Galapagos Finches of Darwin. For the interested readers in the race and genomic diversities, I would like to recommend the following articles as the starting point of study. As for the classic adaptive radiation and speciation please refer to Charles Darwin's *On the Origin of Species*. John Murray, London, 1859.

1. Lisa Gannett, *Racism and Human Genome Diversity Research: The Ethical Limits of "Population Thinking"*, Philosophy of Science, Sept 2001v68 i3 pS479, Page 1-8, http://www.asc.upenn.edu/usr/ogandy/C53704read/Gannett.pdf. Last accessed on July 4, 2014.

2. Priscilla Wald, *Blood and stories: how genomics is rewriting race, medicine and human history*, Patterns of Prejudice, Vol. 40, Nos 4_/5, 2006, p 303-333, https://www.princeton.edu/~publicma/Wald_article.pdf. Last accessed on July 4, 2014.

3. Paul Voosen, *In Research Involving Genome Analysis, Some See a 'New Racism"*, in the section of the Chronicle Review in the Chronicle of Higher Education, March 24, 2014, http://chronicle.com/article/In-Research-Involving-Genome/145397/. Last accessed on July 4, 2014.

4. Leakey, Richard. *The Origin of Humankind* (Science Masters Series), Basic Books, 1996

5. Howell, Clark F. and Bourliere, Francois, (Eds.). *African Ecology and Human Evolution*, Aldine Transaction, 2007

6. Givnish, Thomas J. and Sytsma, Kenneth J. (Eds.), *Molecular Evolution and Adaptive Radiation*. Springer; 2010 edition, 2010

My concern is especially so because the revival of Myanmarism[191] is also accompanied with the claim that Myanmar is the place of human origin. For example, U Kyaw Hsan, in his capacity of Minister of the Information Ministry, declared in 2011

---

[191] Shwe Lu Maung, *The Price of Silence: Muslim-Buddhist War of Bangladesh and Myanmar – A Social Darwinist's Analysis,* DewDrop Arts & Technology, USA, 2005, see the Chapters 4,5,6, and 7.

that the world has recognized that "human origin is at Myanmar", as per reported given by the government official newspapers, Myanmar Ahlin, July 24, 2011, p 9. Myanmar authorities refute the "out-of-Africa" evidence with the assertion that human origin actually is "out-of-Myanmar". Please see the Exhibit-R44A given below. U Kyaw Hsan, the Minister of the Ministry of Information, said that "human-like primate fossils had been found at Pondaung[192] area. These Pondaung Primate fossils[193] were found to be 40 million years old. They were older than those of Africa which were dated to be 33 million years only. Therefore, the world has recognized that 'human origin is at Myanmar'." U Kyaw Hsan, a former Brigadier General, is presently (as of July 2014) is the Minister of the Ministry of Cooperatives.[194] Also, I noticed a piece of news that reported that Burmese archaeologists have determined that human origin is at the Samon Basin of central Burma.[195] The report says, ""Stone Weapons used in Stone Age Period and Advanced Primates, Human-like Primates were excavated at the Samon River Region wide in Myanmar, Stone Age People and Preliminary Stone Age People were Myanmar born that Human evolution growth as Phases of Fauna World in Myanmar, the Human Origin started from the Samon River Valley," exposed Archaeologists." (See Exhibit-R44B). The same news in Burmese was also posted online (Exhibit-R44C).[196] My humble view is that the Myanmar authorities and scientists ought to be more prudent. In the field of science, it is the best to leave such matters of research findings to the peer-reviewed professional journals and Myanmar must have specially trained science journalists. It is important that the scientific findings are not abused in allure of racism and discrimination.

---

[192] See Yaowalak Chaimaneea et. al. *Late Middle Eocene primate from Myanmar and the initial anthropoid colonization of Africa*, PNAS June 26, 2012 vol. 109 no. 26 10293-10297. Abstract at http://www.pnas.org/content/109/26/10293.
[193] Also see Shwe Lu Maung, *The Price of Silence Muslim-Buddhist War of Bangladesh and Myanmar, A Social Darwinist's Analysis*, DewDrop Art & Technology,USA, 2005, pp160-163
[194] See Myanma Ahlin, August 28, 2012, Frontpage.
[195] http://burmeseclassic.org/news_detail.php?id=2652&type=3
[196] http://www.swesonemedia.org/index.php?q=5825

Exhibit-R44A
Myanmar asserts that the Central Burma is the place of human origin

U Kyaw Hsan. Myanma Ahlin, July 24, 2011, backpage and p9. English version is my translation, paraphrased to convey the meaning only.

ရှာဖွေဖော်ထုတ်ချက်အရ ပုံတောင်ပုံညာဒေသ မြိုင်မြို့နယ်နှင့် ပုလဲ မြို့နယ်များတွင် အဆင့်မြင့် လူတူ့ပရိုင်းမိတ်ရုပ်ကြွင်းများ စတင်တွေ့ရှိခဲ့ပြီး နိုင်ငံတကာရှိ အဖွဲ့အစည်းများက ခေတ်မီနည်းစနစ်များဖြင့် စစ်ဆေး ခဲ့ရာ ရှေးနှစ်ပေါင်းသန်း (၄၀)က လူတူ့ပရိုင်းမိတ် ရုပ်ကြွင်းများအဖြစ် သိရှိခဲ့ရကြောင်း၊ ထိုပရိုင်းမိတ်များသည် အာဖရိကဒေသတွင် တွေ့ရှိရ သည့် နှစ်သန်း (၃၃)နှစ် သက်တမ်းရှိ ပရိုင်းမိတ်ရုပ်ကြွင်းများထက် သက်တမ်းပိုမိုစောသည့်အတွက် "ကမ္ဘာ့လူသားအစမြန်မာက"ဟု ကမ္ဘာ ကပင် အသိအမှတ်ပြုလက်ခံခဲ့ကြကြောင်း။

U Kyaw Hsan, the Minister of the Ministry of Information, said that human-like primate fossils had been found at Pondaung area. These Pondaung Primate fossils were found to be 40 million years old, They were older than those of Africa which were dated to be 33 million years only. Therefore, the world has recognized that 'human origin is at Myanmar'.

Exhibit-R44B
Myanmar asserts that the Central Burma is the place of human origin

http://burmeseclassic.org/news_detail.php?id=2652&type=3
accessed on June 05, 2014

Human Source Origin
Started From The Samon River Valley Myanmar
From : Pyi Myanmar News Journal, May 07, 2014

Human Source Origin Started From The Samon River Valley Myanmar

From : Pyi Myanmar News Journal

May 07, 2014

"Stone Weapons used in Stone Age Period and Advanced Primates, Human-like Primates were excavated at the Samon River Region wide in Myanmar, Stone Age People and Preliminary Stone Age People were Myanmar born that Human evolution growth as Phases of Fauna World in Myanmar, the Human Origin started from the Samon River Valley," exposed Archaeologists.

"In the Samon Valley, Myanmar Archaeologists and the *French National Center for Scientific Research* (*Centre national de la recherche scientifique, CNRS*) cooperated excavations from 1998 to 2009 that the Region not only developed Stone Age, Copper Age and Iron Age Eras, there could be proved the Valley was Human Originated Source," said in Samon Valley Research Paper Presentation Seminar held on 3rd May.

Exhibit-R44C
Myanmar asserts that the Central Burma is the place of human origin

http://www.swesonemedia.org/index.php?q=5825
accessed on May 15, 2014

SweSone Media Group

လူသားဇာစ်မြစ်သည် မြန်မာနိုင်ငံ စမုံမြစ်ဝှမ်းက စတင်ခဲ့ဟု ဆို

9
Self-Alienation

While unjust alienation of the Rohingya by the people and *State* of Myanmar is opposed and rejected it is imperative, for all fairness, to examine if the Rohingya are playing a fair or unfair game at their end. In such an examination I found that the Rohingya have been carrying out, knowingly or unknowingly, a process of *self-alienation*. The Rohingya must reject and stop such self-alienation. I fully understand that 99% or even 99.95% of the Rohingya are simple farmers and fishermen. They are illiterate, barely literate, uneducated and absolutely poor. They do not understand the implications of the politics that have been carrying out, in their name, by a fistful of the Rohingya elite who occupy the leadership by the questionable virtue of elitism. There are three actions that self-alienates the Rohingya.

Self-Alienation-1. Mujahid rebellion in 1950s was the first act of Rohingya self-alienation. I have presented the surrender of the Mujahids in the Chapter 4 Pure Gold. The Mujahid's objective of annexing the Mayu region to then Pakistan was an act of Rohingya self-alienation. The political circumstances that shrouded the British withdrawal from the region and formation of India, Pakistan, and Burma compelled the Rohingya into armed insurrection to make their voice heard. The British authorities and the emerging leaders of the Indo-Pakistan-Burman region totally ignored their voice and views. In this respect the Rohingya fell in the same boat with many other Fourth World people (e.g. the Chin, the Kachin, the Shan, the Karenni, the Karen of Burma; the Mizo, the Manipuri, the Naga of the Northeast region of India, and the Chakma and the Mrama of Pakistan). For more discussion in this respect please also see the coming chapter "Citizenship and beyond". As such, it is not fair to squarely put the blame on the armed insurrection of the Rohingya who belong to Fourth World nations.[197] We must also put the blame

---

[197] Also see Shwe Lu Maung, *Burma Nationalism and Ideology*, University Press Ltd., Dhaka, 1989, Chapter 9.

on the authorities who ignored their voices. Nevertheless, rather unfortunately, judgment and decision are made in light of *the face value*, no matter what the circumstances may determine *the face value*. Therefore, we also need to take care of *the face value* that I present here.

The Rohingya's armed insurrection is different, for example, from the Kachin rebellion, in its objective. The Kachin fights for either independence or a genuine federation. The same is true for the other ethnic rebellions of the Shan, the Karen, the Kachin, the Mon, the Karenni, the Chin, and the Rakhine etc. The fight with the cry of either independence or genuine federation of the Kachin, the Karen, and the Mon etc. is considered a fight against Burman colonialism and chauvinism but not a struggle of pro-West, pro-East, or pro-Religion. But the Rohingya Mujahids fought not for an independent state or a genuine federation but with a view of cutting of their region from Myanmar to join another country known as Pakistan *(Islamic Republic of Pakistan)*,[198] in the name of the Muslim Brotherhood. Therefore the Rohingya Mujahid rebellion is seen as pro-Pakistan and Pan-Islamic *protégé* but not pro-independence, nor pro-federation. This is *the face value* of the past Rohingya's armed insurrection that still casts a shadow in Myanmar politics today. This is the reason why the Myanmar rebel alliances such as the National Democratic Front (NDF) and the Democratic Alliance of Burma (DAB) rejected the membership application of *the* Rohingya armed organizations but the DAB accepted the membership of other Muslim armed forces such as All Burma Muslim Union (ABMU) and Muslim Liberation Organization of Burma (MLOB). Please see my book *Burma Nationalism and Ideology*[199] for more information.

With the surrender of the last Mujahid to the Myanmar government in 1961 (see the Chapter 4 Pure Gold) the Mujahid chapter was closed but the ghost of the pro-Pakistan and Pan- Islamic *protégé* keeps haunting not only to the people but also to the State of Myanmar. The ghost of the pro-Pakistan and Pan-Islamic[200] *protégé* or its simplified version *Mujahid ghost* even disturbs Bangladesh to her irritation and dismay. It is a fact that when newly independent

---

[198] Please recall Brigadier General Aung Gyi's speech in the Chapter 4 Pure Gold.

[199] Shwe Lu Maung, *Burma Nationalism and Ideology*, University Press Ltd., Dhaka, 1989.

[200] For more about Pan-Islam see Shwe Lu Maung, The Price of Silence: Muslim-Buddhist War of Bangladesh and Myanmar – A Social Darwinist's Analysis, DewDrop Arts & Technology, USA, 2005, Chapter 2&3.

Bangladesh opened its Consulate at Sittwe (Akyab) in 1972 a good number of Rohingya turned up and staged a protest shouting "Pakistan Zindabad". It is also a fact that Rohingya elite opposed the Bangladesh liberation struggle and remained pro-Pakistan and pro-Jamaat-e-Islami[201] until 1994. I do not know of the relationship between the Rohingya elite and the Islamic parties of Bangladesh in the post 1994. This is the reason that Bangladesh remains cautious and hostile at times to the Rohingya. How do I know about the *inner* feeling of Bangladesh? I lived as a domiciled Bangladeshi for 14 years and with sincerity and gratefulness I served my adopted country as a R&D scientist (Chief Scientific Officer) at her prestigious institute, Bangladesh Institute of Research and Rehabilitation in Diabetes, Endocrine and Metabolic Disorders (BIRDEM), working directly under its president, National Professor Dr. M. Ibrahim, the top physician and a former Cabinet Minister. In virtue of my official status I was privileged to have acquainted and even become friends with a number of Cabinet and State Ministers, and Secretaries, Joint-Secretaries, and Deputy-Secretaries. After publication of my book *Burma Ideology and Nationalism* from the University Press Ltd., in 1989, I was honored to get introduced to a number of leading politicians and journalists. Prominent journalist Mr. Enayetullah Khan[202] happily published my articles in his famed *Weekly Holiday*. My statement of the Rohingya elite and Bangladesh relationship is based upon combination of my own experience and what I learned from those leading citizens of Bangladesh.[203]

Therefore, I can say, most confidently, that it is very important for the Rohingya to get rid of the *Mujahid ghost* in order to establish a new friendly image not only in Myanmar but also in Bangladesh. Let me be candid again; the image of pro-Pakistan and Pan-Islamic *protégé* must be totally erased. I know the image of

---

[201] For more about Jamaat-e-Islami see Shwe Lu Maung, *The Price of Silence: Muslim-Buddhist War of Bangladesh and Myanmar – A Social Darwinist's Analysis*, DewDrop Arts & Technology, USA, 2005, pp 111-128.

[202] Enayetullah Khan (1939-2005), was a leftist intellectual and journalist. Known for his weekly Holiday (Chief-Editor) founded in 1965 and New Age founded in 2003, recipient of Ekushey Padak in 2004 for excellence in journalism, cabinet minister of Bangladesh government (1977-78), ambassador to China, North Korea, Cambodia and Myanmar (1984–1989).
http://newagebd.com/detail.php?date=2012-11-10&nid=29626#.UbZB1srDCPo

[203] Alo see Shwe Lu Maung, *The Price of Silence: Muslim-Buddhist War of Bangladesh and Myanmar – A Social Darwinist's Analysis*, DewDrop Arts & Technology, USA, 2005

protégé was created some 60-year ago in the past but is being still cherished by few elite. As a result, its shadow swallows entire unfortunate Rohingya populace who are virtually voiceless. Therefore, in order to come out of the *shadow* the *image* must entirely be erased.

It must also be recognized that the Mujahid rebellion was rejected by the Rohingya populace at large as I mentioned in my earlier book.[204] I have already mentioned earlier in this book that Brigadier General Aung Gyi, on behalf of the Burmese Government, welcomed last 200 of them in 1961. Today, also the Rohingya, including such big names as the Arakan Rohingya National Organization (ARNO) and the Rohingya Solidarity Organization (RSO), have abandoned armed struggle and they are engaged in peaceful movement for a better democratic society. The leaders like Nurul Islam (ARNO) and Dr. Yunus (RSO) have repeatedly stated that they are for a democratic reform. Therefore, it is reasonable and pragmatic to totally eliminate *the face value, the shadow of the ghost,* and *the ghost itself* of the Mijahid armed insurrection that died 53 years ago.

Having said in favor of democratic reform we must also keep vigilance of such new development presented in the Exhibit-PRO[205] that will harm the non-violent movement.

---

[204] Shwe Lu Maung, *The Price of Silence: Muslim-Buddhist War of Bangladesh and Myanmar – A Social Darwinist's Analysis*, DewDrop Arts & Technology,USA, 2005, p 29.
[205] http://www.stasiareport.com/the-big-story/asia-report/indonesia/story/2-rohingya-leaders-go-shopping-terror-indonesia-20130711; http://www.bt.com.bn/news-asia/2013/07/15/myanmar-denies-rohingya-military-training-reports; http://www.rfa.org/english/news/myanmar/militants-07122013183218.html

Exhibit-PR0
Rohingya Militant False Alert

www.stasiareport.com/the-big-story/asia-report/indonesia/story/2-rohingya-leaders-go-shopping-terror-indonesia-2013

THE STRAITS TIMES

asiareport

| Politics/Diplomacy | Economy | In Transition | Opinion | Editorial |

Greater China > India/South Asia > Japan/Korea > Aseap > Australia/New Ze

Home) Asia Report) Indonesia) Story)

2 Rohingya leaders go shopping for terror in Indonesia

Trip a sign that Myanmar's sectarian clashes are spilling beyond its borders

Published on
Jul 11, 2013

elevenmyanmar.com/business/2753-us-company-to-build-food-factory-in-myanmar

MYANMAR DENIES REPORTS OF ROHINGYAS UNDERGOING MILITARY TRAINING IN RAKHINE

Published on Saturday, 13 July 2013 02:07

http://www.rfa.org/english/news/myanmar/militants-0712201318

Myanmar to Investigate Reports of Rohingya Militants

2013-07-12   Tweet 9   Recommend 23

In this regard my recommendations are:

1. The Rohingya people must make timely statement to clear any false reports and alarm.

2. The Rohingya people must reject any move for a violent struggle. This is of special importance because the Myanmar government and people are creating a situation that pushes the Rohingya into a corner, which will sooner or later become intolerable. When unbearable people, in a desperate attempt, could pick up arms in revolt. This will give an excuse to the Myanmar government to annihilate the Rohingya. The Rohingya must work hard not to give this chance to the Myanmar government.

3.   The United Nations must adopt a binding resolution that makes Myanmar government fully responsible for all what is happening inside Myanmar and to the Rohingya. The international community must actively exercise the Responsibility to Protect as per procedures provided in the 2009 report "Implementing the responsibility to protect" of the UN Secretary General.[206] The report puts emphasis on three pillars of implementation as described below.

---

[206] http://www.un.org/ga/search/view_doc.asp?symbol=A/63/677

"Pillar one
The protection responsibilities of the State (sect. II)
Pillar two
International assistance and capacity-building (sect. III)
Pillar three
Timely and decisive response (sect. IV)"

The three pillars are clarified ad follow.[207]

"The three pillars of the responsibility to protect, as stipulated in the Outcome Document of the 2005 United Nations World Summit (A/RES/60/1, para. 138-140) . . .

1. The State carries the primary responsibility for protecting populations from genocide, war crimes, crimes against humanity and ethnic cleansing, and their incitement;
2. The international community has a responsibility to encourage and assist States in fulfilling this responsibility;
3. The international community has a responsibility to use appropriate diplomatic, humanitarian and other means to protect populations from these crimes. If a State is manifestly failing to protect its populations, the international community must be prepared to take collective action to protect populations, in accordance with the Charter of the United Nations."[208]

It must be mentioned here that Myanmar government so far has failed to protect the Rohingya people. Therefore, the international community must begin taking appropriate action.

Self-Alienation-2. The key feature of a democratic society is multiculturalism and pluralism. When multiculturalism and pluralism is in practice each and every person of the community has responsibility to understand sensitivity of the society as a whole. In this regard, I would like to candidly point out that it is wrong to assert that the Rohingya are the descendants of the ship-wrecked

---

[207] http://www.un.org/en/preventgenocide/adviser/responsibility.shtml
[208] http://www.un.org/womenwatch/ods/A-RES-60-1-E.pdf

Arabian sailors, merchants, and Arabian Islamic missionaries. The claim of the Arabian descent has inflicted fatal injury to the aboriginal origin of the Rohingya. The assertion that *Rohingya* is a derivative of Arabic word *Rahim* finds no lineage of linguistic or traditional culture since the Rohingya speak a dialect of the Indo-European language phylum and at least 95% of them are farmers or fishermen. Due its emphasis of Arabian lineage it again happens to create a second image of Rohingya self-alienation projecting themselves as the Arabian *protégé*.

Exhibit-PR1

Map showing notorious Naungdaw and Manaung Seas where shipwrecks are common to the unfamiliar sailors

There are two notorious areas of the shipwrecks. Please see the map given above. One is called Naungdaw Sea near the islands of Naungdaw Gri and Naungdaw Chay.[209] The other is the Ye Kyun Sea near Ye Kyun island (Exhibit-PR1). I have some experience[210] in these stormy seas. Among the two notorious seas Naungdaw is considered the worst. I learned about these seas from my father since I was a kid as he narrated his experiences of sailing across the sea in 1940s. When I grew up I had opportunity to sail in the local sailing boats[211] as well as to cruise in the motorboats in these seas. I have some knowledge about the local tales and beliefs in the area. These seas are not any worse than other seas in the coast

---

[209] 'Naungdaw' means 'Royal Brother'. 'Gri' means 'big' and 'Chay' stands for 'small'. These are the twin oceans of Big and Small Royal Brothers. Because of the majestic waves they are called Royal Oceans.

[210] I cannot claim that I am a seaman or boatman but I do have some experience of rough water canoeing in the upper Kissapanadi-Meechaung, and sailing in many parts of the Arakan coast and rivers, as an oarsman or a crew. I am not good with the sail or rudder.

[211] Most of them are fishing canoe-style boats 20-30 feet long with single sail and three or four crew. As a zoologist I enjoyed these fishing-sailing trips.

of Myanmar. Local danger is always everywhere to the unfamiliar sailors.

The local people talk about only one shipwreck that brought the dogs from the wrecked ship to the Ye Kyun island. The tale is that the ship wrecked due to "Dragon's anger," which means a tsunami and the dogs were washed up and survived on Ye Kyun island (Exhibit-PR2).

Exhibit-PR2
Dragon's Anger

နဂါးနှိက်လို့ သဘော်၁နစ်တေ
(nagar-nhait-lo thun-phaw-nait-teh)

Dragon's Anger sinks the ship

I incline to think that it could have been at the time of 1762 earthquake and tsunami.[212] The dogs became wild and ferocious. Local people sneak onto uninhabited the island and steal the puppies and sell them with good price as the guard dogs or hunting dogs. The story is that the *Ye Kyun dogs* even fight the tiger! They are bigger, longer (from nose to tail) and taller (at the shoulder) than other breeds. They also fight very bravely. Once I had three dogs of Ye Kyun ancestry. The local people do not talk about any other shipwreck. It may just mean that they do not remember the distant past. Therefore, there may have been shipwrecked and Arabian seaman survivors who settled in the days of Weithali, LeMro and/or Mrauk-U dynasties. There is no doubt that the Arabian merchants and Islamic missionaries must have settled in the Arakan and Myanmar. Human movement and migration is a phenomenon.

The story of the Arabian Rohingya's origin is that the surviving Arabian sailors and settlers got married with the local women and their descendants are known as Rohingya. The argument put up by the Rakhine people is that if they are the descendants of the local women they must call themselves Rakhaingthar.

---

[212] http://news.nationalgeographic.com/news/pf/14871977.html

Exhibit-PR3
A Burmese proverb
of cultural dilemma

အမေကျော် ဒွေးတော်လွမ်းတယ်
'amaykyaw dweytaw lwundae'

Meaning-
'Longing for the auntie beyond
the mother'
This is a literal translation.

Culturally, it means betrayal,
unpatriotic or even treason.

One may debate this topic of what to be called. Nevertheless, the assertion of the Arabian origin of the Rohingya squarely falls in the domain of cultural dilemma (if not of betrayal to the mother), which is powerfully expressed in the Burmese proverb 'amaykyaw dweytaw lwundae' (Exhibit-PR3). Auntie (dweytaw) is the sister of the father; sister of mother is called *dawdaw, adaw, dawlay, dawgyi* or *gyidaw*. The proverb smites a person who is longing for the father's sister in the presence of his or her own biological mother, depiction of a cynical situation– pretty bad in Burmese culture.

We have a saying - 'if you are in Rome be a Roman'. This simplified quote comes from the Latin-
"si fueris Romae, Romano vivitomore; si fueris alibi, vivito sicut ibi" "If you are in Rome, live in the Roman way, if you are elsewhere, live as they do there" attributed to St. Ambrose.[213]

It is important to know and to be sensitive to the local culture when one asserts his or her own. Cultural conflicts lead to war. The Arabian lineage among the Rohingya and Muslim of Myanmar could not be more than 10% of the total Muslim

---

[213] http://wiki.answers.com/Q/Who_said_when_in_Rome_do_as_Romans_do

population, (which is about 5 millions?) in Burma. Therefore, it carries neither statistical nor cultural validity to generalize that the Rohingya are the Arabian descendants. If we were to take the 7th century as the earliest Arabian immigration into Arakan and Burma it is now already more than 1,300 years. When we consider the 19th century as the latest Arabian settlement in Myanmar it is already 200 years. It is high time that the Myanmar Rohingya and Muslims should try to get acclimatized with *amay* (mother) and stop longing for *dweytaw* (father's sister).

In saying so, I, in no way, mean that the Arabian descendents must forget their ancestry. No, I do not mean that. I encourage every body to remember his or her ancestry and cherish the loving memories. By tracing the ancestry the scientists have shown the evidence of human kind's common ancestry, adding great value to our common humanity. Many nights in my childhood I fell asleep with the *Tales of One Thousand and One Nights* that my parents told me. I learned them along with many Burmese folklores when I was a child. I read them when I grew big. Burmese translation of 'The Arabian Nights' or 'Tales of one thousand and one nights' are there in Myanmar. People are not against culture. But, unfortunately, there are things known as politics, nationalism, and patriotism, which will never disappear from human society. I remember that in late 1960s the Red China advised her children abroad to be loyal to their country of residence and citizenship and to live in harmony with the culture of the land. The message, reported in the media, came at a time when Burman-Chinese riots took place at Rangoon and other cities of Burma and Southeast Asian region. My point here is *to adjust* but *not to assert*.

Self-Alienation-3. The third self-alienation of Rohingya comes from the legend of Hanifa. The stage is romantically set as follow.[214]

"In 680 AD after the war of 'Karbala' Muhammad Hanafiya with his army arrived at Arab-Shah Para, near Maungdaw in

---

[214] Mohammed Ashraf Alam. A short historical background of Arakan, posted at http://www.ndphr.net/2004/12/short-historical-background-of-arakan.html. Last accessed on June 11, 2013.

the Northern Arakan, while Kaiyapuri, the queen of Cannibals ruled this hilly deep forest attacking and looting the people of Arakan. Mohammed Hanif attacked the Cannibals and captured the queen. She was converted to Islam and married to him. Her followers embraced Islam en masse. Mohammed Hanif and the queen Kaiyapuri lived in Mayu range. The peaks where they lived were still known as Hanifa Tonki and Kaiyapuri Tonki. The wild cannibals were tamed and became civilised. Arakan was no more in danger of them and peace and tranquility prevailed. The followers of Mohammed Hanif and Kaiyapuri were mixed up and lived peacefully." The descendants of these mixed people no doubt formed the original nucleus of the Rohingya Muslims in Arakan."

This story is said to be based on a book titled Hanifa O Kaiyapuri by Shah Barid Khan in 16th century.[215] Obviously, this *Muhammad Hanafiya* or *Mohammed Hanif* who some Rohingya are honoring as their founding father is *not* Imam Muhammad Al-Hanafiya (638-700 CE), the brave brilliant son Hazarat Ali (599 - 661 CE) with his wife Khawla bint Jafar bib Qais Al-Hanfiya, as I have demonstrated in my book *The Price of Silence*.[216] The Rohingya's *fabled* founding father Mohammed Hanif is a fictional hero from **"Jaiguner Puthi"**, one of the finest examples of DOBHASI PUTHI literature, composed by SYED HAMZA of Udna village in Hughli district in 1797. The following is an account this fictional hero and his mythical origin as described by Wakil Ahmed at Banglapedia.[217] I also give a screen print image after the text (Exhibit-PR4).

"Jaiguner Puthi, one of the finest examples of DOBHASI PUTHI literature, composed by SYED HAMZA of Udna village in Hughli district in 1797. The poem is based on Shah Barid Khan's *Hanifar Digvijay* (16th century) and Muhammad

---

[215] Mohammed Ashraf Alam, A Short Historical Background of Arakan posted at http://www.ndphr.net/2004/12/short-historical-background-of-arakan.html. Last accessed on June 11, 2013.

[216] See Shwe Lu Maung *alias* Shahnawaz Khan, *The Price of Silence Muslim-Buddhist War of Bangladesh and Myanmar, A Social Darwinist's Analysis,* DewDrop Art & Technology, USA, 2005, Chapter 5.3, pp 208-225.

[217] Jaiguner Puthi by Wakil Ahmed at http://www.banglapedia.org/HT/J_0025.HTM, last accessed on June 11, 2013.

Khan's *Hanifar Ladai* (1724) and narrates the story of the battle between Jaigun, princess of the kingdom of Erem, and Hanifa and their subsequent marriage. Jaigun, depicted as a heroic woman, defeats Hanifa in a duel, but Hanifa wins in the end, and Jaigun embraces Islam. The two are engaged to be married. Before their marriage, Jaigun and Hanifa together conquer one kingdom after another, converting their pagan kings to Islam. Hanifa attacks his father's kingdom and converts his father and uncle to Islam. The story ends with the marriage of Hanifa and Jaigun. The objectives of the poem were to describe the heroism of Hanifa and Jaigun and to emphasise the physical prowess that helped the spread of Islam. During British rule, the defeated Muslims looked for consolation in tales of the past glory of Islam, which poems like *Jaiguner Puthi* satisfied. [Wakil Ahmed]"

Exhibit-PR4
Reference on
Shah Barid Khan's *Hanifa digvijay* (16th century)
http://www.banglapedia.org/HT/J_0025.HTM

BANGLAPEDIA
National Encyclopedia of Bangladesh

Jaiguner Puthi one of the finest examples of DOBHASI PUTHI literature, composed by SYED HAMZA of Udna village in Hughli district in 1797. The poem is based on Shah Barid Khan's *Hanifar Digvijay* (16th century) and Muhammad Khan's *Hanifar Ladai* (1724) and narrates the story of the battle between Jaigun, princess of the kingdom of Erem, and Hanifa and their subsequent marriage. Jaigun, depicted as a heroic woman, defeats Hanifa in a duel, but Hanifa wins in the end, and Jaigun embraces Islam. The two are engaged to be married. Before their marriage, Jaigun and Hanifa together conquer one kingdom after another, converting their pagan kings to Islam. Hanifa attacks his father's kingdom and converts his father and uncle to Islam. The story ends with the marriage of Hanifa and Jaigun. The objectives of the poem were to describe the heroism of Hanifa and Jaigun and to emphasise the physical prowess that helped the spread of Islam. During British rule, the defeated Muslims looked for consolation in tales of the past glory of Islam, which poems like *Jaiguner Puthi* satisfied. [Wakil Ahmed]

(Note. The above quote and the screen print, Exhibit-PR4, are downloaded from http://www.banglapedia.org/HT/J_0025.HTM on June 11, 2013. A short description of Puthi Literature can be read at http://www.banglapedia.org/HT/P_0336.HTM, and there is also some information of the poet Syed Hamza (c 1755-1815) at http://www.banglapedia.org/HT/S_0645.HTM).

The story is also mentioned by an author at http://www.indianetzone.com under the subject of the *development of Bengali literature under the Muslim rule*. The complete text given below for good information is downloaded on June 11, 2013 from http://www.indianetzone.com/54/development_bengali_literature_du ring_muslim_rule.htm. Bengali poets in the Arakan courts are also mentioned. 'Hanifer Digvijay' and 'Hanifar Ladai' are highlighted.

Long block quote begins.
"The Nawabs of Bengal gave great encouragement to the writers which led to further development of Bengali literature during Muslim Rule. The writers wrote on Persian themes. This led introduction of several Persian words as well as themes into Literature of Bengal. Shek Subhodaya, a Sanskrit hagiology on Shaykh Dialal al-Din Tabrizi and Niranjaner Rushma, a Bengali ballad by Ramai Pandit indicates the influence of Islamic rule. Sultans of Hussain Shahi Bengal encouraged the development of Bengali literature that is read by both Hindu and Muslim. The Sultans of Pandua and Gaud extended their support to Bengali literature irrespective of caste.

The Bhagavata, Ramayana and Mahabharata were translated into Bengali during their rule. Poets like Vidyapati and Chandidas flourished during this period. Several literary themes were derived from Perso-Arabic culture. Saint-poet Nur Kutb-i Alam of Pandua, introduced the Rikhta Style in Bengali. In this style half the hemstitch was composed in Persian and the other half in Bengali. Muhammad Saghir is the author of the first Bengali romance Yusuf Zulaykha. Other romantic writers were Bahram Khan (Layla Madjnun), Sabirid khan (Hanifa-Kayrapari), Donaghazi (Sayf al-Mulk) and Muhammad Kabir (Madhumalati).

The Muslim writers replaced the invocations to Hindu gods and goddesses by Hamd and Nat. This was a steady practice of all Muslim writers. The important romantic writers were Shah Muhammad Saghir; Daulat Uzir Bahram Khan; Daululat Qazi of Arakan, Alaol (Padmavati), Saiful Mulk Badiuzzamal, Haft Paikar and Sikander Nama; Abdul Hakim (Yusuf -Zuleikah) Querishi Magan (Mrigavati).

Dobhashi literature was used by Muslim writers. In order to develop Bengali nomenclature Muslim writers were being habituated with this practice from early days. However these writings have some features in common like the humanistic love story.

Heroic tradition include Zainuddin's `Rasul Vijay`, Shah Barid's `Rasul Vijay` and `Hanifer Digvijay`, Muhammad Khan's Hanifar Ladai, Gharibullah's Janganama, Heyat Mohammad's Jangnama and Syed Hamza's Amir Hamza. It was substituted in the narratives by a growing practice of escapism, fairy tales, romance and fantastic adventures. This was known as Dobhashi literature.

Elegiac literature developed centering the tragedy of Karbala. It depicts the life and history of the prophet from the creation till the death of the grandson of the Prophet, Imam Hussain at Karbala. The most important works are: Navivangsha of Sayyid Sultan, Maktul Hussain of Mohammad Khan, Maktul Hussain of Muhammad Yaqub and Janganama of Abdul Hakim. One of the major features of this poem was lamentation and the freedom with which the imagination of the poets roams freely and describes the lamentation of trees, skies, the earth, the angels and departed souls.

The medieval age was the period of Muslim cultural development. Sayyid Sultan's Navibangsha, Shab-i-Miraj, Ofat-i-Rasul and Muhammad Khan's Maqtul Hussain and Kiyamatnama speak of the Muslim concept of origin, evolution and destruction of the Earth and the final judgment of good and bad souls. It was an attempt to inform the ignorant about purifying of souls. Other important works are: Neeti-Shahstravasta of Muzammil, Neseehatnama of Afzal Ali, Shariatnama of Nasrullah Khan.

In mystic literary practice there are two categories. It

includes the tradition of philosophical expositions of the theory and practices of religion as well as the Padavalis. Baul and Murshidi were also popular songs. Through symbols different stages of a disciple till the final stage of self illumination are described. Most of the Murshidi songs are found in Bengal. This is followed by the thematic expressions of the Mathnavi of Maulana Jalal Uddin Rumi and of the Mantiq- ut- Taier of Shaikh Fariduddin Attar."

(Last Updated on: 11/06/2011)"
Long block quote ends.

A piece of the web page screen print is given in the Exhibit-PR5.

Exhibit-PR5
Reference on
Shah Barid Khan's *Hanifa digvijay* (16th century)
from
http://www.indianetzone.com/54/development_bengali_litera
ture_during_muslim_rule.htm

← ⟳ www.indianetzone.com/54/development_bengali_literature_during_muslim_rule.htm   ⋄ ⋄ c

▤ Most Visited ⬤ Getting Started 🗋 Hulu 🅽 Netflix - Member Login... 🗋 Suggested Sites 🗋 Watch God of Study on... 🗋 Web Slice Ga

The Muslim writers replaced the invocations to Hindu gods and goddesses by Hamd and Nat. This was a steady practice of all Muslim writers. The important romantic writers were Shah Muhammad Saghir; Daulat Uzir Bahram Khan; Daululat Qazi of Arakan, Alaol(Padmavati)Saiful Mulk Badiuzzamal, Haft Paikar and Sikander Nama; Abdul Hakim (Yusuf -Zuleikah) Querishi Magan(Mrigavati)

Dobhashi literature was used by Muslim writers. In order to develop Bengali nomenclature Muslim writers were being habituated with this practice from early days. However these writings have some features in common like the humanistic love story.

Heroic tradition include Zainuddin's 'Rasul Vijay', Shah Barid's 'Rasul Vijay' and 'Hanifer Digvijay', Muhammad Khan's Hanifar Ladai, Gharibullah's Janganama. Heyat Mohammad's Jangnama and Syed Hamza's Amir Hamza. It was substituted in the narratives by a growing practice of escapism, fairy tales, romance and fantastic adventures. This was known as Dobhashi literature.

Elegiac literature developed centering the tragedy of Karbala. It depicts the life and history of the prophet from the creation till the death of the grandson of the Prophet, Imam Hussain at Karbala. The most important works are: Navivangsha of Sayyid Sultan, Maktul Hussain of Mohammad Khan, Maktul Hussain of Muhammad Yaqub and Janganams of Abdul Hakim. One of the major features of this poem was lamentation and the freedom with which the imagination of the poets roams freely and describes the lamentation of trees, skies, the earth, the angels and departed souls.

Again, the fictional hero Hanifa of Rohingya is not Imam Muhammad Al-Hanafiya (638-700 CE). The brave brilliant son of Hazarat Ali (599 - 661 CE) with his wife Khawla bint Jafar bib Qais Al-Hanfiya, never went out of the Arabia, leave alone coming to Arakan. Please see my book – *The Price of Silence*[218] – for in depth

---

[218] See Shwe Lu Maung, *The Price of Silence Muslim-Buddhist War of Bangladesh and Myanmar, A Social Darwinist's Analysis,* DewDrop Art & Technology, USA, 2005, Chapter 5.3, pp 208-225.

presentation. Briefly, Imman Muhammad Al-Hanafiya is known in various synonyms–Muhammad ibn al-Hanafiyya, Muhammad Ibn Ali, Muhammad Hanif, Muhammad Hanifiah, Muhammad Hanafia, Muhammad Hanafiya, and also as Muhammad Akbar. One Shi'ite tradition tell us that -

"The Kaisánís believe Imam Muhmmad Ibn al-Hanafiya is Imam Mahdi, the Savior or the Just Leader of Humanity, and he will return from Mount Radwa, where they believe that he is living, and not dead (Shahrastani, Milal wa nihal, Vol. 1, p. 232; Nawbakhti, Firaq al-shi'a, Najaf edition, p. 27., cited by http://www.al-islam.org/mahdi/nontl/Chap-2.htm#n1). The poem below, which is re-produced from Donaldson's *The Shi'ite Religion*, page 101, testifies the hope of a Shi'ite sect, the Kaisánís, for the arrival of Mahdi Muhammad Ibn al-Hanafiya on his horse and lead his horse men to liberate them from the evils of oppression.

> Four complete are the Imams,
> of Kuraish, the lords of Right:
> Ali and his three good sons,
> each of them a shining light.
> One was faithful and devout;
> Kerbala hid one from sight;
> One, until with waving flags,
> his horsemen he shall lead to fight,
> Dwells on Mt. Radwa, concealed;
> honey he drinks and water bright."[219]

Imam Muhammad Al-Hanafiya's burial place is reproduced from my book *The Price of Silence*, p 222, and presented below.

---

[219] See Shwe Lu Maung, *The Price of Silence Muslim-Buddhist War of Bangladesh and Myanmar, A Social Darwinist's Analysis*, DewDrop Art & Technology, USA, 2005, Chapter 5.3, p 221.

Exhibit-PR6
Imman Muhammad Al-Hanafiya's burial place reproduced
from my book The Price of Silence, p 222,

Imam Muhmmad Ibn al-Hanafiya was buried at Jabal Radwa, but a Shi'ite sect, the Kaisânis, believes that he is Imam Mahdi and is still alive, living there and waiting for the right time to emerge again for the salvation of humankind. Jabal Radwa is west of Medina in Saudi Arabia. Map is from Microsoft Encarta 97 World Atlas.

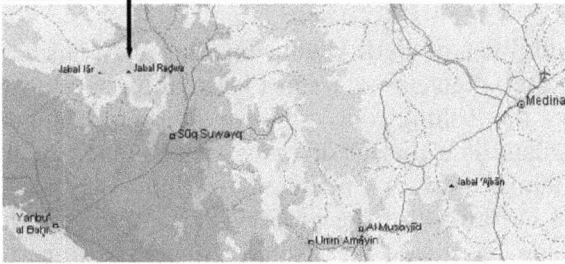

The Battle of Kerbala (61AH/680 CE). It was the battle that made the decisive division of the Sunni and the Shi'ite, never to be friends again. In recent days, Iran(Shi'ite)-Iraq(Sunni)

It will be fatally wrong if the Rohingya continue to build their nationalism on a fiction written in a genre of Bengali literature known as Dobhasi Puthi because it is another act of self-alienation.

If the Rohingya wants an amicable solution to the crisis it is important to abandon the fictional descriptions of their origin. Nobody wants to add more fuel to the fire. Nobody wants more bloodshed. Please note that Wakil Ahmed at Banglapedia pointed out that these heroic poems are "to emphasise the physical prowess that helped the spread of Islam." Especially the tale of Hanifa conquering the northern Rakkhapura in the 7th century and converting the indigenous people into Islam simply makes the Rakhines furious. The tale also adds more grin to the view that the Muslims spread Islam by swords. Depiction of the Rohingya as the descendants of the invaders makes them as the undesirable elements to the Myanmar nationalism. If the Myanmar people were to put up the resistance to *the invaders* coming from a far away land it will be difficult to put the blame on them. It will be seen as a legitimate national defense.

Again, mythology and fiction in the origin of the people and nations are common features everywhere. Myanmar chronicles have abundance of fictions. I have given good account of Myanmar mythical, fictional, superstitious politics in my earlier books,[220] and pointed out that these myths, fictions, and superstitions form fundamental fabrics of Myanmar Ultranationalism and play a big role in Myanmar's failure of nation building, all along her history. It is the best to stay away from the failed path. Simple maxim is "keep fiction as fiction."

Final Part of Self-Alienation. Serious consideration must be given to the language program. Please allow me to be frank and open. Today, the Rohingya do not have a written language and their spoken language is a dialect of Indo-Aryan branch of Indo-Iranian language family, which belongs to Indo-European language phylum.[221] I am aware of the programs trying to introduce written Rohingya language using the Arabic alphabets. Arabian languages belong to the Central Semitic Languages of Semitic Languages phylum.[222] Considering the 'mother tongue' cultural sensitivity, for example "Ekushey of Bangla," it is predictable that a bloody reaction will occur if the Rohingya language is Arabized and used in Myanmar. There is no doubt that the ordinary Rohingya in Myanmar will be the victims whereas no harm will come to the elite abroad who are carrying out the program.

If the Rohingya dialect is Arabized Rohingya's self-alienation will come to its completion and the apocalypse that I described in my book "The Price of Silence" would be accelerated and more dramatized.

Among the Muslims there is a view that Arabic is language of God and with only Arabian culture Muslimhood is complete. Seriously, we should learn lessons from the experience of Bangladesh. There was a time that the Bengali of Arabian lineage were the dominating elite and they asserted Arabian culture over the Bengali traditions. It went to such an extreme that even long-cherished Bengali traditions were classified 'un-Islamic'. It was even

---

[220] Shwe Lu Maung, *Burma Nationalism and Ideology*, University Press Ltd., Dhaka, 1989, Chapter 8.6 and Shwe Lu Maung, *The Price of Silence: Muslim-Buddhist War of Bangladesh and Myanmar – A Social Darwinist's Analysis*, DewDrop Arts & Technology, USA, 2005, Chapters 4.5 and 4.6.

[221] http://en.wikipedia.org/wiki/Indo-Aryan_peoples

[222] http://en.wikipedia.org/wiki/Central_Semitic_languages

attempted to replace the Bengali alphabets with the Arabic letters in the style of Urdu.[223,224] The result was the birth of 'Ekushey Movement' in 1952, and consequently independent Bangladesh emerged in 1971 at a huge cost. Today, 'International War Crimes Tribunals' is going on in Bangladesh, trying the 'pro-Pakistan collaborators'. Therefore, one must know the cultural sensitivity and its limit. This is high time that the Rohingya elite stop self-alienation and explore ways to help the majority common Rohingya get into the main stream of Myanmar society.

It is best to highlight common heritage in light of common humanity in the process of confidence-building for unity. I have presented substantial evidence of 'commonness' upon which Rohingya can also stand in their struggle for equal rights in Myanmar society.

---

[223] For example see Bengali Language movement at
http://en.wikipedia.org/wiki/Bengali_Language_Movement
[224] Also see Tazeen Mahnaz Murshid, *Women, Islam and the State in Bangladesh subordination and resistance* at
http://www.swadhinata.org.uk/document/WomenBdeshTazeen.pdf

10
Crimes Against Humanity

No matter what the violence against the innocents cannot be tolerated and justice must be done in the interest of humanity.

US President Barack Obama, breaking the boycott and sanctions, visited Burma in November 2012, and he delivered a speech at the Convocation Hall of Rangoon University on November 19, 2012. He said:[225]

"No process of reform will succeed without national reconciliation. (Applause.) You now have a moment of remarkable opportunity to transform cease-fires into lasting settlements, and to pursue peace where conflicts still linger, including in Kachin State. Those efforts must lead to a more just and lasting peace, including humanitarian access to those in need, and a chance for the displaced to return home.

Today, we look at the recent violence in Rakhine State that has caused so much suffering, and we see the danger of continued tensions there. For too long, the people of this state, including ethnic Rakhine, have faced crushing poverty and persecution. But there is no excuse for violence against innocent people. And the Rohingya hold themselves -- hold within themselves the same dignity as you do, and I do.

National reconciliation will take time, but for the sake of our common humanity, and for the sake of this country's future, it is necessary to stop incitement and to stop violence. And I welcome the government's commitment to address the issues of injustice and

---

[225] I downloaded the full text on November 25, 2012 from
http://thoughtsandpolitics.blogspot.com/2012/11/obama-delivers-speech-at-yangon.html. It was still there when I accessed it on June 29, 2014.

accountability, and humanitarian access and citizenship. That's a vision that the world will support as you move forward."

His speech was enlightening. He reminded me of U Nu. It was on a drizzling day of June 1960 that I listened to Prime Minister U Nu who welcomed us, the freshmen, known as the Freshers in Burma, to Rangoon University and enlightened us with his vision of peaceful and prosperous future, and urged us to study well and to stand out in the world. It was very exciting to see and meet a historical figure and head of a government. U Nu was an inspiration for me. Similarly, Obama and his speech were inspirational.

Indeed, **"there is no excuse for violence against innocent people."**

The charge that the Rohingya are the Illegal Bengalis is a political blunder that Myanmar has to answer for many ages to come.

Alienation of the Rohingya under the charge that they are Bengali is a human rights violation that Myanmar will be scorned for years to come.

Rejection and termination of the citizenship of the Rohingya under the charge that they are Bengali is a human rights violation that Myanmar will be seen as the sinners for years to come.

Discrimination of the Rohingya under the charge that they are Bengali is a human rights violation that Myanmar will be responsible for years to come.

Oppression of the Rohingya under the charge that they are Bengali is a human rights violation that Myanmar will be accountable for years to come.

Displacement of the Rohingya under the charge that they are Bengali is another human rights violation that Myanmar will be liable for years to come.

Killings of the Rohingya under the charge that they are Bengali is a genocide that Myanmar will be counted as criminals for years to come.

The sum total of the systematic alienation, de-citizenization, discrimination, oppression, displacement, and killing of the Rohingya is a crime against humanity that Myanmar will have to face the international tribunal in the years to come.

No matter what, the United Nations will never go for a tribunal. The United States is just eager to counter balance China. The EU will try to make a few dollars more out of Myanmar natural resources. Who in the world is in a position to bring about justice? Under this helpless scenario we can seek comfort in the ageless saying that 'no crime goes unpunished'. In deed, situation can change abruptly, especially so in these days of digital globalization and greater awareness of 'common humanity'. The concept of 'planetary citizenry' is taking roots across the world. Due to the mounting international demand from the traumatic experiences of Rwanda genocide 1994[226] and Kosovo Račak massacre 1999[227] the United Nations in 2009 adopted the *Resolution A/RES/63/308 Responsibility to Protect*.[228] Therefore, we may dispel despair and move forward in force to protect the hapless Rohingya of Myanmar and bring about justice in that land.

The questions are:
How can Myanmar reconcile over these crimes?
How can Myanmar live with a clear conscience over these crimes?

While we search our souls to find answers for these questions we also need to be practical and realistic to analyze the case so that we can formulate a rational answer that will eventually lead to reconciliation and clear conscience.

When Myanmar became an independent country in 1948 she was stepping into a new world of republics with all her heritage of feudalism, monarchism, racism, religionism, and colonialism. Please note I call it a country not a nation. Myanmar is a failed nation, so far.[229] In the new born Myanmar the republican concept of *we-the-people* was infantile and hapless. Myanmar independence

---

[226] http://en.wikipedia.org/wiki/Rwandan_Genocide
[227] http://en.wikipedia.org/wiki/Ra%C4%8Dak_massacre
[228] http://www.unric.org/en/responsibility-to-protect/26981-r2p-a-short-history
[229] See Shwe Lu Maung, *Burma Nationalism and Ideology*, University Press Ltd., Dhaka, 1989

struggle began with Young Men Buddhist Association (YMBA) around 1910.[230] Its ideology (Exhibit-PR7) was *wunthanu rakkhita taya* (Patriotic Defense Principles) for the defense of *amyo-batha-tharthana* (race-language-religion).

Exhibit-PR7
YMBA Ideology

ဝံသာနု ရက္ခိတ တရား
wunthanu rakkhita taya
Patriotic Defense Principles

အမျိုး �‌ဘာသာ သသာနာ
amyo-batha-tharthana
race-language-religion

In 1964, with two friends, I attended the annual conference of YMBA at Yangon. My friend, Soe Thein (not the original name) was a YMBA member and he wanted us to join the association. He believed that YMBA could be instrumental to dislodge the military government. Khin Win (not the real name) and I were given YMBA permission to go with him as the observers. At that time we were resurrecting the All Burma Student Union (ABSU) and Rangoon University Student Union (RUSU). I was a member of the recruit committee. After the 1962 coup d'état General Ne Win and his colonels dissolved the student unions and dynamited the Rangoon University Student Union Building on the 7th of July 1962. We built a bamboo cottage and reestablished the student union. Soe Thein and I were the RUSU members.

The YMBA conference was attended by more than 300 delegates from all over Burma, all were Burman (Bama), very lively and disciplined. Its members were forty and above, all well dressed, well spoken, very eloquent, very cultured, and educated. They were the cream of the society. We met its out-going secretary and he was very welcoming and encouraged us to join the association with an

---

[230] Ibid. p102

emphasis that the young generation was missing in his association but that YMBA was very selective. I considered them orthodox and it was my first and last YMBA conference. Nevertheless, it was an unforgettable experience because they were the most cultured Burmese I have ever met. I still wish I were a cultured person like them but I remain rugged and wild.

It was in 1988 that YMBA came back into my mind when Aung San Suu Kyi called the 1988 uprising *second independence struggle* in her Shwedagon Pagoda rally speech on 26 August, 1988. The vanguard of the 1988 uprising was the *Sangha* (monk community) while the students formed the front. Myanmar Buddhist monks have been in politics at all time. Similarly, *wunthanu rakkhita taya* (Patriotic Defense Principles) has been there in Myanmar society even though YMBA may appear insignificant. During the 2012 Buddhist-Muslim riots a number of associations bearing the name *wunthanu* emerged and *wunthanu* network was established. It was then that the hate-billboards and URLs calling for the extermination of the Bengali illegal Muslim immigrants populated the cities and the internet, inside and outside Myanmar. This is nothing new. I have described the rise of Neo-Nazism in Myanmar in my book *The Price of Silence*.[231] It is painful to recall it but I need to mention it again for the sake of clarity.

Myanmar Nazism, revived with General Ne Win when he took over state power, dissolved the 1947 Constitution, and introduced Burmese Way to Socialism. The doctrine Burmese Way to Socialism is *the Myanmar National Socialism*; and *national socialism is Nazism*.[232] Ne Win was a core member of BaSein-TunOke faction (national extremists) of *Dobama Asiayone*.[233] Professor Aye Kyaw, one of the most respected scholars of Myanmar, an ethnic Rakhine, summarized the *wunthanu rakkhita taya* (Patriotic Defense Principles) as follows.[234]

---

[231] Shwe Lu Maung, *The Price of Silence: Muslim-Buddhist War of Bangladesh and Myanmar – A Social Darwinist's Analysis*, DewDrop Arts & Technology,USA, 2005.

[232] http://en.wikipedia.org/wiki/Nazism and
http://en.wikipedia.org/wiki/National_Socialism_disambiguation

[233] See Doe-Bhama Asi-Ayone in Shwe Lu Maung, *Burma Nationalism and Ideology*, University Press Ltd., Dhaka, 1989, p 71 & 102. and http://en.wikipedia.org/wiki/Thakins

[234] Also see Shwe Lu Maung, *The Price of Silence: Muslim-Buddhist War of Bangladesh and Myanmar – A Social Darwinist's Analysis*, DewDrop Arts & Technology, USA, 2005, p 232.

"Ethnic Minorities vs. Non-ethnic Minorities

With respect to the definition of an ethnic minority, Dr. Maung Maung, a lawyer and a State Councilor, who later became president of Burma invited Professor U San Tha Aung, Director General of the Department of Higher Education, and myself as Rakhaing representatives in 1979. Present at that meeting in his office was U Kyaw Nyein who later became Minister of Education. I submitted my proposal that those people who appeared in the Inquest (census) of King Bodawpaya taken in the 1880s[235] ought to be regarded as ethnic minorities. Through the discussion, we agreed that those people who were in Burma before the end of the First Anglo-Burmese War in 1826 should be regarded as ethnic minorities. Those people who came along with the British colonial administration were regarded as non-ethnic minorities.

This definition is in line with the principle defined by General Aung San, father of the Nobel Laureate Daw Aung San Suu Kyi. This definition is historical valid and sound, thereby not creating any further problem.

We have accepted this definition. In April 2001, the Arakan League for Democracy (in Exile) held its third conference in New Delhi, India. This conference laid down, among others, a principle, which was very important for shaping the destiny of Burma. This principle is called the Bhumi Rakkhita Putra Principle. Bhumi means land; Rakkhita taking care of, Putra sons and daughters. Those who were in Rakhaingland, and who have been cherishing, maintaining, and taking care of this land generations after generations before the end of the first Anglo-Burmese War ought to be given priority and preference." The excerpt ends here.

The above excerpt is from the *position paper of the Arakanese perspective*, by Professor Aye Kyaw at the Oslo Burma Seminar on January 15-17, 2004. The position paper, *The Burma We Love*, is published in Arakanpost, Issue-5, July, 2004, p13. An ethnic Rakhaing, late Dr. Aye Kyaw, a US citizen, was a professor of history and highly respected in the Rakhaing as well as Myanmarese community abroad and at home. He was a key figure in the

---

[235] The year 1880 must be a typesetting error. It must be 1780. King Bodawpaya died in 1819. He brutally annexed Arakan in 1784. The First Anglo-Burman War broke out in 1824, with victory to the British in 1826. Arakan was handed over to the British under the Rantapo Treaty in 1826.

formulation of racial policy of Arakan League for Democracy (ALD, in exile) and Arakan National Council. Now ALD and RNDP (Rakhine Nationalities Development Party) have merged in the name of Rakhine National Party (RNP). More hostility can be expected.

Therefore, "the politics of Bengali illegal Muslim immigrants," which is being played against the Rohingya people by the Myanmar nationalists is not mere bigotry but a viable toxic fruit of Myanmar ultra-nationalism– *Bhumi Rakkhita Putra Principle*; it is in line with YMBA's *amyo-batha-tharthana* (race-language-religion) and is *the foundation* of the Burma Citizenship Act 1982. It is strong, powerful, and ultra. Today, 969 Buddhist *Rakkhita* movement led by a powerful Monk U Wirathu,[236] the abbot of historically influential Mandalay Ma-soe-yein monastery, has resulted in series of cleansing of ethnic Muslims in 2012 and 2013.

How do we liberalize the Myanmar ultra-nationalism that now thrives in its Nazi-phase?

It will be suicidal if Myanmar ignores the charges of crimes against humanity. Here, I give three examples of the charges in Exhibit-PR8 and web links.

1.
http://www.oxfordburmaalliance.org/uploads/9/1/8/4/9184764/ichr_r ohingya_report_2010.pdf. (Last visit on November 6, 2014).
2.
http://www.hrw.org/reports/2013/04/22/all-you-can-do-pray-0. (Last visit on November 6, 2014).
3.
http://www.burmacampaign.org.uk/images/uploads/AI-Crimes-against-humanity.pdf. (Last visit on November 6, 2014).

Meanwhile, it will be pragmatic and humanistic for Myanmar to heed the call, on June 20, 2013, of the twelve Nobel Peace Laureates for ending to violence against Muslims in Burma.

---

[236] http://www.huffingtonpost.com/burma-journal/buddhist-monk-wirathu-lea_b_3481807.html and http://www.independent.co.uk/news/world/asia/killing-with-kindness-burmas-religious-battleground--and-the-monks-at-the-heart-of-it-8627571.html

They also call for an international independent investigation of the anti-Muslim violence. Their words are reproduced below from http://nobelwomensinitiative.org/wp-content/uploads/2013/06/NobelWomen_Burma-Statement-June-20-2013_FINAL.pdf.[237]

Exhibit-PR8
Crimes against humanity in Myanmar

Irish Human Rights Group
http://www.nuigalway.ie/human_rights/document
s/ichr_rohingya_report_2010.pdf

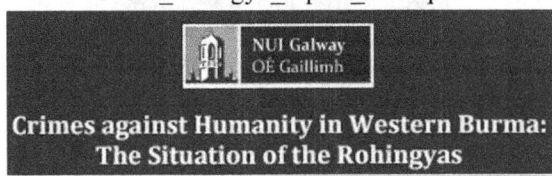

NUI Galway
OÉ Gaillimh

**Crimes against Humanity in Western Burma:
The Situation of the Rohingyas**

Human Rights Watch, USA
http://www.hrw.org/reports/2013/04/22/all-you-can-do-pray-0

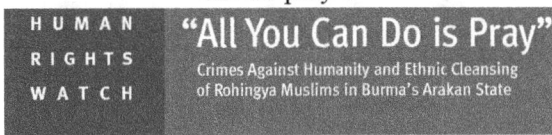

H U M A N   **"All You Can Do is Pray"**
R I G H T S   Crimes Against Humanity and Ethnic Cleansing
W A T C H   of Rohingya Muslims in Burma's Arakan State

Burma Campaign UK
http://www.burmacampaign.org.uk/images/uploa
ds/AI-Crimes-against-humanity.pdf
Crimes against humanity
in eastern Myanmar
"We lost whatever remained of our peace"[1]

---

[237] Also see The Rakhine State Violence, Volume 1: The Rakhaing Revolution, p 264-268.

"There needs to be an international, independent investigation of the anti-Muslim violence in Burma. It is critically important that the Burmese government show leadership in implementing any recommendations from such an investigation to ensure accountability to end this cycle of violence. We urge President Thein Sein strongly to follow through on the commitment he made to allow the U.N. High Commissioner for Human Rights to open an office in Burma. Having an independent UN body present in Burma to monitor human rights violations is an important step towards realizing the fulfillment of those international human rights principles."

The twelve brave Nobel Peace Laureates are:[238]

1. Mairead Maguire, Nobel Peace Laureate (1976) — Ireland
2. Betty Williams, Nobel Peace Laureate (1976) – Ireland
3. Adolfo Pérez Esquivel, Nobel Peace Laureate (1980) — Argentina
4. Archbishop Desmond Tutu, Nobel Peace Laureate (1984) — South Africa
5. Oscar Arias, Nobel Peace Laureate (1987) – Costa Rica
6. Rigoberta Menchú Tum, Nobel Peace Laureate (1992) — Guatemala
7. José Ramos Horta, Nobel Peace Laureate (1996) — East Timor
8. Jody Williams, Nobel Peace Laureate (1997) — USA
9. Shirin Ebadi, Nobel Peace Laureate (2003) — Iran
10. Muhammad Yunus, Nobel Peace Laureate (2006) – Bangladesh
11. Leymah Gbowee, Nobel Peace Laureate (2011) — Liberia
12. Tawakkol Karman, Nobel Peace Laureate (2011) – Yemen

The Myanmar must lead and take initiative to completely erase her deep-rooted ultra-nationalism and reformat her ideology in line with the norms of universal human rights. The international community can help. Yes, *we the people* are ready to help.

---

[238] Also see The Rakhine State Violence, Vol. 1: The Rakhaing Revolution. p 264-268.

Exhibit-PR18
An ancient Myanmar teaching
Thread of Love

ချစ်စကိုရှည်စေ
chitsa ko sheyse
Make the thread of love long

ရန်စကိုတိုစေ
ransa ko tohse
Make the thread of quarrel short

11
The Victims of Civilization

In 1965, when I was a senior student at Rangoon University, I read a Burmese short story in a monthly magazine.[239] It was a love story of two Rangoon University students. Both the girl and the boy came from the high society and were the high school sweethearts. The girl became egalitarian and she became involved in the social work, helping the children of the hawkers in the university locality. She found time to go to the slums and taught the kids reading, writing, and arithmetic, known as the 3R. The boy disapproved her work and accused her of becoming a leftist, incompatible with their background of aristocracy. The girl explained to the boy that she was simply helping the unprivileged children and it had nothing to do with any ideology. Her social work happened to keep her away from the boy and eventually, the boy warned her that she was letting herself down and he would be compelled to depart. She said to him, "Perhaps, I am like water that naturally flows from high to low. I am not letting myself down but I am simply providing water to those who are badly in need of it. You have to take me as I am." The boy was not satisfied with her reasoning and eventually they got separated. Undeterred, the girl kept up with her social work. The title of the short story was "a girl who is like water" (ရေနှင့်တူသော မိန်းကလေး). Similarly, I consider that "I am simply providing water to those who are badly in need of it" when I render my support to the Rohingya people in their struggle for human rights and an equitable place in the society.

The Rohingya are the victims of the civilizations.

When the modern political and national identities, in the post-British colonial era of the Islamic Republic of Pakistan, the Republic of India, and the Union of Burma, were born dividing their land, Arakan and her people also became divided into the three regions, like all other inhabitants of the region. The People's Republic of Bangladesh took the place of East Pakistan in 1971. Of

---

[239] I am sorry that I do not remember the name of the author or the magazine, *Shu-ma-wa*, *Mya-wa-dy*, *Thwe-thauk*, and *Sanda* are four magazines of my time. The author was a new comer.

course Arakan is home to many ethnic peoples, but the Rohingya are worst affected. The triangular region of the India-Bangladesh-Burma is their nomadic land for millenniums. They move about the rivers and coastal regions and live on *Jhum* or shifting cultivation and fishing. Even today, they move about all the time. Perhaps, they are the most mobile people in the South and Southeast Asia. Now they were all over the world. How do they manage without passports or visas in these days of tight border securities? They manage it in their simple nomadic ways!

They do not even have a written language. Their spoken language, which is considered to be in the family of Indo-Aryan languages, is enriched with many vocabularies of Indian, Bengal, Burmese, and Arabic words. Dr. Muhammad Firdaus, M.D., FACP, an American physician of Rohingya ancestry, in USA, told me that the Rohingya can understand the Chakma language and vice versa, suggesting an affinity between the two languages of two most ancient peoples in the region. Sometime in the history, the Islamic missionaries were able to convince them that Islam should be their religion. This is how the Arabic words get a hold in their language in addition to the local ones. I believe the Rohingya, being most oppressed and marginalized at all time, find that Islam is most egalitarian among the prevailing religions of the region. Islam, despite having rigid laws and disciplines, is least hierarchical among the religions. For example, Theravada Buddhism or Elder Doctrine of Burma and Sri Lanka is highly hierarchical.

Nevertheless, by becoming a Muslim, a person does not necessarily become liberated, but unknowingly becomes the hostage of the Pan-Islam.[240] One good example of "the hostage of the Pan-Islam" is East Pakistan and her people who ended up in a bloody fight against the Islamic Republic of Pakistan to liberate themselves into a new identity of Bangladesh, in 1971. In 2014, even after 43 years of independence Bangladesh is still searching her soul and prosecuting the war criminals in the International Crimes Tribunal (ICT), Bangladesh.[241] I do not think Bangladesh will ever be liberated from the web of pan-Islam. In a similar style, the Rohingya people unknowingly became the hostage of Muslim-Buddhist

---

[240] See Shwe Lu Maung, *The Price of Silence: Muslim-Buddhist War of Bangladesh and Myanmar – A Social Darwinist's Analysis,* DewDrop Arts & Technology, USA, 2005, Chapters 2, 3, 5, and 6.

[241] http://en.wikipedia.org/wiki/International_Crimes_Tribunal_(Bangladesh)

politics of Burma and the world when the Mujahideens got into the cloak of Rohingya in 1961, (see the Chapter 4). Now, they are not only caught in the Burmese ethnic conflicts but also in the Muslim-Buddhist conflict. It is a double jeopardy for them.

The Rohingya live a very simple life in a simple farming and fishing societies. Who would have thought of that these simple subsistence farmers and fishermen would become the victims of the Muslim-Buddhist conflict?

Although there now are highly educated Rohingya who are professors, scientists, doctors, engineers, and professionals in Europe, USA, Canada, and Arabian countries, the 99.9% (i.e. 999 out of 1000) of the Rohingya in Myanmar are the simple farmers and fishermen who have been living as *the nomads* for millenniums. They are the migrant people living in the region of today India-Bangladesh-Myanmar border, exclusively along the riverine farm land and coastal regions. The Rohingya are not found on the mountain plateaus or mountain valleys. The people belonging to the Chakma, Dainet, Khmee, Rakhine, and Chin ethnic groups can be found on the mountain plateaus and valleys.[242] This is also one reason why I am convinced that they were the descendants of the original 'out-of-Africa' settlers who populated entire world via the coastal migration, as described in the previous chapters.

Kingdoms rose and fell, and civilizations gone with the wind. The kings and the lords never bothered with these nomadic people and their presence was never recorded in any archive or chronicles because the archives and chronicles were (and are) written by the ruling class and elite. The Rohingya were also too small and insignificant to get an attention. Nevertheless, their existence has been recorded by two Bengali Poets Daulat Qazi and Alaol of the Arakan Palace at Mrauk-U in the 17th century and a Scottish physician named Dr. Francis Buchanan in 1799.

I found three strong historical evidences of existence of the "term-Rohingya" in Arakan, the eastern territory of which is now known as the Myanmar Rakhine State.

(1) A Bengali poet named Daulat Qazi served the Rakhaing king Thiri Thu-Dhamma Raja (r.1622-1638 CE). The

---

[242] I have extensive living and traveling experience in the country–from Southern Taungup to all Arakan, Southern Chin State, Mizoram-Manipur-Maghalaya area in India, Chittagong District and Hill Tracts in Bangladesh.

poet Daulat Qazi in his epic poem 'Satî Mainâ' mentioned that Arakan is known as Roshang.

(2) Another famous Bengali poet named Alaol served in the royal palace in the days of Rakhaing kings Narapadigyi (r.1638-1645CE), Thado Mintar (r.1645—1652 CE), and Sanda-thu-dhamma (r.1652-1684 CE) also described Arakan in the name of Roshang.

(3) Dr. Francis Buchanan in 1799 recorded in his publication that "The Mahommedans settled at Arakan, call the country Rovingaw."

The first and second evidence came from a Bangla-language book titled *Arakan Rajsabhay Bangla Sahitya (1600-1700 AD)* or *Bengali Literature in the King's Court of Arakan (1600-1700 AD)* by Dr. Muhammad Enamul Huq and Sahitya-sagar Abdul Karim Sahitya Visarad, Gurudas Chattaopdhyay and Sons, Kalikata, 1935, it is mentioned During the 17th century AD when Muslim in Arakan nurtured Bengali Literature, the Muslim poets of that time identified the country as Roshang. The scholars mentioned that a Bengali poet named Daulat Qazi served the Rakhine king Thiri Thu-Dhamma Raja (r.1622-1638 CE). The poet Daulat Qazi in his epic poem 'Satî Mainâ' mentioned about the king and his kingdom as follow.

"To the east of the river Karnafili there is a palace, Roshang
City by name – like the Heaven.
There rules the glorious king of Magdha descent a follower
of the Buddha,
Name being Sri Sudhamma Raja, renown for his justice.
His power is like the morning sun, famous in the world,
Grooms the subjects like his own children.
Reveres the Lord [Buddha] and purely religious,
One's sins are forgiven when one sees his feet..."

Another equally famous Bengali poet named Alaol served in the royal palace in the days of kings Narapadigyi (r.1638-1645 CE), Thado Mintar (r.1645—1652 CE), and Sanda-thu-dhamma (r.1652-1684 CE). He wrote many epic poems and also translated

Persian poems into Bengali. I quote below from the translation of Alaol's work.

"Syed Saud Shah, Qazi of Roshang.
Agreed to [foster] me, finding in me a little learning.."
(Sikandar Nama)
"People from every country, hearing the magnificence of Roshang,
Took shelter under the King.
Arabian, Michiri [Egyptian], Shami, Turkish, Habsi
[African], Rumi Khprachani and Uzbek.
Lahuri, Multani, Sindi, Kashmiri, Dakkhini (Deccanese),
Hindi, Kamrupi [Assamese] and Bangadeshi [Bengali],
Ahopai Khotanchari (?), Karnali, Malayabari,
From Achi, Kuchi [Cochi] and Karnataka.
Countless Sheik, Soiyadjada, Moghul, Pathan warriors,
Rajput, Hindu of various nationals.
Avai [Inwa], Burmese, Siam [Thai], Tripura, Kuki to name
How many more should I elaborate. [?]
Armenian, Olandaz [Dutch], Dinemar, Engraj [English],
Castiman and Français.
Hipani[c], Almani, Chholdar, Nachhrani,
Many a races including Portuguese.'
(Padmavati).

The authors explained the term Roshang as follow.

"During the 17th century AD when Muslim in Arakan nurtured Bengali Literature, the Muslim poets of that time identified the country as "Roshang" [npp:Roshâng] (corrupt Bengali for "Rakhaing")[later 'Rohang' has been coined to identify another community with different (non-Buddhist) faith]. Therefore, they did not create this name, "Roshang" but it is the ancient name of Arakan. For this reason we prefer to call Arakan as "Roshang" and in fact we have used this name throughout the book."

Since the article I am citing here is very important and unique I have taken liberty to present its complete facsimile images as the appendix. See the Appendix-2 Roshang. It is evident that the Rohang-ya or the Myanmar corruption 'Rohing-ya' are the Muslim descendants of the Arakan Empire (1430-1784 CE). In the subject of the Muslim settlement in Burma since 7th century CE the reader may consult Moshe Yegar's book *The Muslims of Burma: a Study of a Minority Group*. Wiesbaden: Harrassowitz, 1972. He is an Israeli scholar and can be considered as a neutral person, meaning non-Myanmar or non-Muslim.

The third evidence of Rohingya had been described by Dr Jacques P. Leider[243] came from the publication of Dr. Francis Buchanan in 1799. A British medical man Dr. Buchanan took interest in the langauges and published his experience in his article "A Comparative Vocabulary of Some of the Languages Spoken in the Burma Empire."[244]

He wrote "The proper natives of Arakan call themselves Yakain, which name is also commonly given to them by the Burmas. By the people of Pegu, they are named Takain. By the Bengal Hindus, at least by such of them as have been settled in Arakan, the country is called Rossaum, from whence, I suppose, Mr. Rennell has been induced to make a country named Roshaum occupy part of his map, not conceiving that it would be Arakan, or the kingdom of the Mugs, as we often call it. Whence this name of Mug, given by the Europeans to the natives of Arakan, has been derived, I know not; but, as far as I could learn, it is totally unknown to the natives and their neighbours, except such of them as, by their intercourse with us, have learned its use. The Mahommedans settled at Arakan, call the country Rovingaw; the Persians call it Rekan."

In another article "An account of the Frontier Between Ava and the Part of Bengal Adjacent to the Karnaphuli River (1825)," Francis Hamilton (also known as Francis Buchanan) mentioned the term 'Arakan or Roang', in his description of Chakma. This article was first published in The Edinburgh Journal of Science (Vol. 3, April-October, 1825, pp 32-44). The copy I read is from the SOAS Bulletin of Burma Research Vol. 1, No. 2, Autumn 2003, ISSN 1479-8484, at https://www.soas.ac.uk/sbbr/editions/file64285.pdf, p11-18. I downloaded the article from the website on June 20, 2014.

---

[243] Leider, Jacques P. (July 9, 2012). Interview: *History Behind Arakan State Conflict*. The Irrawaddy. http://www.irrawaddy.org/archives/8642. Retrieved October 30, 2012 2012.
[244] Asiatic Researches 5: 219–240. http://www.soas.ac.uk/sbbr/editions/file64276.pdf. Retrieved October 30, 2012

The excerpt given below is from page 14 of the bulletin;   the highlighted emphasis is mine.

> "The people called Muggs, at Calcutta, are scarcely known by that name in their native country. By the Bengalese, they are commonly called Chakma or Sagma, or in ridicule, Dubades, (two-languaged) because they have in general forgotten their original language, which is the same with that of Arakan or Roang, as they call it, and have attained a very imperfect knowledge of the Bengalese, although several of them read and write this dialect. They all, however, retain some words of the Roang language, especially their names; and their priest use both the character and language of Arakan, little different from that of Ava. They all follow the doctrine of the Boudhas, but have engrafted on these many Hindu superstitions and ....."

It is interesting to note that the evidence came from two poets of the 17th century and from the curiosity of a doctor in 1799, but not from the historians.[245]

In deed, the Rohingya came to the spotlight in 1958 afterward only when a few Rohingya became elite and revealed that they were the Rohingya and they wanted a voice and a choice−equal rights like any other people of Burma. The Burmese, especially the Rakhines, view that the Muslim elite invented 'Rohingya'. Nothing can be more wrong than this view. No, it was not an invention but it strongly signified the Rohingya's coming to the age from their abyssal existence, an event of the emergence of a Fourth World.[246] This was a case of 'historical materialism'[247] in the sense that a group of long ignored people demanded a place in the society. It is legitimate to oppose the totalitarianism but we cannot dismiss the class struggle, class war, and historical materialism.

The Rohingya were simple commoners who never minded

---

[245] My impression is that the historians are mostly bias. All the Myanmar chronicles such as *Glass Palace Chronicles, U Kala Maha Razawin, Dyannyawadi Razawine Thit* (A New History of Dyannyawadi Hisory) are so bias in favor of the ruling king and race.

[246] Shwe Lu Maung, *Burma Nationalism and Ideology*, University Press Ltd., Dhaka, 1989, Chapter 9, pp103-111

[247] See http://www.marxist.com/historical-materialism/ and http://en.wikipedia.org/wiki/Historical_materialism

who the king, the ruler, or the lord was. They just cared their farm and fishing gears and kept moving for the better land and fishing water, just like in the good old days of the 'out-of-Africa' migration! I have lived in the Rohingya villages and rowed or sailed in their fishing boats. When I was a guerrilla (1966-67) they gave me food and protection, in the same manner and kindness that was rendered to me by other rural people of Rakhine, Mro, Khmee, Dainet, Thet, and Chin of Arakan. They are humble and intelligent but very simple.

Now:
Please imagine a world before the divisions of the political geography, in particular the region of the interest in this presentation, as shown in the Exhibit-VC1, Map 1.

Now please consider the periods of the Palaeolithic, Mesolithic and Neolithic cultures, some 12,000 to 3,000 years ago. Today, if the travelers were to go around the Bangladesh borders with Myanmar and India they will find an area known as the tribal belt, the Exhibit-VC1, Map 2. Below, I list some of the tribes as recorded in the Wikipedia.[248]

The tribes in Jharkhand, (Northwest to West Bengal), India:
Mal Pahariya, Parhaiya, Sauria Paharia, Agariya, Damor, Damaria, Sahariya, Saharia, Seharia, Sehria, Sosia, Sor, Koya, Bhine Koya, Rajkoya, Hill Pulaya, Malai Arayan, Palleyan, Palliyar, Biar, Biyar, Bhunjia, Koya, Bhine Koya, Bhumia, Omanatya, Chhalya, Thangluya
The tribes in West Bengal
Bedia, Bediya, Bhutia, Sherpa, Toto, Dukpa, Kagatay, Tibetan, Yolmo, Chakma, Lepcha, Lodha, Kheria, Kharia, Mal Pahariya, Parhaiya, Sauria, Paharia

The tribes in Bangladesh
Khashea, Jaintia, Chakma, Marma, Santals, Garo, Manipuri, Tripuri, Tanchangya, Mro, Mru, Mooran, Khasi, Khajon

---

[248] http://en.wikipedia.org/wiki/List_of_Scheduled_Tribes_in_India and http://en.wikipedia.org/wiki/Indigenous_peoples_in_Bangladesh

The tribes in the Myanmar Rakhine State

(Note: As per Myanmar official classification they are known as the Rakhine national races. The synonyms in the brackets are my insertions).

Rakhine, Daing-net, Thet (Chakma), Kaman, Mra-mar-Gyi (Marma), Khamee, Myo (Mro, Mru, Mooran).

Exhibit-VC1
India Bangladesh Myanmar without borders (Map 1)
and with tthe tribal belt (Map 2)

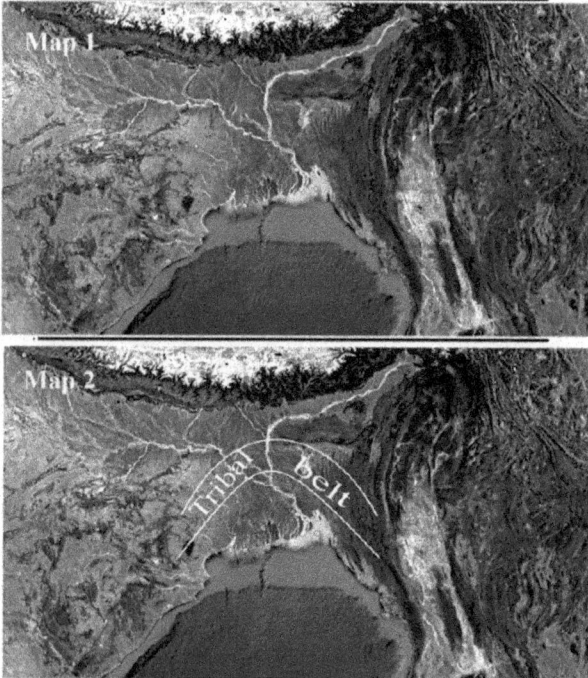

Base map credit: google earth Image landsat

There are three significant factors that I would like to highlight.

1. The tribal regions are the remote areas that are squeezed between the urbanized areas. These tribal areas are the remote

regions that are left isolated, without incorporating in the journey toward modern days.

2. A local tribal populations got divided into three parts by the post-1947 international borders.

3. There are a number of tribes with names ending with 'ya', such as Parhaiya, Agariya, Koya, and Bediya. And there are many tribes with the names that rhyme with 'ya', such as Damaria, Dukpa, Chakma, and Marma.

In light of the above three significant factors, there exists a possibility that the Rohingya are a tribe that long-existed in the tribal belt of *today* India-Bangladesh-Myanmar border. They were so insignificant, small, and humble that nobody has cared to list them in the records and chronicles. The records and chronicles are sanctioned and patronized by the ruling class and the royals. (This tribal theory does not nullify my earlier discussion of the Rohingya presented in the Chapters 6, 7, and 8, but is a variant presentation from a different angle of view).

Nevertheless, the post-WWII geopolitics of the region cruelly alienated them and forced them to look for a place in the civilization. The problem began here. What the heck is a citizenship on this planet of humankind?

In the old days of monarchy and feudalism, they had no problem because they were simple subjects of the Crown, wherever they lived—West or East of Naaf River. There never was a question of 'citizenship' or 'green card.' As long as a person paid due tax it was OK. In modern demarcation of the borders along the midstream of the Naaf River after the WWII, they came to face the identity crisis. It is not their creation. They simply do not understand what the hell is going on with the so-called nations of India, Pakistan, Bangladesh, and Burma aka Myanmar. Where shall they live and what shall they be? They simply do not know. They are the innocent victims of modern political and national identity in the post-British Third World colonialism. Due to their proximity with Chittagong, which became a major Islamic missionary center, they became Muslims at a junction of the history. As such, they also became the victims of religious expansionism. One good event is that due to the common religion the Rohingya of Pakistan were absorbed into the main stream of Pakistan national life. In contrast, they became the victims of Myanmar colonialism. They deserve the rights of *we-the-people*, having a choice and having a voice. And, it is the duty of the privileged to help them. Denial of a choice and a voice to the unprivileged Rohingya by the privileged Rakhine and Myanmar people, when compounded with mass killing and displacement, is beyond doubt a big question of civilization–not a mere technical issue of citizenship. Under the international law[249] it comes under the category of 'crimes against humanity.'

Exhibit-PR12

A common poster in my student days

နှင်းပြား (ninpya)

pounded and flattened

နှင်းပြားဘဝမှ လွတ်မြောက်ရေး

(ninpya bawa hma lwut myauk yeh)

ရုန်းကန်ကြ တိုက်ခိုက်ကြ။

(yonkankya tike-khike kya)

For freedom from
the pounded and flattened life
Struggle and fight.

---

2. Ninpya. The leftist or the left-of-the-center parties like ANLP and ACP are more sympathetic to the Rohingya with a view that they are purely property-less, oppressed, and underprivileged proletarians and peasants. Such people are known as *Ninpya,* meaning 'pounded and flattened people', see the Exhibit-PR12. The Rohingya are being exploited by the religionists, capitalists, and colonialists; therefore, they must be liberated.

The Rakhine leftists view that a nation is a form of conglomerate, in which the duties are assigned and divided

---

[249] See (Nürnberg) Principles of International Law in the *Yearbook of the International Law Commission*, 1950, vol. II, para. 97, and at
http://untreaty.un.org/ilc/texts/instruments/english/draft articles/7_1_1950.pdf.

according to the principle of "from each according his ability to each according to his work." In light of this principle they give due honor and recognition of the contribution of the Rohingya as the farmers, fishermen, and laborers in national food production and economy through ages. *The Rohingya are the comrades at work.* I agree with them. My agreement with this view of the Arakanese leftists became solidified when I became a US Citizen. I came to the United States with a H1B visa, which is issued for the specialty professionals. With due contribution to economy and development of the United States, I eventually became a US citizen. It took five years to get the 'green card' and another five years for the 'naturalization' or 'citizenship', a total of ten years! The Rakhaing leftists sound like the Americans.[250]

It was the Rohingya and the other Muslims forces that made Burma the rice bowl of Asia during the British days. Today also, the Rohingya's agricultural land are most productive in Myanmar. The Muslim fishermen and women of Kyaukpyu Kala Paikseik (meaning Kala *fishing village*) are the most skilled in Myanmar. It was a sinister design that their village was burned to ashes and they were sent to the concentration camps near Sittwe. For more details of atrocities against the Rohingya and Muslims please read the reports by Human Rights Watch (hrw) at

http://www.hrw.org/reports/2013/04/22/all-you-can-do-pray-0 and

http://www.hrw.org/news/2012/10/26/burma-new-violence-arakan-state

I am still intrigued by the view of ACP Chairman Shwe Tha who was a teacher monk, *Dhamma Cariya*, before he quit monkhood and joined the Red Flag Communist Party of Burma led by Thakin Soe.[251]   To be a Dhamma Cariya, a monk or nun, has first to pass elementary, middle, and higher *pathamam* (prerequisite) courses in Three Buddhist Canons *(Tripitaka)* and then the Dhamma Cariya examination, which is equivalent to Bachelor of Arts in Buddhism and duly recognized by the Government of Burma (Myanmar) and Rangoon University. Any body can be a Dhamma Cariya and does not have to be a monk, nun or Buddhist. Yes, a Muslim can also be a Dhamma Cariya.

---

[250] Remember the East-West 'convergent theory' of Pitirim Sorokin in his *Russia and the United States* (Oxford University Press, 1942)!

[251] See about Thakin soe in Shwe Lu Maung, *Burma Nationalism and Ideology*, University Press Ltd., Dhaka, 1989, pp 26, 31, 44, 98, 101.

It is very interesting that we have a good number of monk-communist (a person who was a monk or nun and later became a communist) and communist-monk (a communist who later became a monk or nun).[252] I worked closely with Chairman Shwe Tha and his party from 1978 to 1994. His party's Joint Secretary Oo Khin Maung[253] is a close friend of mine.

According to Red Comrade Chairman Shwe Tha the recognition of the Rohingya is not only humanistic but also proletarian. When he mentioned this in a discussion at the Bangladesh-Burma border in 1986 I looked at his eyes blankly and said, "Oh, c'mon! Ako Shwe Tha? I disagree equating of humanism to ideology. To me, humanism transcends ideology as well as religion."

"Comrade Shwe Lu Maung," he replied and gave me an eloquent discourse of ideology. Red Comrades who are the disciples of Thakin Soe are very good in giving ideological discourses. His discourses can be briefed, "The humanity exists only in a classless society." I was introduced to the circle of the Red Comrades in 1963 when we were re-establishing the Rangoon University Student Union. I used to frequent their office at Rangoon downtown in 1963 and 1964.[254] Red comrades incline to explain everything according to their 'big book' of proletarianism. I love listening to their eloquent ideological discourses. Their leader, Thakin Soe was the first and only person who translated Karl Marx's *Capital, the Manifesto of Communist Party, Dialectical materialism,* and *Historical Materialism* into Burmese.[255] At least eighty percent of the modern Burmese leftist political vocabulary was invented by him. I may or may not agree with their 'big book' but I do agree with them in the assertion that recognition of the Rohingya rights is not only

---

[252] Also see Shwe Lu Maung, *The Price of Silence: Muslim-Buddhist War of Bangladesh and Myanmar – A Social Darwinist's Analysis,* DewDrop Arts & Technology, USA, 2005, pp 206-207.

[253] Also see Ibid. p 189, 204.

[254] The Association of Former Red Comrades, disciples of Thakin soe, was at Barr Street (now Maha Bandula Garden Street), if I remember correctly. They got a row with General Ne Win in 1964 and the association disappeared. I wish they revive it now.

[255] I do not think his translation of Karl Marx's *Capital* got published due to WWII and civil war but his disciples learned from him in the secret meetings and revolutionary camps during the WWII, and Fascist Revolution, and Burmese Civil War. Members of the Arakan Communist Party learned Marx's Capital from him in the revolutionary camp before ACP split off from his party in late 1950. His revolutionary head quarter was in Arakan.

humanistic but also right politics, in our own perspectives.

Unfortunately, I do not believe that there will ever arrive a perfect Utopian classless society on this planet. Humanity and human rights have to be woven into the matrix of the imperfect society. Such a society will facilitate advancement of respect for humanity and human rights across all spectra. Only when there is respect for humanity and human rights a sense of responsibility toward each other across the social spectra will prevail. In a society where there is a sense of responsibility we can expect the prevalence of relative peace and harmony. Indeed, nothing is absolute.

12
Citizenship and Beyond
(A historical materialism)

If the Rohingya were given the Myanmar citizenship today the problem will be solved today!?

No, because the ethnic cleansing and apartheid are the well-known colonialist policies.

Therefore, *I determined that recognition of the Rohingya is a process of the 'decolonization of Burma'.* [256]

If I were to condemn the British colonialism will it be right for me to glorify the Rakhine colonialism or the Myanmar colonialism?

No. The answer is a clear-cut 'no'. It is not right.

That is why my fight, my struggle, and my movement were and are for the decolonization of Burma (Myanmar).[257]

The decolonization of Myanmar is the final frontier in the democratization of Myanmar.

Let us see.

Today's Myanmar concept that the cleansing of the Rohingya and the Muslims from Myanmar means the cleansing of the British colonialism once and for good from the land of Myanmar is embedded with the features of (1) Palingenetic ultranationalism of Roger Graffin,[258] and (2) National Anarchism,[259] in addition to the classic Third World Colonialism.[260] I have summarized the features of the Myanmar ultranationalism in the Chapter 5.

---

[256] See Shwe Lu Maung, *The Rakhine State Violence*, Vol. 1: the Rakhaing Revolution, Shahnawaz Khan Publication (USA), 2014, p 246 and Shwe Lu Maung, *The Price of Silence: Muslim-Buddhist War of Bangladesh and Myanmar – A Social Darwinist's Analysis*, DewDrop Arts & Technology, USA, 2005, Chapters 4 to 7, for more features of Myanmarsim or Myanmar colonialism.

[257] Ibid. In this volume, I presented the strategies and tactics of our struggle for the decolonization of Burma.

[258] http://en.wikipedia.org/wiki/Palingenetic_ultranationalism

[259] http://en.wikipedia.org/wiki/National-Anarchism

[260] See Shwe Lu Maung, *Burma Nationalism and Ideology*, University Press Ltd., Dhaka, 1989, especially the Chapter 9.

The features of the Myanmar palingenetic ultranationalism are (1) Aung San Suu Kyi's declaration of "the second struggle for national independence" in her 1988 Shwedagon Speech,[261] (2) the well-known so-called Saffron Revolution 2007,[262] (3) the recent rise of Buddhist nationalism (e.g. 969 movement),[263] (4) violence against the Rohingya and Muslims, and (5) military warlordism in politics.

The Wikipedia article[264] highlights that "National-Anarchism is a radical, anti-capitalist, anti-Marxist, anti-statist, right-wing political and cultural ideology which emphasizes ethnic tribalism. National-Anarchists seek to establish autonomous villages for neo-völkisch communities and other forms of new tribes, which have seceded from the state's economy and are no-go areas for unwelcomed groups and state authorities." The on-going ethnic violence, religious violence, and anti-everything, which is non-Burmese or non-Buddhist, constitute the "national-anarchism."

I do not encourage the ethnicity-based politics, but I am for the *we-the-people*. Nevertheless, I honor and respect the rights to self-identification and self-determination. The rights to self-identification and self-determination are the fundamentals of the decolonization. Therefore, I here make an attempt to strengthen my view that '*the recognition of the Rohingya is a process of the 'decolonization of Burma.'* Nothing more, nothing less. The philosophy of decolonization of Burma is a synthesis of the Rakhaing Revolution, as described in the Volume 1.

Our philosophy is very simple. We draw a clear demarcation line at 1948, the year the Union of Burma was born as an independent republic with the 1947 Constitution of the Union of Burma, under the Nu-Attlee Agreement 1947. Pre-1948 was feudal and colonial but post-1948 is democratic and republican. In the feudal and colonial days of pre-1948 there was no *people* but only *the subjects of the Crown*. At the advent of newborn republics in 1947-48 the *people* came into existence, at least theoretically. *It is a colossal political task to make the theoretical existence of the 'people' into a reality of life.* Although the Burmese 1947 Constitution was not up to our expectation its philosophy was 'we-

---

[261] Aung San Suu Kyi, Speech to a mass rally at the Shwedagon Pagoda, August 26, 1988, http://www.ibiblio.org/obl/docs3/Shwedagon-ocr.doc
[262] http://en.wikipedia.org/wiki/Saffron_Revolution
[263] http://en.wikipedia.org/wiki/969_Movement
[264] http://en.wikipedia.org/wiki/National-Anarchism

the-people'. We are happy with 'we-the-people' because *sovereignty emanates from we-the-people.* It can be contrasted from the 1974 military-socialist constitution in which *sovereignty emanates from we-the-working-people,* signifying a form of sectarian dictatorship. The 1947 *we-the-people* constitution also contrasted from the present 2008 constitution in which *sovereignty emanates from we-the-national-people,* again signifying a form of sectarian chauvinism. Both 1974 and 2008 constitutions, having an adjective in front of 'people,' create inequality. The 1982 Citizenship Act of Burma is a good example of inequality. The citizens are divided into various classes.[265] Under such condition that we, the 1960-generation, who have been struggling for a more perfect Union of Burma with the ideology of we-the-people, became alienated, marginalized, faced the threats in Burmese politics and nationalism.

""The problem is to find a form of association which will defend and protect with the whole common force the person and goods of each associate, and in which each, while uniting himself with all, may still obey himself alone, and remain as free as before." This is the fundamental problem of which the Social Contract provides the solution."

The above most familiar quote is from "the social contract or principles of political right" (1762) by Jean Jacques Rousseau (Exhibit-Ct1). The source of the quote (Book I:6. The Social Compact) that I downloaded on July 10, 2014, is from 1782 translation by G.D.H. Cole, which is posted at http://www.constitution.org/jjr/socon.htm.

'The social contract' of Jean Jacques Rousseau[266] is reflected in the Preamble of the US Constitution, 1787.

"We the People of the United States, in Order to form a more perfect Union, establish Justice, insure domestic

---

[265] Shwe Lu Maung, *The Rakhine State Violence*, Vol. 1: the Rakhaing Revolution, Shahnawaz Khan Publication (USA), 2014, pp 210-213, and Shwe Lu Maung, *The Price of Silence: Muslim-Buddhist War of Bangladesh and Myanmar – A Social Darwinist's Analysis*, DewDrop Arts & Technology, USA, 2005, p 159.

[266] https://en.wikipedia.org/wiki/Jean-Jacques_Rousseau

Tranquility, provide for the common defence,[267] promote the general Welfare, and secure the Blessings of Liberty to ourselves and our Posterity, do ordain and establish this Constitution for the United States of America."[268]

Exhibit-Ct1
Jean Jacques Rousseau (1712-1778)
Portrait in 1753, by Maurice Quentin de La Tour
posted at
https://en.wikipedia.org/wiki/Jean-Jacques_Rousseau
The portrait is in public domain in USA

Indeed, the recognition of Rohingya faces powerful opposition, including death threats. I will list some of my experience during my Burmese days[269] here.

1965: One Rakhine youth leader, who was one of my mentors, told me that the Mujahiden uprising was a manipulation of the Burma Army to backstab the Rakhaing revolutionaries like U Seinda, Bogri Kra Hla Aung, Bonpauk Tha Kyaw, and Chairman Kyaw Zan Rhee. Unto today, after 50 years, I have not gained any knowledge to accept or reject his assertion. Nonetheless, I live up to his advice that the Rakhaing survival depends on the friendship with the Rohingya and vice versa.

1966-67: I joined the Arakan National United Party (ANUP) of Bogri Kra Hla Aung and also met and worked with Chairman

---

[267] Yes, the original spelling is 'defence' not 'defense'.
http://www.archives.gov/exhibits/charters/constitution_transcript.html.
[268] The official text copied on July 10, 2014 from
http://www.archives.gov/exhibits/charters/constitution_transcript.html
[269] Officially and constitutionally I am not a Burmese since 1978.

Kyaw Zan Rhee of Arakan Communist Party (ACP). Both of them are for the rights of the Rohingya people. In our party, ANUP, we had about 50 Muslim members.

1974-2000: Revolutionary parties–the Arakan National Liberation Party (ANLP) led by Chairman Maung Sein Nyunt, the Arakan Communist Party (ACP) led by Chairman Kyaw Tha, the Arakan Independence Organization (AIO) led by Chairman Kyaw Hlaing, the National United Party of Arakan (NUPA) led by Chairman Khin Maung and the Amyotha Party (AP) led by Major (retired) Tun Kyaw Oo (1990 election) recognize the Rohingya rights.[270]

1999-2001. I extended my recognition of the Rohinyga in my capacity of the Diplomatic Representative of Arakan League for Democracy (ALD) in exile. I was immediately expelled from ALD.[271]

Of course, all the parties listed above that recognize the Rohingya rights are now either annihilated or marginalized. In 1990 Major (retired) Tun Kyaw Oo[272] was imprisoned with a 12-year sentence for his recognition of the Rohingya and his party was dissolved by the military authorities. But the question remains–why do they recognize the Rohingya rights? And, why do I agree with them? These are what I know:

The label "illegal Bengali" or "illegal Chittagonians" has been tagged to the Rohingya by the people and government of Myanmar. Myanmar recognized them as the British era immigrants from the Chittagong region of Bengal in the days of the British rule. Under this accusation the Myanmar people and government are cleansing up the "Illegals," without giving them a chance to defend before a judge. In this particular aspect, the Myanmar action against the Rohingya violates the Articles 10 and 11 of the Universal Declaration of Human Rights, that are given below, in both Burmese and English.[273]

---

[270] Also see *The Rakhine State Violence*, vol. 1: The Rakhaing Revolution, Chapter 16.

[271] Ibid.

[272] I do not have any information of Major Tun Kyaw Oo since his imprisonment in 1990.

[273] Please also see the Chapter 3.

Article 10.

• Everyone is entitled in full equality to a fair and public hearing by an independent and impartial tribunal, in the determination of his rights and obligations and of any criminal charge against him.

အပိုဒ် ၁၀

အခွင့်အရေးများနှင့် တာဝန် ဝတ္တရားများကို အဆုံးအဖြတ်ခံရာတွင် လည်းကောင်း၊ ပြစ်မှုကြောင့် တရားစွဲဆိုစီရင် ဆုံးဖြတ်ခံရာတွင် လည်းကောင်း၊ လူတိုင်းသည် လွတ်လပ်၍ ဘက်မလိုက်သော တရားရုံးတော်၏ လူအများ ရှေ့မှောက်တွင် မျှတစွာ ကြားနာစစ်ဆေးခြင်းကို တူညီစွာ ခံစား ပိုင်ခွင့်ရှိသည်။

Article 11.

• (1) Everyone charged with a penal offence has the right to be presumed innocent until proved guilty according to law in a public trial at which he has had all the guarantees necessary for his defence.

• (2) No one shall be held guilty of any penal offence on account of any act or omission which did not constitute a penal offence, under national or international law, at the time when it was committed. Nor shall a heavier penalty be imposed than the one that was applicable at the time the penal offence was committed.

အပိုဒ် ၁၁

(၁) လူအများ ရှေ့မှောက်၌ ဥပဒေအတိုင်း စစ်ဆေး၍ ပြစ်မှုကျူးလွန်သည်ဟု ထင်ရှား စီရင်ခြင်းခံရသည့် အချိန်အထိ ပြစ်မှုနှင့် တရားစွဲဆိုခြင်း ခံရသူတိုင်းသည် အပြစ်မဲ့သူဟု၍ ယူဆခြင်းခံထိုက်သည့် အခွင့်အရေးရှိသည်။ ထိုအမှုကို ကြားနာစစ်ဆေးရာဝယ် စွပ်စွဲခံရသည့် ပြစ်မှုအတွက် ခုခံချေပနိုင်ရန် လိုအပ်သော အခွင့်အရေးများကို ထိုသူအား ပေးပြီး ဖြစ်စေရမည်။

(၂) လူတစ်ဦးတစ်ယောက်အား နိုင်ငံ ဥပဒေအရဖြစ်စေ၊ အပြည်ပြည်ဆိုင်ရာ ဥပဒေအရ ဖြစ်စေ၊ ပြစ်မှုမမြောက်သော လုပ်ရပ် သို့မဟုတ် ပျက်ကွက်မှုအရ ဆွဲဆိုပြစ်ပေးခြင်း မပြုရ။ ထို့အပြင် ပြစ်မှုကျူးလွန်စဉ်အခါက ထိုက်သင့်စေနိုင်သော အပြစ် ဒဏ်ထက်ပိုမိုကြီးလေးသော အပြစ် ဒဏ်ကို ထိုက်သင့်ခြင်းမရှိစေရ။

The accusation of being "illegal Bengali" or "illegal Chittagonians" is flawed, illogical, and amount to arbitrary persecution based on race and religion. The US-based rights group known as Human Rights Watch has put out a comprehensive report on the matter (Exhibit-Ct2),[274] with a strong message that it is a crime against humanity.

Exhibit-Ct2
Human Rights Watch's report 2013
on the Rakhine State Violence

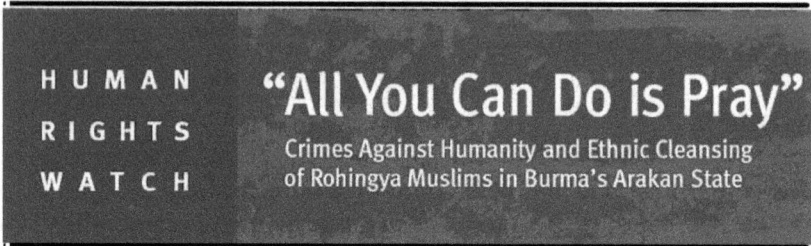

HUMAN
RIGHTS
WATCH

"All You Can Do is Pray"
Crimes Against Humanity and Ethnic Cleansing
of Rohingya Muslims in Burma's Arakan State

http://www.hrw.org/reports/2013/04/22/all-you-can-do-pray-0

In the earlier chapters I have presented the available evidence, which lead to the reasonable conclusion that the Rohingya are the aborigines of the region and one of the oldest tribes that has been a victim of civilization for millenniums. But, could the Rohingya be an 'illegal Bengali' or 'illegal Chittagonian' of the British colonial era? In this regard, a piece of ICS U Kyaw Min's statement renders a logic worthy of discussion.

In Myanmar, there will hardly be anybody who does not know U Kyaw Min, born in 1899,[275] one of the eight I.C.S. (prestigious Indian Civil Service) of the British Era in all Burma and a Member of Parliament from 1951 to 1962, and a founding father of Arakan National United Organization (ANUO or Ra-Ta-Nya, 1948-1962). I would like to post a piece of excerpt from his article, "The Arakan State," that is housed at the Cornell University Library (Call No. Wason DS485 B892 K77+, ASIA), and I downloaded it on July 14, 2013 from–
http://www.archive.org/details/cu31924022999126, (Exhibit-Ct3).

---

[274] http://www.hrw.org/reports/2013/04/22/all-you-can-do-pray-0.
[275] I do not know when he passed away.

It reads as follows.

"The problem of the Arakanese was the Chittagonian problem, not the Burmese. The Chittagonians, however, came to Arakan as servants and labourers and as such they were wanted in Arakan. They never were really a serious problem for they kept their place as servants and labourers and in the mofussil, where they came as peasants, there was enough room for them because of the lack of Arakanese farmers. The relations were always cordial. The first clash between them was with the advent of the Japanese in early 1942. But that is a story apart."

Exhibit-Ct3

The Arakan State by U Kyaw Min, M.P., ICS (Retd.), Barrsiter-at-law

The problem of the Arakanese was the Chittagonian problem, not the Burmese. The Chittagonians, however, came to Arakan as servants and labourers and as such they were wanted in Arakan. They never were really a serious problem for they kept their place as servants and labourers and in the mofussil, where they came as peasants, there was enough room for them because of the lack of Arakanese farmers. The relations were always cordial. The first clash between them was with the advent of the Japanese in early 1942. But that is a story apart.

This piece of ICS U Kyaw Min's view must be given very important consideration. First, he wrote "The problem of the Arakanese was the Chittagonian problem." But, he later said, "The relations [between the two communities] were always cordial. The first clash between them was with the advent of the Japanese in early 1942. But that is a story apart." Let us keep in our mind that the

Rakhaing people have been living next to Bengal for thousands of years without any communal conflict. The imperial and royal wars were recorded in the history, but not single incidence of racial or religious communal violence. As ICS U Kyaw Min wrote, " The first clash between them was with the advent of the Japanese in early 1942. But that is a story apart." I wish ICS U Kyaw Min is with us to tell 'the story apart'. In his absence, I will try to construct the "story apart" in this presentation.

Today, Myanmar and Rakhine ultranationalists are trying to expel the Rohingya with the note that they were illegal immigrants of the British colonial era. However, ICS U Kyaw Min clearly stated that there was a distinct group of people known as the Chittagonians, but not the Rohingya, who came to the Arakan Division of British Burma as the legal migrant workers. *Most importantly, his statement "as such they (the Chittagonians) were wanted in Arakan" is a strong and valid evidence of their legal status.* That is to say that they were not illegal. It is highly possible that due to religious, racial, and linguistic affinity the migrant workers from the Chittagong region became integrated with the local Rohingya communities. It is also highly possible that they actually were the returning Arakanese Muslims who escaped into the British Bengal when the Burmese King Bodawphaya seized Arakan in 1784. We know very well that the Muslims of today Central Burma, who are living in Meiktila and adjacent areas, are the descendants of the Arakanese Muslims who were abducted by the Burmese conquerors and used as the slave-labor in digging the Meiktila Lake. Meiktila (*cf.* Mithila or Maithila of Ancient India) is the city where a bloody Buddhist-Muslim conflict took place from March 20 to 22, in 2013, leaving more 40 dead, 60 injured and 9,000 displaced, most of them Muslim.[276] We also know that the 'Myedu Muslims' of the central Burma are also the Arakanese Muslims abducted by Burmese King Bodawphaya after his conquest of Arakan in 1784. They were used as the slave labor in digging (Myedu) and as such they earned their identity–the Earth Diggers or Myedu.

More importantly, the term 'Chittagonian', that was originated by the British in the 19th century, simply refer to a person living in the city of Chittagong or in the District of Chittagong under the British Administration. It is a relatively modern word. It is like

---

[276] http://en.wikipedia.org/wiki/2013_Burma_anti-Muslim_riots, accessedon June 19, 2014.

the term New Yorker, a term that refers to a person living in the New York City or New York State. A New Yorker can be a Puerto Rican, Ethiopian, Jamaican, Italian, German, Russian, Mongolian, Japanese, Chinese or English *et cetera*. There are more than 200 ethnic groups in New York City, perhaps almost all ethnic groups of the world, including the Native Americans.

Similarly, there are many ethnic groups in Chittagong City and Chittagong District. Therefore, when ICS U Kyaw Min said "the Chittagonian" it does not necessarily mean a Bengali, but could well also be a Rohingya. (Please refer back to the Brigadier Aung Gyi's speech given in the Chapter 4). As a matter of fact, there exists an argument that Chittagong City and Chittagong District were not part of the Bengal main land, historically and politically speaking. The Chittagong area hosted ancient city kingdoms such as Samatata and Harikela.[277] Please note the striking resemblance of the today's Rakhine State emblem and symbols of the ancient coins from the City Kingdoms of Samatata, Harikela, Veisali, and Pyu, with the symbol of Śrīvatsa (Exhibit-Ct4A and Exhibit-Ct4B). As a matter of fact, they are the same! I will leave the reader alone so that you may ponder why they are the same.

The pictures in the Exhibit-Ct4A are downloaded on July 7, 2014 from:
1. The Rakhine State emblem and Veisali coin are from: http://en.wikipedia.org/wiki/Rakhine_State

2. The Samatata coin from: https://www.vcoins.com/en/stores/coinindia/36/product/india_akaras _of_samatata_ramakara_ar_64ratti_very_rare/80523/Default.aspx, and

3. The Harikela coin from: http://www.historyfiles.co.uk/KingListsFarEast/IndiaSamatata.htm

4. The Pyu coin from:

---

[277] http://www.banglapedia.org/HT/S_0065.htm, and
http://www.banglapedia.org/HT/A_0354.htm, and
http://www.banglapedia.org/HT/H_0086.htm, and
http://www.historyfiles.co.uk/KingListsFarEast/IndiaSamatata.htm

http://www.seasite.niu.edu/burmese/Cooler/Chapter_2/Chapter_2.htm

Exhibit-Ct4A

Today's Rakhine flag emblem and ancient Veisali,
Samatata, Harikela, and Pyu coins (7th-9th century)
Please note that they are the same. Also see Exhibit-Ct4B.

Rakhine State Emblem   Rakhine Veisali Coin

Bengal Samatata Coin   Bengal Harikela Coin

Pyu Coin

Please note the Śrīvatsa symbols signify connectivity of
the ancient Bengal, today Rakhine State,
and ancient Myanmar.
For the references, please see the text.

Exhibit-Ct4B
Map showing the ancient kingdoms of
Samatata, Karikela, Veisali, and Pyu, where the same coins
with the symbol of Śrīvatsa (see Exhibit-Ct4A) were found

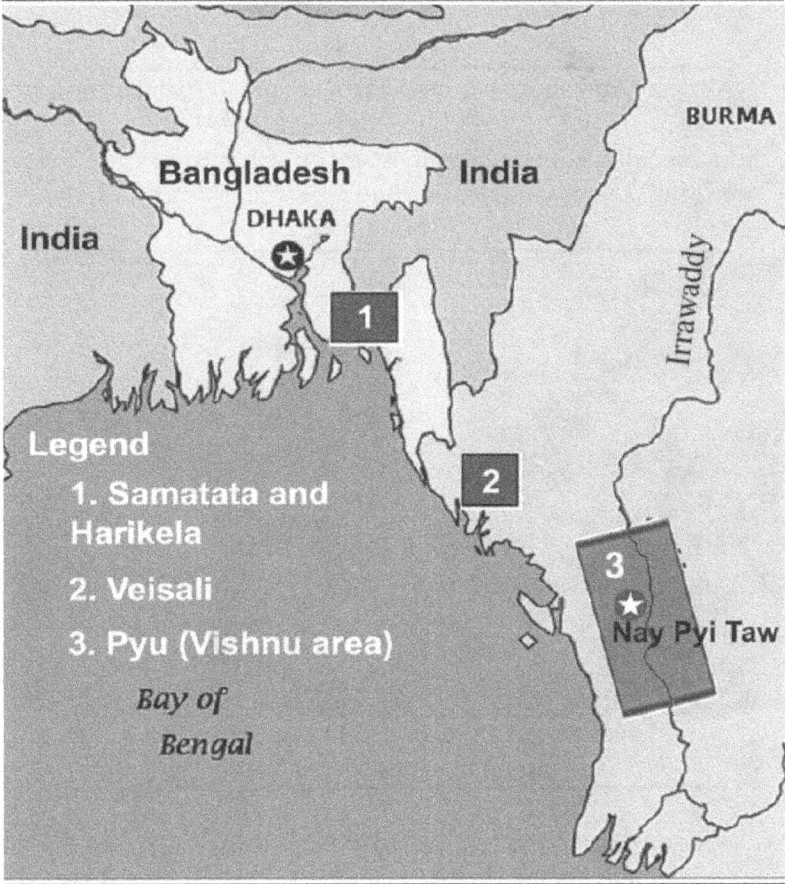

Chittagong City was the most important international port city and was occupied by various rulers and powers of the region in the history.[278] The area became part of Bengal only in the days of Mughal conquest in 1666. The Mughal Emperor Aurangzeb (r.1658-

---

[278] See Dr. Suniti Bhushan Qanungo, *History of Chittagong* Vol. 1 and 2, published by Dipankar Qanungo, Chittagong, 1988 and http://en.wikipedia.org/wiki/History_of_Chittagong

1707)[279] seized it from the Rakhaing King Sanda Thudhamma (r.1652-1684).[280] The popular open source encyclopedia known as wikipedia even has a colorful painting, depicting the Mughal assault of the Rakhaing Fort by an unknown artist. The painting in grayscale is shown in the Exhibit-Ct5. The original painting is housed in the Chittagong University Museum.

Exhibit-Ct5

Mughal-Arakanese battle on the Karnaphuli river in 1666
Public Domain
http://en.wikipedia.org/wiki/History_of_Chittagong#mediavie
wer/File:Mughal-Arakanese_battle_on_the_Karnaphuli_river
_in_1666.jpg

Unknown - Chittagong University museum.
Commons uploader: Rahat

According to the historian Suniti Bhushan Qanungo the city name Chittagong, among many possibilities, came from a stone pillar inscription made by the Veisali King Tsu-la-taing Tsandaya who conquered Chittagong in 952 CE and erected the stone pillar with the inscription that read "Tset-ta-gaung," meaning "to make war is not proper."[281] From what I learned from the Rakhaing oral traditions

---

[279] http://en.wikipedia.org/wiki/Aurangzeb
[280] Shwe Lu Maung, *The Price of Silence: Muslim-Buddhist War of Bangladesh and Myanmar – A Social Darwinist's Analysis*, DewDrop Arts & Technology, USA, 2005, p 245
[281] See Dr. Suniti Bhushan Qanungo, *History of Chittagong* Vol. 1, published by Dipankar

the stone pillar inscription says, "Tsite-thi-gaung," which means "War must end." For many years the Chittagong region was under the rule of the Rakhaing kings. For example, a map of the ancient Arakan posted at http://www.arakanland.com/index_3.html shows that the Chittagong Region was in the Arakan Kingdom (Exhibit-Ct6).

Exhibit-Ct6
A map of Ancient Arakan posted at http://www.arakanland.com/index_3.html

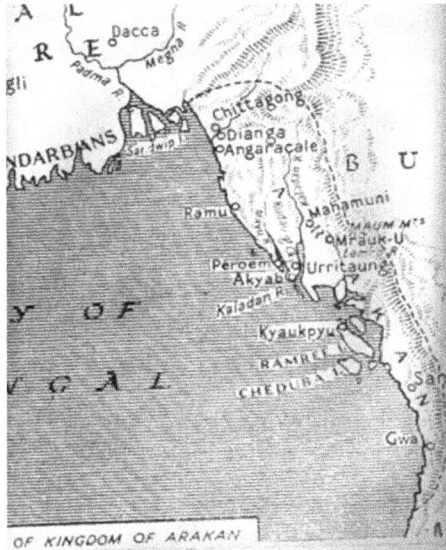

Arakan Kingdom is demarcated by the broken lines.

Above all, what intrigues me most is the assertion of Pamela Gutman that King Min Bin (also spelled Mun Bargri, Mun Pa Gri, Mong Ben) had Bengali wives. She wrote as follows in her 2008 article *"Between India and Southeast Asia- Arakan, Burma's Forgotten Kingdom."*[282] The highlighted emphasis placed by me.

"The Shitthaung shrine, built by King Mong Ben after he conquered Bengal in 1536, was the magnificent statement

---

Qanungo, Chittagong, 1988, p 17.
[282] Just by accidence, I found the article at
-http://arakankotawchay.blogspot.com/2011/06/between-india-and-southeast-asia-arakan.html.
Last accessed on July 7, 2014.

of a cakravartin Buddhist king who had conquered Islam. An arched screen on the western side and the arrangement of stupas on the roof recall the mosque architecture of 16th century Gaur in east Bengal. Surrounding the central image are circumambulatory passages, on the outer of which the king is depicted as a god with the attributes of a cakravatin king, some derived from the iconography of Vishnu the Preserver. He is flanked by his Bengali and Arakanese wives, distinguished by their dress, and by depictions of his power and the prosperity he has brought to his country."

(Please note: "cakravartin" means king of the universe. 'cakra' means the round one or universe and 'vartin' means the controller. There are 10,000 worlds in the universe. In the Myanmar Buddhist concept only an Embryo Buddha can be a "Cakravartin." Every king in Arakan and Burma was poised as a "Cakravartin". The Cakravartin is symbolized with *Swastika*, which was adopted as the Nazi symbol in the Hitler's Germany).

King Min Bin (r.1531-1553) also adorned a Muslim title Zabuk Shah.[283] The picture of the king and his wives can be found at http://en.wikipedia.org/wiki/Min_Bin, as of July 07, 2014. His names and his shrine, the most famous and historic Shitthaung Pagoda, testifies that the Muslims and Islam actually had enriched the Rakhaing culture and Buddhism, in contrast to the today's Islamophobia in Burma.

Why am I showing these ancient lineages? My point is very simple. The Rakhaing colonized 12 cities of Bengal[284] for 130 years, from 1536 to 1666 CE, and the Rakhaing king even had Bengali wives. Therefore, it is very logical and natural to have the Chittagonians or Bengalis in today's Myanmar Rakhine State, which is nothing but the Eastern Territory of the Arakan Kingdom.

More–
We should not forget the slavery in the Imperial Arakan or Rakhaingpraygri. It is vividly described by Maurice Collis in his

---

[283] See Shwe Lu Maung, *The Price of Silence: Muslim-Buddhist War of Bangladesh and Myanmar – A Social Darwinist's Analysis*, DewDrop Arts & Technology, USA, 2005, p 212.
[284] The Rakhaings glorify themselves as the rulers of the Bengal 12 Cities.

book *The Land of the Great Image* (1943).[285] The scanned image of Maurice Collis's narration his book is given in the Exhibit-Ct7.

Exhibit-Ct7
The slavers of Arakan
From: Maurice Collis, *The Land of the Great Image* (1943),
New Directions Publishing;
Reprint edition (November 17, 1985), p 111

Among the Slavers of Dianga

We have an excellent description of what these raids were like, written by the Mogul historian, Shiab-ud-din Talish. 'The Arakan pirates, who were both Portuguese and native, used constantly to come by water and plunder Bengal,' he writes. 'They carried off such Hindus and Moslems as they could seize, pierced the palms of their hands, passed thin slips of cane through the holes and shut them huddled together under the decks of their ships. Every morning they flung down some uncooked rice, as we do for fowl. . . . Many noblemen and women of family had to undergo the disgrace of slavery or concubinage. . . . Not a house eventually was left inhabited on either side of the rivers leading from Chittagong to Dacca. . . . The sailors of the Bengal flotilla were so terrified of the pirates that if a hundred armed boats of the former sighted but four of the latter, their crews thought themselves lucky if they could save themselves by flight. . . . Half the pirates' booty went to the King of Arakan.'

These were the ruffians among whom Friar Domingos had lived for seven years; and we can well understand the reason for his loneliness. Manrique was a man of tougher fibre. As will later appear, he was able to win the confidence of the mercenaries and undertake on their behalf important responsibilities.

It reads as follows.

"We have an excellent description of what these raids were like, written by the Mogul historian, Shiab-ud-din Talish, 'The Arakan Pirates, who were both Portuguese and native, used constantly to come by water and plunder Bengal,' he

---

[285] Maurice Collis, *The Land of the Great Image* (1943), New Directions Publishing; Reprint edition (November 17, 1985).

writes. 'They carried off such Hindus and Moslems as they could seize, pierced the palms of their hands, passed thin slips of cane through the holes and shut them huddled together under the decks of their ships. Every morning they flung down some uncooked rice, as we do for fowl. . . . Many noblemen and women of family had to undergo the disgrace of slavery or concubinage. . . . Not a house eventually was left inhabited on either side of the rivers leading from Chittagong to Decca. . . . The sailors of the Bengal flotilla were so terrified of the pirates that if a hundred armed boats of the former sighted but four of the latter, their crews thought themselves lucky if they could save themselves by flight. . . . Half the pirates' booty went to the King of Arakan.'

These were the ruffians among whom Friar Domingos had lived for seven years; and we can well understand the reason for his loneliness. Manrique was a man of tougher fibre. As will later appear, he was able to win the confidence of the mercenaries and undertake on their behalf important responsibilities."

The Land of Great Image by Maurice Collis was based upon the diaries of the Portuguese Augustinian friar Sebastião Manrique's[286] visit to the Palace of Arakan King Thiri Thudhamma in 1628.[287] Friar Manrique went to the King of Arakan as the envoy of the Portuguese pirates who were contracted by the King of Arakan for the defense of the Arakan frontier with the Mughal Empire. His job was to dispel the accusation that the Portuguese mercenaries were plotting against the Arakanese King and to solicit the King's continued support to the piracy. Friar Manrique was accompanied by the senior pirates and they had 53 'Indian' captives, both Hindu and Muslims, as the gifts for the Arakanese King.[288]

---

[286] Also see *"Travels of Fray Sebastien Manrique 1629-1643"* : a translation of the Itinerario de las missiones orientales / with introduction and notes by C. Eckford Luard ; assisted by H. Hosten Manrique, Sebastião, d. 1669. See the section for the travel into Arakan.

[287] Manrique's travelogue is well known in Arakan because it gave a very good account of the Arakan Royal Palace and coronation of the king. The Rakhaing people highly regard it as the evidence of the Glorious Mrauk U. They also boast the slavery and piracy as the prowess of their might.

[288] Maurice Collis, *The Land of the Great Image* (1943), New Directions Publishing; Reprint edition (November 17, 1985), p 124

Maurice Collis narrated the conversations between the Muslims captives (to be enslaved in Arakan) and Manrique.[289] From these conversations it can be seen that the religious antagonism of the Islam, Christianity, and Buddhism was already taking place in the year 1628! Maurice Collis described it as follows.[290]

"These men, Moslem residents of the riverine villages of eastern Bengal, had been kidnapped by the Christian slavers and sold by them to the [Buddhist] King of Arakan for labour in his rice-fields. On the way to their servitude they are invited [by Manrique] to adopt the religion of their kidnappers on the ground that it is a higher religion. God is compassionate and merciful, they reply: how can we prefer your religion which permits you to act so cruelly against us?"

Now is the time to make my points, based on the above presentations.

A. The Rakhine colonialism:

1. The Rakhine Empire ruled over eastern Bengal for 130 years, from 1536 to 1666 CE, and the Rakhaing king even had Bengali wives.

2. In those years of the Rakhine colonialism, the Bengali people were kidnapped and put into slavery in Arakan (Rakhaingpraygri), to work in the rice-field—a similar situation of the cotton fields of America in the 18th and 19th centuries.

3. In addition, we also know that there were Bengali nobles, intellectuals, poets, and soldiers in the Arakan Royal Service in those days (refer back to the Chapter 11, pp 173-174).

It is undeniable that the Rakhine Colonialism must be held responsible for these people because, enslaved or free, they all were the subjects of the Rakhine colonialism.

B. The Myanmar colonialism:

The Burmese occupied Arakan in 1403 CE for the second time. It was in 957 CE that the Burmese occupied Arakan Veisali for the first time. In the 1403 occupation "the Rakhaing King Narameit

---

[289] Ibid. pp 128-132 and p 137
[290] Ibid. pp 130-131

Hla took refuge with Sultan Ghiasuddin Azam Shah (r.1399-1409 CE), at Gaur. He became renowned there for his wisdom and knowledge, and widely known as King Solomon (Mun Sawmon) in the Islamic Palace of Bengal Sultan. After 27 years of his service as a minister and soldier, Sultan Jalal Uddin (r. 1415-1433 CE), a Hindu-convert-Muslim, gave him a 30,000-strong Muslim Army to restore his throne in Rakkhapura. Why a Muslim army? Because there virtually was no Rakhaing of prime age left to be soldiers. Such was the history."[291] This was the time that a large number of Bengali settlement took place. The Burmese annexed Arakan in 1784, putting Arakan independence to an end.

The Myanmar colonialism must be held responsible for this event.

C. The Islamic colonialism:

The King Narameit Hla's (also known as King Solomon or Mun Saw Mwan) restoration of his throne with the help of Bengal Sultan Jalal Uddin is interpreted as the Muslim Conquest of Arakan by the Islamic historians.[292] Since then the Pan-Islamists have been planning and plotting to restore the Islamic Kingdom of Arakan. The Pan-Islamist's romanticism of a 'global Ummah' under one Caliph[293] (*cf.* One nation under God) equally victimizes both the Buddhists and the Muslims of Arakan and the Rakhine State. This is also a cause of the Rakhine State Violence.

Therefore, the Islamic colonialism must be held responsible for this scenario.

D. The British colonialism:

The British occupied Arakan and lower Burma in 1826 after defeating the Burmese king in the First Anglo-Burman War (1824-1826). The entire Burma fell into the British rule in 1885. Arakan and Burma became part of the British India. The British made Burma

---

[291] Shwe Lu Maung, *The Price of Silence: Muslim-Buddhist War of Bangladesh and Myanmar – A Social Darwinist's Analysis*, DewDrop Arts & Technology, USA, 2005, p 173 and also see http://en.wikipedia.org/wiki/Bengal_Sultanate

[292] See Shwe Lu Maung, *The Rakhine State Violence*, Vol. 1: the Rakhaing Revolution, Shahnawaz Khan Publication (USA), 2014, pp 303-305 and http://en.wikipedia.org/wiki/Bengal_Sultanate

[293] In 2014, the reader will be familiar with today's Islamic State of Iraq and Syria (ISIS), its Caliphate and global significance.

"the rice bowl of Asia."[294]

I would also like to cite an article of Burmese agricultural researcher U Khin Win. Please see U Khin Win, *A century of rice improvement in Burma*, International Rice Research Institute, Manila, Philippines 1991, online at–
http://burmalibrary.org/docs4/A_Century_of_Rice_Improvement_in _Burma.pdf. I accessed it on July 11, 2014. If the link does not work please copy and paste the URL in the web browser.

Exhibit-Ct8

Rice Production increase in the British days
from: U Khin Win, *A century of rice improvement in Burma*,
International Rice Research Institute, Manila, Philippines 1991.
http://burmalibrary.org/docs4/A_Century_of_Rice_Improvement_in _Burma.pdf, p 15

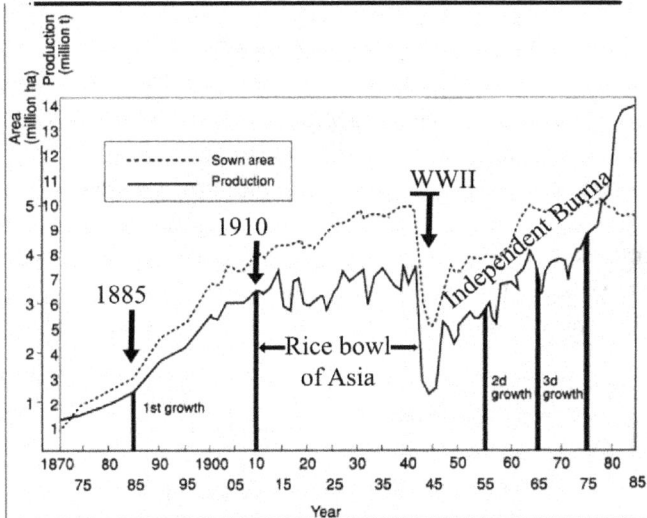

1. Trends in rice area and production.

Note. I have added a few legends to indicate
the colonial era, WWII, and independent era.
The "rice bowl of Asia" began in 1910 and
ended in 1941 at the onset of the WWII.

---

[294] see U Khin Win, *A century of rice improvement in Burma*, International Rice Research Institute, Manila, Philippines 1991, online at
http://burmalibrary.org/docs4/A_Century_of_Rice_I
mprovement_in_Burma.pdf. I accessed it on July 11, 2014.

"The rice-sown area of 1.5 million ha in 1885 increased to 4 million ha in 1910. While the yield remained almost the same, the rapid area expansion increased production from 2 million to 6 million t. As a result, rice exports also rose from a few hundred thousand to 1.5 million t."

I also reproduce one of his graphs here (Exhibit-Ct8) for clarity; see page 3 (15 in pdf) of his research article.

In the project of rice production in Burma the British brought in agricultural laborers from India, most from South India and Bengal area. Agricultural land were also leased to the petty landlords who were also from India. There was no Burmese with money to lease the land because Burma was ridden with wars since 1752 (Mon-Bama War) to 1885. Rather, many Burmese sold their land to the Indian and Chinese investors.

As cited above, when ICS U Kyaw Min wrote (Exhibit-Ct3), "The Chittagonians, however, came to Arakan as servants and labourers and as such they were wanted in Arakan," he was referring to the British era slave labor. This was the slave labor that made Burma "the rice bowl of Asia."[295] He was polite to call them the Chittagonians but not *Kala, which the Burmese use everyday to discriminate and despise the people of Indian subcontinent.*

In the system of the colonial slavery, they were not human but were the commodities and transferred from one colonial ruler to another, ruthless and brutal. The Burmese colonialism came into Arakan in 1784, and British colonialism in 1826. The British officially abolished slavery in Burma only in 1926.[296] The slavery known as the Phya-kyuan (Slave of Buddha) was finally abolished by U Nu in 1960.[297]

If the British colonialism is made responsible for the influx

---

[295] see U Khin Win, *A century of rice improvement in Burma,* International Rice Research Institute, Manila, Philippines 1991, online at
http://burmalibrary.org/docs4/A_Century_of_Rice_I
mprovement_in_Burma.pdf. I accessed it on July 11, 2014.
[296] http://www.history.ac.uk/ihr/Focus/Slavery/articles/sherwood.html
[297] Shwe Lu Maung, *The Price of Silence: Muslim-Buddhist War of Bangladesh and Myanmar – A Social Darwinist's Analysis,* DewDrop Arts & Technology, USA, 2005, p 134

of agricultural laborers into Burma, then the Rakhine and Myanmar colonialism must also be accountable for the earlier influx of the people from India. The good part is that the Indian (Bengali included here) petty landlords and the bureaucrats who migrated into Burma since 1430 (the days the Arakan Empire) were absorbed into the mainstream of Myanmar politics, economy, and culture. They were all in the affluent Rangoon and adjacent areas. Many of my professors at Rangoon University were of Indian origin. The sad part is that the poor people, who are still toiling as the subsistence farmers, laborers, and fishermen, were alienated as the 'Illegals', and blamed for the economic hardship and cultural decay. Shit flows downhill. This is outrageous.

The punishment (alienation, apartheid, IDP concentration camps, derivation of food, healthcare and education) inflicted upon the Rohingya and the Muslims of Burma with the charges that they are the British colonial era settlers is not the decolonization of Burma, but rather a practice of Myanmar colonialism.

In the view that colonialism is the worst form of slavery, I wrote in 2005, "Launching of the Rohingya nationalism is the Burmese Muslim's struggle to escape from the modern slavery [known] as *the Kala*."[298] Today, not only in Myanmar but also in many Southeast Asian countries the Rohingya are trafficked and conducted into the slavery. The ASEAN! Is it a neo-liberalism or neo-slavery?

I support the abolition of slavery in all forms and manifestations. Don't you?

In overview, it is imperative to look beyond the citizenship toward an equitable civil society where there will be–

1. Equality, liberty, and justice,
2. Respect and honor of the human rights,
3. Economic emancipation, and
4. A government of the people, by the people, for the people.

---

[298] Shwe Lu Maung, *The Price of Silence: Muslim-Buddhist War of Bangladesh and Myanmar – A Social Darwinist's Analysis*, DewDrop Arts & Technology, USA, 2005, p 250

13
Bangladesh and International

Without a concerted international cooperation, especially with Bangladesh, Myanmar cannot solve the Rohingya crisis, Islamic Extremism, or Buddhist radicalism.

It is especially so because the Rohingyas and other Muslims are being persecuted for their being Bengali, regardless of their citizenship status. Citizen or non-citizen (illegal) Rohingyas and Muslims are persecuted with the charge that they are Bengalis. Thus, Bangladesh, West Bengal (India), and Bengalis across the world have been implicated. This is such a serious racial violation that it will not be a simple case of *forgive-and-forget*. It will be hard to forget and forgive unless justice is duly done.

Bangladesh has flatly said the Rohingyas are not Bengalis, and surely not Bangladeshis either.

It is then that Myanmar has to sit face to face with Bangladesh and sincerely discuss the crisis, frankly and openly with good neighborliness. Myanmar has to take Bangladesh into confidence just like childhood friends. Without Bangladesh, Myanmar will be able to resolve neither the Rohingya crisis nor Myanmar Muslim dilemma. Now it appears that Bangladesh-Myanmar friendship has become cold, if not strained. It is crucial not to make the situation worse. It will depend on how Myanmar plays the card.

Bangladesh Prime Minister Sheikh Hasina visited Myanmar from December 5 to 7, 2011, and met the newly elected President Thein Sein. Some comments on her visit will shed some light on Bangladesh-Myanmar relation.

Brig Gen (Retired) Md Abdul Hakim Aziz, psc,- in his article "Recalibrating Bangladesh-Myanmar relation", published by the leading media, the Daily Star, at http://www.thedailystar.net/newDesign/news-details.php?nid=214402, on Saturday, December 17, 2011, wrote as follow.

"THE relation between Bangladesh and Myanmar officially

began on January 13, 1972, the date on which Myanmar recognised Bangladesh as a sovereign state. However, the relation between these two close neighbours has never been smooth and has undergone frequent ups and downs over the last 40 years on a few issues. Both countries have not been able to build a pragmatic relationship with each other despite having a lot of potentials. Myanmar being closed to the outside world for more than 50 years shows few distinct patterns of behaviour in developing effective bilateral relations with Bangladesh. These are: Myanmar capitalised Bangladesh's geographical vulnerability, being remained under the umbrella of China was reluctant to count her small neighbour, being always stubborn in their attitude and behavior to solve the disputes and more inclined towards India and China. As such Bangladesh was discouraged and lost interest to charter a course to bring Myanmar into a negotiation table for developing meaningful relation with her. On the contrary, India and China have taken the full advantage of Myanmar's isolation and developed a deep relationship with her.

The issues that dominated their relations are the influx of Rohingya refugees, demarcation of land and maritime boundary, illegal drug trafficking and alleged cross border movement of insurgents. The relation deteriorated severely in 1991 when Myanmar armed forces launched a surprised attack and ransacked the then Bangladesh Rifle's border outpost at Rejupara in Cox's Bazar district. Myanmar forces killed three members of Bangladesh Rifles and looted their arms and ammunition. However, a major regional conflict was averted because of exercising restrains by Bangladesh." The quote ends.

In his article, Brigadier General Aziz asserted further, "During the visit, the prime minister of Bangladesh raised the issue of Myanmar refugees living in Nayapara and Kutupalong camp and the huge number of undocumented Myanmar nationals living in Bangladesh and stated that early resolution of these issues will help strengthen the bilateral relations to a great extent. The president of Myanmar expressed his desire to cooperate with Bangladesh in resolving the issue."

Another leading citizen of Bangladesh, Barrister Harun Ur

Rashid, former Bangladesh Ambassador to the UN, Geneva, in his article "PM's visit to Myanmar: New opportunities unfolding" at http://archive.thedailystar.net/newDesign/news-details.php? nid=213161, on Thursday, December 8, 2011, expressed his thoughts as follow.

"Somehow or other, Bangladesh and Myanmar have not consolidated its bilateral relations as much as it deserves . . .

The amount of bilateral trade is meager. It is reported that in 2010-11 Bangladesh's exports stood at $9.65 million and imports from Myanmar at $175.7 million . . .

One of the bilateral issues that often cause a misunderstanding is the issue of Rohingya refugees. It first cropped up in 1978. Within a year, it was resolved amicably with Myanmar. Another flow of refugees came to Bangladesh in 1991 and in 1997. About 38,720 refugees reportedly remained in Bangladesh and negotiation on the issue continues still.

The migration of the Rohingya people to Bangladesh is a complex matter. It should not be seen merely as a refugee problem; partly because many militant Rohingya groups including the Arakan Rohingya National Organisation and Arakan Rohingya Islamic Front have been reportedly fighting for decades for a separate land in Rakhaine state.

Bangladesh cannot support the secession movement in a neighbouring country. Given the background, both countries may jointly develop an effective border management to prevent the flow of migration of Rohingyas to Bangladesh." The quote ends.

Another leading citizen, the columnist Nizam Ahmed candidly asked "Should Bangladesh believe Myanmar?" in his article published at–
http://www.ebangladesh.com/2012/07/27/should-bangladesh-believe-myanmar/, on July 27, 2012. He reported:

"The newly appointed Myanmar Ambassador Myo Myint Than while meeting Foreign Minister Dipu Moni on Wednesday once again pledged like his predecessors that all registered and unregistered Rohingya refugees would be taken back after proper verification . . .

"We have noted the pledge, but wondering how we can believe it, when Myanmar had failed to verify particulars of some

21,000 Rohingya refugees since 1998," a senior official of the Bangladesh foreign ministry said.

The number of these registered refugees in two camps at Kutupalang and Nayapara under Cox's Bazar district swelled to more than 30,000 early this year as Myanmar did not take them back despite of repeated pledges and promises. The registered Rohingya refugees at the camps are the remnants of 250,000 Rohingya who had fled into Bangladesh in late 1991 following persecution under the then military regime in Myanmar. Most of the refugees that had crossed into Bangladesh in late 1991 and early 1992 were repatriated from some 20 refugee camps in Cox's Bazar district until 1998.

Meanwhile the Rohingyas alleging communal persecution continued to cross into Bangladesh and so far nearly 400,000 of them, dubbed as local people as economic refugees, have anchored in squalid shanties scattered in Cox's Bazar and Bandarban districts. Had Bangladesh authorities not taken adequate steps to seal border during the communal riot in Myanmar's western Rakhine state in June hundreds of thousands more would have fled into the country – a traditional safe haven for the Rohingya Muslims. Though the stance of Bangladesh is a bit harsh in humanitarian view, impoverished Bangladesh is really unable to take the burden of more Rohingyas."

Nizam Ahmed wrote the article in July 2012 while the Rakhine State riot was at its peak. According to him there are 400,000 Rohingya refugees in Bangladesh. President Thein Sein was planned to visit Bangladesh in July 15, 2012 but was postponed due the emergency arising from the Buddhist-Muslim riots but as of today, July 28, 2013, the visit is still postponed. The visit cancellation was widely reported, even by the Pakistan defense forum at–

http://www.defence.pk/forums/bangladesh-defence/191712-myanmar-president-cancels-dhaka-tour.html.

Besides the Rohingya issue there was also a maritime dispute between the two countries. The dispute (Case No. 16) was brought to the International Tribunal for Law of the Sea at Hamburg, Germany. The judgment made on March 14, 2012 (http://www.itlos.org/index.php?id=108#c964) was in favor of Bangladesh. Was it why President Thein Sein cancelled his visit to

Bangladesh? This may be my wishful thinking! But the maritime dispute was a serious one with the two navies confronting each other. Now both countries are enlarging and modernizing their navies. It is dangerous. Tension along the Bangladesh-Myanmar border is high and unpredictable. The reader may go to the border and spend about a month as an innocent tourist. Then you will understand my point here.

Another trifle, as reported by–

http://www.newagebd.com/detail.php?date=2012-11-13&nid=29876#.Uc37-crDAWs, is that "Myanmar, which had earlier showed interest to export electricity to Bangladesh, has now rejected the proposal saying that the country itself has been suffering from power shortage."

It may sound stupid to think sequential that in March 2012 Myanmar lost the maritime case to Bangladesh, Buddhist-Muslim riots took place in June, President Thein Sein postponed his July visit to Bangladesh (still to be re-scheduled!), and in November Myanmar swallowed her spit saying "No electricity for you" to Bangladesh. All are connected?!

On the other hand, I am pretty sure that Bangladesh will not be giving full board to 400,000 *aliens* in her home forever. One day, Bangladesh will say, "Enough is enough." Then what?

Meanwhile, Myanmar comes up with the rants of Islamic militants taking over Myanmar and show hysteria that Muslims are converting all Myanmar persons through marriage. Interestingly, the Chins (~ 2 millions in all Myanmar), the Kachins (~3-4 millions in all Myanmar), and about 25% of the Karen (1.5 millions out of 6 million Karens in all Myanmar)[299] are Christians who have been converted by the Christian missionaries during and after British colonialism. It makes up a total of 7.5 million Christians among the Myanmar population of 51 millions, without counting the Christians of other ethnic groups. Myanmar Muslims, including Rohingya, maybe at most 5 millions. Then, why the brunt at the Muslims? The Buddhist fundamentalists led by U Wirathu complained that Muslim extremists and radical Islamists are taking over Myanmar. *If so, it*

---

[299] The clause 'in all Myanmar' is used to contrast with the specific regions like the Chin State, the Kachin State, or the Karen State, etc.

will be the best for Myanmar to work with Bangladesh because no country but Bangladesh has opposed and fought against the Muslim extremists, radical Islamists, and Islamic Fundamentalism. Just to get an idea of what I say here the reader may please read my book *The Price of Silence.* Today, Bangladesh is trying the extremists at the International Crimes Tribunal (Bangladesh). It is a daring quest of Bangladesh against the odds of a civil war but she is determined. Please visit the Bangladesh Foreign Ministry to learn more about the tribunal at-

http://www.mofa.gov.bd/index.php?
option=com_content&view=article&id=692&Itemid=177

Exhibit-BD1
Bangladesh Fertility Rate achievement
google search result on June 28, 2013

2.20 births per woman (2011)

Bangladesh, Fertility rate

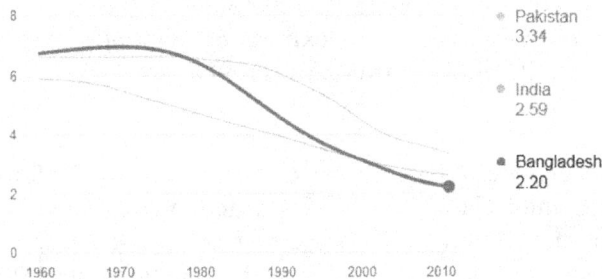

Pakistan	3.34
India	2.59
Bangladesh	2.20

Explore more

Sources include: World Bank

Myanmar is also afraid that the Bangladesh population will spill over into Myanmar. This fear is logical but harboring hysteria without an attempt for a solution is counter productive. It is not right for a *state*. A citizen may harbor fear from a problem but the *state* has to solve the problem. The Bangladesh population problem can be solved. For example–

Bangladesh Millennium Target Goals[300] achievements are

---

[300] http://www.unmillenniumproject.org/goals/gti.htm

remarkable.

Please visit–

http://www.sid.gov.bd/wp-content/uploads/2013/02/Millenium_Development_Goals.pdf.

With regard to population growth, the emphasis here is in the fertility rate. Please see the Exhibit-BD1 that I found in the Google search (June 28, 2014) and the Table-BD1 that I constructed based on the information available, on June 31, 2014, at–http://en.wikipedia.org/wiki/List_of_sovereign_states_and_depen dent_territories_by_fertility_rate. Since 2011, Bangladesh fertility rate has come down below the world average.

The fertility rate improvement is an astounding drop from about 7.0 births per woman in 1970 to 2.20 births per woman in 2011 (Exhibit-BD1). This is a tremendous achievement for Bangladesh. Nilratan Halder in his article *Poverty alleviation and development goals* published on Friday, 28 June 2013 at–

http://www.thefinancialexpress-bd.com/index.php?ref=MjBfMDZfMjhfMTNfMV82XzE3NDQyNw==, reported as follow.

"Bangladesh recently received a special 'Diploma Award' from the United Nations (UN) Food and Agriculture Organisation (FAO) in recognition of its achieving one of the key millennium development goals (MDGs) well ahead of the target year 2015."

This is something we have to congratulate Bangladesh. It is a great achievement for *humanity*. It is a very promising example set in a country which once was dubbed "bottomless basket" by Henry Kissinger, US Secretary of State from 1969-1977.[301] It was a revolution for Bangladesh. She was the first Muslim country to officially adopt the family planning. It was an uphill for Bangladesh against the ferocious attacks after attacks inflicted by the orthodox Imams from across the world. However, by 1980s, the Islamic world came to Bangladesh to learn about the family planning.

---

[301] http://en.wikipedia.org/wiki/Henry_Kissinger

Table-BD1			
Fertility Rate Comparison			
Births per woman			
Country	2009	2011	2014
1 Algeria	2.38	2.264	2.78
2 Argentina	2.25	2.211	2.25
3 Australia	1.79	1.92	1.77
4 Bangladesh	**2.83**	**2.245**	**2.45**
5 Brazil	1.74	1.678	1.69
6 China	1.73	1.598	1.55
7 Croatia	1.35	1.46	1.45
8 France	1.89	2.000	2.08
9 Germany	1.41	1.39	1.43
10 India	2.60	2.47	2.51
11 Indonesia	2.18	2.117	2.18
12 Iran	2.04	1.670	1.85
13 Japan	1.27	1.39	1.42
14 Kenya	4.96	4.78	3.54
15 Malaysia	2.60	2.635	2.58
16 Mexico	2.21	2.32	2.29
17 Myanmar	**2.07**	**2.002**	**2.18 (Burma)**
18 Nigeria	5.32	5.525	5.25
19 Pakistan	3.52	3.423	2.86
20 Russia	1.34	1.54	1.61
21 Saudi Arabia	3.35	2.811	2.17
22 Sri Lanka	1.88	2.313	2.13
23 Thailand	1.85	1.579	1.50
24 United Kingdom	1.82	1.94	1.90
25 Unites States	2.05	2.100	2.01
26 World	**2.55**	**2.451**	**2.60**
27 Zimbabwe	3.19	3.29	3.56
The table is based on the information available, as of July 31, 2014, at Wikipedia, see the text full the URL link.			
2009 data is by the United Nations			
2011 data is by the World Bank			
2014 data is *an estimate* by the CIA(USA)			

This is one outstanding example of Bangladesh   that Myanmar must take into account   when considering Bangladesh to be a partner in tackling the religious conservatism and dogma. Bangladesh is also doing good in food autarky. A blogger happily reported as follow.

"Dear readers,
How are you today?
Few Newspapers today published a news headline that the US Ambassador Dan W Mozena, on Wednesday, 16th January, 2013 in a programme, Mozena criticized the former US secretary of state Henry Kissinger's 'insulting terming' of Bangladesh as a basket case. Mozena was speaking at a workshop on Food Security organized by the USAID at a hotel in Dhaka city.

He redefined that at present Bangladesh is "a country with food revolution".

Mr. Mozena said that the remark is belied by the fact that the basket is now filled with crops. He also said that he believes, Bangladesh will gain food autarky within the next one decade. Bangladesh is now a 'Basket of Food' and not a "Bottomless Basket", by dint of millions of hardworking farmers in the country, he observed."
(http://profilebd.blogspot.com/2013/01/bangladesh-is-basket-of-food-not.html, I accessed it on June 28, 2013).

Prime Minister Sheikh Hasina has been pushing to get food autarky by 2013.[302] With a population of 150 millions (2011 estimate)[303] in that small little land (~150,000 square kilometers) of floods, landslides, and tropical storms it is an achievement of near miraculous.   Myanmar with an area of about 680,000 square kilometers is more than four times bigger than Bangladesh. Her population of 51 millions is about three times smaller than Bangladesh. Still, Myanmar faced a famine in 1967! Her rice export, in order to earn hard currency, is at the expanse of the demanding domestic need. One day Myanmar will have a large population like Bangladesh. It will be beneficial for Myanmar to learn from

---

[302] http://archive.thedailystar.net/newDesign/news-details.php?nid=148388
[303] http://www.google.com/#bav=on.2,or.r_qf.&fp=fa3e032282d157b4&q=Bangladesh+population

Bangladesh experience and prepare how to feed her people when her population hits 100 millions.

Exhibit-BD2
BIMSTEC
A cooperation of 7 countries
Please se the text for more.

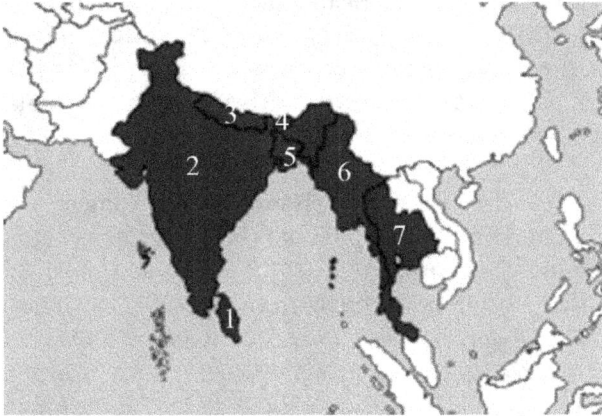

1. Sri Lanka, 2. India, 3. Bhutan, 4. Nepal,
5. Bangladesh, 6. Myanmar, 7. Thailand
Map from: http://www.bilaterals.org/spip.php?rubrique84

In light of the above discussion, it is the best for Myanmar to work with Bangladesh in solving (1) Rohingya crisis, (2) religious extremism, (3) food and population concerns, and (4) global warming and rising sea. The rising sea will submerge 4 to 10% of the coastal areas of all countries in the Bay of Bengal. Myanmar is no exception. They are already members of BIMSTEC (The Bay of Bengal Initiative for Multi-Sectoral Technical and Economic Cooperation) that groups Bangladesh, Bhutan, Myanmar, India, Nepal, Sri Lanka and Thailand to work together for the regional development and peace (Exhibit-BD2).[304]   It is high time that BIMSTEC puts the focus on the climate change and rising sea, and seriously work together to tackle the regional crisis that will definitely arise from the climate change and rising sea.

---

[304] See http://www.bilaterals.org/spip.php?rubrique84 and http://en.wikipedia.org/wiki/Bay_of_Bengal_Initiative_for_Multi-Sectoral_Technical_and_Economic_Cooperation

One more important point. Myanmar has expressed its concern of Buddhism's future in Myanmar. Bangladesh, although an Islamic nation, has been nurturing Buddhism. The government of Bangladesh patronized Dhamarajika Buddhist Temple, Kamalapur, Dhaka, and other Buddhist monasteries in Chittagong, Cox's Bazar, Bandarban and other Buddhist communities of Bangladesh. There is even a Buddhist university in the capital city of Dhaka. Although, now and then, the Buddhist establishments suffer attacks from the extremists, the government sincerely does a good job in helping them replenished. Cooperation between Myanmar and Bangladesh will also benefit Bangladeshi Buddhists.

Today, the Rohingya issue is no longer confined to Myanmar geographical or political boundary. For example, the United Nations,[305] on June 10, 2014, reported that more than 86,000 Rohingya fled Myanmar on boats from July 2012 to June 2014. The displaced Rohinygas are all over the world–Thailand, Malaysia, Indonesia, Australia, Korea, Japan, Canada, USA, Europe, Arabian Gulf States, Pakistan, India, and Bangladesh. The Rohingya issue is no longer a local issue, but it is an international one with serious implications for humanity. Muslim-Buddhist killings, atrocities, and destructions have become common in many countries.

I may sum up in this way. It is wrong for Myanmar to implicate Bengali and Bangladesh in Myanmar Rohingya and Muslim crisis. It will greatly benefit both Myanmar and Bangladesh if Myanmar sits down with Bangladesh and just informally discuss the matters of mutual interest. If Bangladesh-Myanmar dialogue is upgraded to an international round table it surely will help avoid an apocalypse, which is looming over the horizon.

The fate of Nayak Mizanur Rahman of Border Guard Bangladesh (BGB) sets an example. The BGB Corporal Rahman was shot and killed by Border Guard Police (BGP) of Myanmar while on a routine patrol along the Naikhyongchhari border on May 28, 2014. Two other Bangladesh Border Guards were wounded, as per media reports.[306] The news said that Myanmar Border Guard Police shot at the BGB men because they were mistaken as the Rohingya armed

---

[305] http://www.unhcr.org/5396ee3b9.html
[306] See http://observerbd.com/details.php?id=24129,
http://www.dhakatribune.com/bangladesh/2014/jun/02/mizanur-laid-rest, and
http://www.bangladeshchronicle.net/index.php/2014/06/bad-news-at-the-border/

personnel, belonging to the Rohingya Solidarity Organization (RSO). Bangladesh denied the existence of such an armed group in its borders. Bangladesh gave Corporal[307] Rahman a state funeral. There were angry voices in Bangladesh. An example is given at the Exhibit-BD3.[308] However, it was comforting that Bangladesh and Myanmar resolve the situation diplomatically at the level of the Director General. The bilateral meeting was held on June 10-12, 2014 at Nay Pyi Taw and an accord of cooperation in the border security was signed by BGB Director General Major General Aziz Ahmed and Myanmar Police Major General Zaw Win.[309]

It is urgent and crucial for Myanmar and Bangladesh to elevate the border cooperation into the highest level of national cooperation and coordination. I can give two vital reasons for the urgency.

1. Myanmar has concentrated more than one million Rohingya people in the camps, which are known as the Internally Displaced Persons (IDP) camps and in an open prison known as the Buthidaung-Maungdaw area. They were charged with illegal entry from Bangladesh to Myanmar, with an intent of Islamizing Myanmar! This incredible accusation is an open secret that everybody knows.

2. Bangladesh, as described above,[310] reported that there are nearly 400,000 (or more than 500,000)[311] Myanmar Rohingya Muslims, who have fled persecution in Buddhist Myanmar, at Cox's Bazar area and they are a burden on Bangladesh in many ways, including serious social, economical, and political concerns.

---

[307] I understand 'Nayak' or 'Naik' is a 'Corporal'. See
http://en.wikipedia.org/wiki/Naik_(military_rank)
[308] http://www.bangladeshchronicle.net/index.php/2014/06/bad-news-at-the-border/
[309] http://observerbd.com/details.php?id=25542 and
http://www.elevenmyanmar.com/index.php?option=com_content&view=article&id=6436
[310] http://www.ebangladesh.com/2012/07/27/should-bangladesh-believe-myanmar/
[311] See http://bdnews24.com/bangladesh/2014/07/10/rohingya-bangladeshi-marriage-illegal

Exhibit-BD3
Bad news at the border
http://www.bangladeshchronicle.net/index.php/2014/06/b
ad-news-at-the-border/

Bad news at the border

June 3, 2014 | Filed under: Opinions | Posted by: bdchronicle

Mohammad Ali Sattar

Turning to our borders with Myanmar, we observe a hostile and offensive stance
taken by Yangon

• The killing needs to stop

Situations that can be seen from all quarters suggest that we have lost our guts and morale
in standing against the ills of the world.

The picture depicts the Border Guards Bangladesh personnel
preparing for the official funeral of Nayak Mizanur Rahman

Thus, according to Bangladesh, it is the Myanmar citizens who are illegally entering into Bangladesh. But, according to Myanmar, it is the Bengali people illegally entering into Myanmar. Meanwhile, the emergence of East and West Arakan, in the style of East and West Bengal, permanently segregating the people in the racio-religious line, will be detrimental to the regional stability. If Myanmar and Bangladesh fail to cooperate and solve the problem, *the Muslim-Buddhist War of Bangladesh and Myanmar* that I have depicted in my book *The Price of Silence*[312] will come true.

---

[312] Shwe Lu Maung, *The Price of Silence: Muslim-Buddhist War of Bangladesh and Myanmar – A Social Darwinist's Analysis*, DewDrop Arts & Technology, USA, 2005

Epilogue

Ethnic selfishness paralyzes not only the Rakhine State but also Myanmar as a whole, raging with endless wars and sickened with deep hatred. Wherever we go we find people of all kinds. War and peace, quests and conquests, colonialism and liberation, trades and explorations, and migration and immigration *et cetera*, across the mountains, oceans, and deserts, bring diversities to every nook and corner of the world. It is a natural, cultural, and social phenomenon of humankind. Is it any wrong to have diversified peoples in the Rakhine State or in Myanmar? Countries arise and countries disappear. Civilizations flourish and civilizations vanish. Peoples are born and peoples are dead. No matter what, humankind strives for peace and prosperity. I wish I am a poet or philosopher, but I am neither. Still, I love poems and philosophy. That is why I fancy that I am "The Brook" of Alfred Tennyson (1809-1892 CE).[313]

> "And out again I curve and flow
> To join the brimming river,
> For men may come and men may go,
> But I go on forever."

And, there was a Greek philosopher named Heraclitus (*Herakleitos*, 535–475 BCE)[314] who said that we cannot jump into the same river twice. Perhaps, I over simplify his philosophy. Let us see.

Heraclitus's philosophy *Panta rhei* "everything flows" is mentioned in many ways. The following expressions are taken from http://en.wikipedia.org/wiki/Heraclitus.[315]

1. "Ever-newer waters flow on those who step into the same rivers."[316]

---

[313] Alfred Tennyson (1809-1892) was a very famous poet of England. His poem "The Brook" can be read at many web sites. But I read it at http://www.poetry-archive.com/t/the_brook.html. Last accessed on July 13, 2014.

[314] http://en.wikipedia.org/wiki/Heraclitus, accessed on July 13, 2014.

[315] Ibid.

[316] DK22B12, quoted in Arius Didymus apud Eusebius, Praeparatio Evangelica, 15.20.2, http://en.wikipedia.org/wiki/Heraclitus.

2. "All entities move and nothing remains still."[317]

3. "Everything changes and nothing remains still ... and ... you cannot step twice into the same stream."[318]

4. "We both step and do not step in the same rivers. We are and are not."[319]

I became interested in Heraclitus's *Panta rhei*, "everything flows", when I try to understand stupidity of life. I was and still am a student of biological science and "everything flows" meets the process of evolution that I learned. We, *Homo sapiens*, are still evolving or 'flowing.' Similarly, a nation flows and evolves.

Time flies as the earth revolves around the sun with the speed of 460 meters per second (~1028 mph), and there came this great person who one day came into the classroom and wrote down on the blackboard "$E=mc^2$." He was the one who explained my childhood's puzzle why the moon raced with me whenever I ran.[320] I came to understand the phenomenon of the "moon-chase" when I learned Albert Einstein's *theory of relativity*[321] at Rangoon University.

Then, the space programs and the human genome project, accompanied with the digitalization, globalization, energy crisis, and climate change became part of our human life.

No matter what, Rohingya or Bengali, Rakhine or Bama, Burma or Myanmar, English or American, New Yoker or Yankee, as long as *relativity* is misunderstood or abused Myanmar will be in problem.

. . .

So will be the world.

---

[317] Cratylus Paragraph Crat. 401 section d line 5, http://en.wikipedia.org/wiki/Heraclitus.

[318] Cratylus Paragraph 402 section a line 8, http://en.wikipedia.org/wiki/Heraclitus.

[319] DK B49a, Harris 110. Others like it are DK B12, Harris 20; DK B91, Harris 21, http://en.wikipedia.org/wiki/Heraclitus.

[320] Also see Shwe Lu Maung, *The Price of Silence: Muslim-Buddhist War of Bangladesh and Myanmar – A Social Darwinist's Analysis*, DewDrop Arts & Technology, USA, 2005, Dedication page and p 18.

[321] Albert Einstein, *Relativity: the special and the general theory*, Wings Book, New York, 1961. Also see http://en.wikipedia.org/wiki/Albert_Einstein

Appendix-1: Open Letter to Dr. Dipu Moni

This is an open letter I wrote in 2009 and published by the News From Bangaldesh.

When Dr. Dipu Moni goes to Myanmar on May 15: Responsibility to Protect

News From Bangladesh
Open Letter
Thursday May 14 2009 12:20:16 PM BDT
http://newsfrombangladesh.net/view.php?hidRecord=263475

By Dr. Shwe Lu Maung, USA

Being aware of that:(1) Bangla-Mynamar relationship is being strained by the infantile disorders of Myanmar ultranationalist democracy. Maritime border dispute, border fencing, and Rohingya issues are the roadblocks in the advancement of friendship and cooperation between the two countries while understanding and joint effort are in urgent and immediate need to face the regional problems being posed by the global warming and rising sea level. Coming years will mark the days of struggle for survival for both Bangladesh and Myanmar.

(2) The people of Bangladesh warmly adore Myanmar for her immediate recognition of Independent Bangladesh in 1971. As such, Myanmar is loved as a good neighbor by the Bangladeshis. The senior Bangladeshi people still remember the good old days when the people of India Subcontinent and Burma together fought against the British Colonialism. The Bangladesh people and government wish Myanmar healthy, happy, and prosperous. With this good will, Dr. Dipu Moni goes to Myanmar to promote the common interest, representing the Bangladesh people and de jure peoples government-

I would like to take this privilege to request Dr. Dipu Moni to kindly take the following thoughts of mine into kind consideration.

1. Border, especially maritime border dispute is a common feature

for the nations separated by a flowing river and ever-changing current. However, when it comes to the determination of economic zone and development of the natural resources and industries in the disputed area tension could grow high and border wars have occurred in the world.

2. Border fencing is a hysteria created by previously Rangoon and now Naypyidaw. On the other hand it has become a phenomenon in the world as per examples set by China Great Wall and recent India and American fences. Since 1978, the Bangla-Myanmar border tension has been created by the fallout of Burmese internal war between the ethnic Rohingya-Rakhine and Rangoon forces. More than two hundred thousand Myanmar Muslims were driven out into Bangladesh, with the charges that they are the Bengali illegal immigrants. This is a serious accusation and Dr. Dipu Moni must be prepared to face it firm and strong. Recently, the Myanmar authorities, as usual, refused to accept the responsibility of the Rohingya boat-people with the limp excuse that they are the illegal Bengali in the Rakhine State of Myanmar.

A Myanmar Consulate General by the name of Ye Myint Aung at Hong Kong went further to say that they cannot be Myanmar because they are dark-brown and ugly as ogres. When we pull the string it can be construed that the diplomat said Bengali are dark-brown and ugly as ogres. In this regard, the Irrawadday News Magazine at http://www.irrawaddy.org/cartoon.php?art_id=15109 has put up a good punching cartoon, featuring Dr. Ibrahim Gambari who is the United Nations Special Envoy to Myanmar. Nonetheless, it is pleasing to see that the international community does not pay any serious note to these Myanmar racial slurs. Myanmar is considered handicapped due to her congenital infantile disorders of right-wing ultranationalist democracy. Had an American diplomat uttered such racial slurs there would be uproar all over the world.

3. The question now is how long the Rohingyas will be able to tolerate. If pushed to the extreme a revolution could and would break out destabilizing the region. They are the Muslim descendants of the Arakan Empire which onetime ruled from Dhaka in the West to Pegu in the East. The Arakan Empire was founded in 1430 C.E. by a

Rakhaing King named Saw Mwan alias Narameithla with the help of 30,000 Bengali soldiers provided by Bengal Sultan Jalaluddin Shah.

The Arakan Empire lasted until 1666 when its commercial center, Chittagong, was seized by the Mogul. In those two hundred plus years of Arakan Empire, there is no question that there existed Bengali settlement in the mainland of Arakan, which is now the Rakhine State of Myanmar. World historians recorded the Muslim settlement in Arakan and Burma long before the days of Arakan Empire. Those Muslims who settled in the Arakan Empire are now known as the Rohingyas, a term derived from Rakkhapura which is the ancient name of Arakan. The descendants of Rakkhapura Kingdom are known as the Rakhine, Rakhaing, or Rakhaingthar. The terms 'Rohingya' and 'Rakhaingthar' are two sides of a coin.

Both words, Rakhaingthar and Rohingya, derive from the Sanskrit word Rakshak, which is the variant of the Pali word Rokkha/Rokkhi. Both "Rakshak" and "Rokkha/Rokkhi" mean defense or military. In India, the Indian Military is called Bharat Rakshakâ. In Bangladesh Proti-Rokkha means ˜National Defence and Rokkhi Bahani means Defence Militia.

In terms of Sanscrit and Pali language, a Rakhaing/Rakhaingthar, Roshang/Rohangya, or Rohong/ Rohongya simply mean a soldier, a comparable term to Rakkha Chaylay (herd boy or guard boy) of Bangladesh. In view of history it is noteworthy that Rakkhapura means a soldier village or a military cantonment. It probably originated as a military outpost of the Brahmaputra Civilization in the ancient past. Bangladesh historians and archaeologists are now finding evidence of the Brahmaputra Civilization in Rajshahi city of northern Bangladesh.

In the Buddhist chronicles, the Brahmaputra Civilization is known as the Mizzimadesh, pronounced Mizzima deytha in Burmese, and it begins at Magadha and ends at Arakan Mountains. Rakkhapura or Arakan was not associated with Burma until the Burmese King Maung Wynne occupied it in 1784, violating the Arakan-Burma border treaty signed by the Arakan King Khari alias Ali Khan and the Burmese Ava King Narapiti in 1454 CE. In a Bangla-language book titled "Arakan Rajsabhay Bangla Sahitya (1600-1700 AD)" by Dr. Muhammad Enamul Huq and Sahitya-sagar Abdul Karim Sahitya Visarad, Gurudas Chattaopdhyay and Sons, Kalikata, 1935, it is mentioned During the 17th century AD when Muslim in Arakan nurtured Bengali Literature, the Muslim poets of that time identified the country as Roshang.

Therefore, Roshangya or now Rohingya (a Myanmar corruption) is an ancient term, not an invention of the Arakanese Muslims 1958 as per Myanmar authorities and historians claim. The terms date way back to pre-Bengal and Pre-Myanmar era. A visit to Rashahi Varendra Research Museum and other museums in Dhaka and Chittagong will render good evidence in support of the above statement. On the basis of the Myanmar 1990 election data, I calculated that there were 1.87 million Rohingya Muslims and 2.13 million non-Rohingyas in the Rakhine State (see my book *The Price of Silence*, p252).

4. The negation of the Rohingya people is not confined to the junta. To great dismay the Myanmar democratic forces such as the heavy-weight National League for Democracy (NLD), Arakan League for Democracy (ALD), United Nationalities League for Democracy (UNLD), National Coalition Government of Union Burma (in exile), National Democratic Font (NDF), and Rakhine academician-historians jumped up and sided with the military junta, committing the political genocide to the Rohingya people. Therefore, Dr. Dipu Moni cannot expect that the Rohingya issue would or could be solved in 2010 or later. The problem will persist for the decades to come.

5. It is the nature of the Myanmar authorities to back their political actions with the military might. Bangladesh has experienced it frequently. At present, Myanmar bullies around the region with army of 500,000 soldiers. Dr. Dipu Moni should make the Myanmar authorities understand that Bangladesh can raise her fighting force to a million-strength overnight and Bangladesh Navy and Air Force are superior to Myanmars.

At Naypyidaw, the Bangladesh delegation will see three famous

Myanmar Kings, Anawratha, Bayinnaung, and Alaungpyaya.[322] Please remember that Bayinnaung's Second Myanmar Empire (1540-1599 CE) was put to an end by the Arakanese King Razagri *alias* Salim Shah Sultan in 1599. He was known as the Emperor of Pegu. Major portion of the Arakan Royal Army was made up of the Rohingya and Portugese soldiers. This is one of the reasons why the Myanmar military government and pro-democracy forces alike are negating the Rohingyas. Vindictive they are! The Rakhine people are now totally Burmanized and do not pose any threat to Myanmar neo-empire, but the Rohingyas do because they were the people who liberated Arakan from the hands of Burmese in 1430 and founded the Arakan Empire.

Please allow me to refresh Dr. Dipu Moni's knowledge bank that Arakan King Razagri, as per tradition of the feudal conquerors, married Bayinnaung's grand daughter Princess Khin Ma Hnaung and, upon her request, appointed her brother as the Governor of Chittagong. The descendants of the Burmese Prince are now the chieftains of Bandarban and known as the Bo Mun and well placed in modern Bangladesh. Myanmar government and people should appreciate that Bangladesh and Bengali people have preserved their Emperor Bayinnaung blood.

6. Dr. Dipu Moni may kindly remind the Myanmar authorities that the Union of Myanmar (Pyihtaungsu Myanmar Naingan) was the outcome of the united struggle of the people, including the Muslims, of British Burma. Therefore, the Burma Citizenship Act 1982 is feudal and colonial in nature and as such shall be repealed. The Union of Myanmar is a nation-state but not a continuation of the feudal Myanmar or tribal nations. Accordingly, Myanmar shall duly recognize the Rohingya cultural identity, which is a mix of Bengal-Myanmar culture. More than six hundred years after their original settlement in Arakan in 1430 CE they are now more Burmese than Bengali. Their loyalty is with Myanmar. They should be given equal rights like other ethnic people of Myanmar and allowed to enter into the main stream of national and political life. If the Myanmar authorities still insist that they are Bengali and continue

---

[322] In the original letter it was Anawratha, Kyansitttha, and Bayinnaung, It was a mistake. I have corrected here.

dehumanization and ethnic cleansing, then Bangladesh and Bengali people will have no choice but provoke the Responsibility to Protect (R2P). This could sadly mean a repetition of 1430!

7. Finally, when no more bearable probability is high that a Rohingya revolution could and would break out. If so, Myanmar must bear full responsibility of the consequences.

End and thank you.

Appendix-2: Roshang

Appendix- Roshang -1

Arakanese Research
Journal

Vol. III

Arakanese Research Society of Bangladesh (ARSB)
Buddha Mandir, Teknaf Pourashava
Cox's Bazar-4760, Bangladesh.
e-mail : u_bodhinyana@yahoo.com

Appendix Roshang - 2

အာရက္ခနိုင်(ငံ) ရိုတာ(ချ) ဂျာနာ(လ်)
ရခိုင်သုတေသန ဂျာနယ်
အတွဲ (၃)

ထုတ်ဝေ
ဂျူ(၃၀) ၂၀၀၅

အယ်ဒီတာ
ဉီးဗောဓိဉာဏ

အတိုင်ပင်ခံအယ်ဒီတာ
ဉီးမောင်စိန်ပြူ နှင့် ဉီးစောထွန်းဦး

လက်ထောက်အယ်ဒီတာ
ဓမ္မဒဿ

စာစီနှင့်ဒိုင်း
သန်းဝင်း

ထုတ်ဝေသူ
အာရက္ခနိုင်(ငံ) ရိုတာ(ချ)ဆိုဆိုင်ယတီ
အော်(ဗ) ဘင်္ဂလာဒေ(ချ) ARSB
[ဘင်္ဂလာဒေ(ချ) ရခိုင်သုတေသနအဖွဲ့]

ထောက်ပံ့ တန်ဖိုး
US 5.00 ဒေါ်လာ

**Arakanese
Research Journal**
Vol. III

Published on
July 30, 2005

Editor
U Bodhinyana

Consulting Editors
U Maung Sein Pru
U Saw Tun Oo

Assistant Editor
Dhammadassa

Composed & Design
Than Wan

Published by
Arakanese Research Society
of Bangladesh (ARSB)

Complementary Price
US $ 5.00

Appendix Roshang - 3

Contents / မာတိကာ / সূচী

Editorial Notes — 1

Ārakān Rājsabhāy Bangālā Sāhitya — Dr. Muhammad Enamul Huq & Abdul Karim Sahitya Visarad. — 4

Arakan: A Promised Land — A S Nayaka — 19

Initation Ceremony: in Arakanese Society — Venerable U Bodhinyana — 34

ရခိုင်ကိုးတော်သာသနာ အခြေအနေ — ဦးဗတ္တင် (၇ိုင်ပြည်) — 53

ရခိုင်ကိုးတော်လယ် ရခိုင်စာရိုးဟန်သုံးမျိုး — ဦးလောင်ဘာသိန်း — 61

ရခိုင်ပြည်အား ပြန်လည် ရှာဖွေတွေ့ရှိခြင်း — ဒေါက်တာ ဂျက် ပီ လိုက်ဒါ — 70

ရခိုင်စာပေကောက်နှုတ်ချက်များ — ပြည်ထောင်စုပြန်ခန်းကော်မတီ — 76

মুসলিম উপাধিধারী বৌদ্ধ রাজন্যবর্গ... ব্রক-উ যুগে মুসলিম প্রভাবের উপর সংক্ষিপ্ত আলোচনা — ড: জাক্ পি লাইডার — 99

Appendix Roshang - 4

Ârakân Rājsabhāy Bangālā Sāhitya
(1600 – 1700 AD)*
[Bengali Literature in the Kings' Court of Arakan]

Translated from Bengali by: Maung Sein Pru* *

Chapter I
The Kings' Court of Ârakan* **

The inhabitants of Ârakān [thereafter written as Arakan]⊕ are generally known as "Mag" or "Magh"1 in Bengal. The Arakanese [Rakhaing/ Rakhine] people of Mongoloid race do not identify themselves as such; they are not even acquainted with this name. No doubt, the Bengalis being inexperienced with ethnology wrongfully call them as "Magh"2 . But there is good reason to name some of the ancient Arakanese (who are called as Rajbanshi [Rajbangsi/Rājvamsi] and

---

* The original book was written in Bengali by Doctor Muhammad Enamul Huq, M.A., Ph. D.,and Sahitya-sagar Abdul Karim Sahitya Visarad. Published by Sahitya-sagar Abdul Karim Sahitya Visarad, Village : Shuchakradandi, Post: Patiya, Chittagong, Bangladesh (then East Bengal). From: Gurudas Chattaopadhyay and Sons, 203/1/1 Cornwallis Street, Kalikata. 1935 AD. Printed at Atindra Nath Chowdhury, Phinix Printing Works, No. 29 Kalidas Singh Lane, Kalikata, [India]

** He is presently engaged in GRAUS,a local NGO, stationed in his native town, Bandarban. He can be reached at email: himavanti05@yahoo.com

*** Out of seven chapters of the book the 1st chapter has been translated for the readers. The condensed version was once included in the high school curriculum of Bengali literature in Bangladesh. The message seemed unheard-of in one of our neighbouring countries where the largest size of Rakhaing/ Rakhine reside and also among its cohabitant coined after the word 'Roshang' professing different faith.

⊕ The words/text mentioned within 'third brackets' in the paper are those of the editor.

1 There is no doubt that the word "Magh" spread from Chittagong. The Chittagonians use both "Mag" and "Magh" to pronounce the word, while reading and writing the year they write Maghi Shon [the Magh Calender]. That is why while writing the word it is wise to be written as "Magh".

2 History of Burma – Lt. Col. A.P.Phayre (1184, London), pp 47 – 48.

Appendix Roshang - 5

5   *Arakanese Reaserch Journal Vol. III*

live in the southern parts of Chittagong) as "Magh". Their ancestors are supposed to have migrated to Arakan from "Magadha" and for some time ruled there. For this reason they may have called both as "Rajbangshi" and "Magh". These "Rajbangshi" from Chittagong and Arakan were racially Aryan and clan "Mag" or "Magh"[3]. Later since their [Rajbangshi] causes were inseparably mingled with that of Arakan as a whole, all the Arakanese people were generally identified as "Magh".

These "Magh" or Arakanese are not known to the Bengalis for their fame. Till now the Bengalis utter the name of "Magh" with fear and displeasure. In Bengali collocation "Magher Muluk" [land/country/ kingdom of the Maghs] is very familiar. In the 15th and 16th centuries AD the "Maghs" or Arakanese as pirates caused severe disturbances in the coastal districts of Bengal, though three centuries has passed, the Bengalis sacrificed their lives and riches, till now they have not forgotten the oppressor and pirate "Maghs". {Continued as in page 2 of the book and shall hereafter be written as 'Cont: p-..'} Though we know the "Magh" by their bad name, our introduction to another side of the "Maghs" today would at least help us to partially remove the ill reputation.

When in the period between the middle of the 16th and the end of the 17th century AD, parts of the west and north Bengal were full of the Vaishnavite literature, the famous Vaishnavite poets including Narahari Sarkar (1478 – 1540), Govinda Das (1537/1525 – 1612), Gyandas (born 1530), Jadunandan Das (born 1537), Premdas and Kavi Shekhar were busy dealing on the love story of Radha – Krishna, and their works were filled with the charming syntax of Vaishnavite passions and other side of the Bengali literature was banished from the scene, the Bengali literature took refuge in the distant hills of Arakan. The Bengali literature was received with honour in the Kings' Court of

---

[3] Ibid.

Appendix Roshang - 6

the "Magh" who are known to the Bengalis as barbarians, uncivilised, and pirates. The Bengali literary goddess-Banga Bharati, no less liked the green woods and hilly landscape of Arakan. The way Bangali flourished in the court of the 17th century Arakan, nothing of that sort is found in its [Bengal's] own soil. It is surprising that during the exile of Bengali language in Arakan, it was greatly appreciated by the Muslim courtiers of the Arakanese kings and the Muslim poets of East Bengal, especially those of the [greater] Chittagong Division. Later we will see the Bengali language received new form and inspiration from the Muslim poets in the Kings' Court of Arakan. To properly understand the development of the Bengali literature in the hands of foreigners of a foreign land we need to know first the Arakanese history of the 17th century and Muslim influence on it. With this aim in mind we have introduced the following short history of Arakan and the Muslim influence on it.

The province east of [greater] Chittagong district that we call "Arakan" today was not known to the Arakanese by this name. They used to call the country as "Rakhaing"[4] ?[and also Rakhine]. The word is derived from Sanskrit "Rakkha" and Pāl "Yakkha"; the Buddhists called the indigenous inhabitants by this name before conquering Lanka or Ceylon; it seems that the Indian Aryans used to call the Arakanese as "Dravid" and "Mangal" [Mongol] people by their names before they were converted to Buddhists; even now, though the Arakanese mean the word "Rakhaing" as *doitya* [demon] or *rākhasa* [cannibal, mythically one of a non-Aryan anthropophagous race of India]; they do not hesitate to name their land as "Rakhaing-tainggyi" or the land of demons.[5]

---

[4] JASB, Vol.XIII, part 1, 1844, p 24.
[5] i. Ibid.
ii. History of Burma - Lt. Col. A. P. Phayre (1884, London), p. 43. *[In fact "Rakhaingpyi" has been mentioned in page 41 of the referred book not 'Rakhaing-tainggyi' as has been designated in the paper. Ed.]*

Appendix Roshang - 7

7

Arakanese Reaserch Journal Vol. III

{Cont: p-3.} During the 17th century AD when Muslim in Arakan nurtured Bengali Literature, the Muslim poets of that time identified the country as "Roshang" [npp: Roshàng](corrupt Bengali for "Rakhaing")[later 'Rohang' has been coined to identify another community with different (non-Buddhist) faith]. Therefore, they did not create this name, "Roshang" but it is the ancient name of Arakan. For this reason we prefer to call Arakan as "Roshang" and in fact we have used this name throughout the book.

The Muslim influence in Roshang and modern Chattagram [Chittagong] has been noticeable from ancient times. The Arab traders established trade link with the East Indies in the eighth and ninth century AD. During this time Chittagong, the lone seaport of East India, became the resting place and colony of the Arabs. We know from the accounts of the ancient Arab travellers and geologists[6] including Sulaiman (living in 851 AD), Abu Jaidul Hasan (contemporary of Sulaiman), Ibnu Khuradba (died 912 AD), Al-Masudi (died 956 AD), Ibnu Howkal (wrote his travelogue in 976 AD), Al-Idrisi (born last half of 11th century) that the Arab traders became active in the area between Arakan and the eastern bank of the Meghna River. We can also learn about this from the Roshang national history: when Roshang King, Maha Taing Chandra (788 – 810 AD) was ruling in the 9th century, some shipwrecked Muslim traders were washed ashore on "Ronbee" or " Ramree" Island. When they were taken to the Arakanese king, the king ordered them to live in the village (countryside) in his country[7]. Other historians[8] also recognised the fact that Islam and its influence developed in Arakan in the 9th and 10th century AD. From this period of time {After the tenth century the country was professedly Buddhist, notwithstanding the spread of Mahomedanism which reached Achin in

---

[+] Elliot and Dowson, Vol. 1.
[7] J A S B, Vol. X, part 1, 1844, p 36.
[8] History of Burma – G E Harvey, ICS, 1925, p 137.

Appendix Roshang - 8

1206 and dotted] the coast from Assam to Malay with the curious masques known as Buddermokan reverenced by the Buddhists and China-men as well as Mahomedans". The Arabic influence increased to such a large extent in Chittagong during mid 10th century AD that a small Muslim kingdom was established in this region, and the ruler of the kingdom was called "Sultan". Possibly the area from the east bank of the Meghna River to the Naf [npp: Nâf] was under this "Sultan". We can know about the presence of this "Sultan" in the Roshang national history. [Cont: p-4.] In 953 AD Roshang King, Sulataing Chandra (951 – 957 AD) crossed his border into Bangla (Bengal) and defeated the "Thuratan" (Arakanese corrupt form of Sultan), and as a symbol of victory set up a stone victory pillar at a place called "Chaik-ta-gong" and returned home at the request of the courtiers and friends[10]. This Chaik-ta-gong was the last border of his victory, since according to Roshang national history – "Chaik-ta-gong" means "war should not be raised"[11]. Many surmise that the modern name of Chittagong district originated from "Chaik-ta-gong"[12].

In this way the religion of Islam spread and the Muslim influence slowly extended from the eastern bank of the Meghna to Roshang Kingdom in the 8th and 9th centuries. From the travelogues of the Egyptian traveller to India, Ibn Batuta (14th century AD) and from the accounts of the Portuguese pirates in the 16th century, the influence of the "Moors" or Arabs was waxing till then. So it is evident that long before the Muslim race was established in Bengal in the 13th century, Islam reached to this remote region of Bengal. A conclusion may easily be drawn that after the establishment in Bengal, Islam further spread in

---

[*] Ibid. [The English extract herein presented within second bracket is the verbatim from the reference book, which was referred vaguely by the authors in their book. Ed.]

[10] J A S B, Vol. XIII, part I, 1844, p. 36

[11] Ibid. [The editor has serious reservation over the word and its meaning.]

[12] Eastern Bengal District Gazetteers – Chittagong, 1908, p 1.

Appendix Roshang - 9

the region. That is why Bengali literature was for the first time cultivated among the Muslim of the region. Since the 15th century onwards the Muslims of this region began to engage themselves in the study of Bengali, that is, began to write books in Bengali, of which we have lots of proofs.

The study of Bengali literature that the Muslim initiated reached perfection under the aegis of the courtiers of the Roshang kings. It is needless to say that the Kings' Court of Roshang got filled up with Muslim influence long before this. From the beginning of the 15th century AD the Kings' Court of Roshang by luck was compelled to heartily receive the Muslim influence. Roshang king Meng-tsau-mwun (1404 – 1434 AD) (known as Narameikhla in the Burmese history[13]) after ascended the throne in 1404 AD forcibly gained possession of a lady named Tsau-bongyo, the sister of the chief called Anan-thiu. {Cont: p-5.} The brother, determined on revenge, went to the king [court] of Ava Meng-tshwai=Minhkaung (1401 – 1422 AD). Minkaung with a strength of 30,000 troops attacked Roshang and defeated Mang Saw Mwan in 1406 AD. Mang Saw Mwan fled and took refuge under the Sultan of Gaur[14] [also written as Gaud by some historians]. At that time Sultan Shamsuddin II (1406 - 1409) of Ilyas Shahi lineage was ruling Gaur. He cordially received Roshang King Mang Saw Mwan and granted him asylum. The Roshang King lived there for twenty-four years till 1430 AD. Meanwhile there was a rebellion in Gaur; King Ganesh (1409 – 1414 AD) occupied the throne of Gaur; Sultan Ibrahim Shah Sharki of Jounpur attacked Bengal to oust King Ganesh. Probably the Roshang King assisted the Sultan of Gaur during the rebellion[15]. After the revolt, Jalaluddin Muhammad Shah (1414-1431 AD) ascended the throne of Gaur; peace was established. Jalaluddin

---

[13] History of Burma – G. E. Harvey, I.C.S. 1925, p. 130.
[14] J A S B, Vol. XIII, part 1, 1844, p 44.
[15] i. Ibid – p 45.
ii. History of Burma – Lt. Col. A P Phayre, [1844 London], pp 77 – 78.

Appendix Roshang - 10

Muhammad Shah sent a general, Wali Khan (Ulu-Kheng in Roshang history) with Mang Saw Mwan to regain Arakan in 1430 AD. Wali Khan betrayed his trust and joined with an Arakanese feudal lord, Tsenka [or Tse-u-ka according to Phayre] and imprisoned Mang Saw Mwan. Roshang King tactfully escaped and fled to Bengal; again the Sultan sent two more generals with the Roshang King to regain Arakan. The two generals killed the traitor Wali Khan and reinstated Mang Saw Mwan to the throne of Roshang in 1430 AD[16]. The Roshang king got back his kingdom but became tributary to the Sultan of Gaur[17]. His Mahomedan followers built Sandihkan mosque at Mrohaung [18] [Mrauk-u].

Mang Saw Mwan or Narameikhla (1430 – 1434) by regaining his lost kingdom remained tributary to Gaur for four years. Thereafter it is common for the kings, though Buddhists, to use Mahomedan designations in addition to their own names, and even to issue medallions bearing the [Islamic] *kalima*, [the Mahomeden confession of faith] in Persian script...[19]. {Cont: p-6.} Narameikhla may have introduced and supported the practice as a tributary to Muslims; but history testifies that though the kings after him were independent, they did not gave up the practice. That is why we see Narameikhla's brother Meng Khari (1434 – 1459 AD), though independent is known as "Ali Khan"[20]. More could be seen:-

Buddhist name	Muslim name	Reigning period
Basawpyu	Kalim Shah[21]	1459 – 82 AD
Mengbeng=(Min-bin)	Sultan[22]	1531 – 53 "

---

[16] i. Ibid
    ii. History of Burma – Lt. Col. A P Phayre, [1844 London], p. 78
[17] J A S B, Vol. XIII, part 1, 1844, p 46.
[18] History of Burma – G. E. Harvey, I.C.S. 1925, p. 130.
[19] Ibid. p 140
[20] Ibid.
[21] J. A. S. B., Vol. XV, 1846, p. 232.
[22] History of Burma – G. E. Harvey, I.C.S. 1925, p. 140.

Appendix Roshang - 11

Meng-Phalaung Sikandar	Shah[23]	1571 – 1593 "
Meng-Radza-gyi	Salim Shah[24]	1593 – 1612 "
Meng-Kha-moung	Husain Shah[25]	1612 – 1622 "
Thiri-thu-dhamma	*Illegible Persian name[26]	1622 – 1638 "
Narapadigyi	* –do–[27]	1638 – 1645 "

It can be seen from the above list that from 1434 to 1645 AD, for a period of about two hundred years, the independent Arakanese Kings used Muslim names in their coins. There was no good relation at all between the Kings of Arakan and the Muslim forces of Bengal during these two centuries. But they followed Muslim traditions and culture at home. The reason is: [that] the Arakanese Kings could not be free from the influence of the Muslim civilisation, politics and cultures, which is superior to theirs. We can learn from the seventeenth century Bengali literature – though the relation between the Arakanese Kings and Bengal Muslim royal-powers was not at all good, they did not show any sign of hostility towards the Muslim community but in its place they nurtured sincere admiration. For this reason they entrusted the chief administrative posts of the government departments including that of the defence to the Muslims.

[Cont; p-7] In short, the powerful intrusion of the Muslim influence that penetrated into the Kings' Court of Roshang in the fifteenth century AD grew all the more in the following centuries. This influence gradually grew so strong that it reached the highest point in the seventeenth century. The Bengali literature in this century shows the full picture of the Muslim influence in the King's Court of Roshang. The picture of the Muslim influence on the King's Court of Arakan portrayed in the Bengali literature has been presented below.

---

[23] History of Burma – Lt. Col. A P Phayre, [1844 London], p. 173
[24] J. A. S. B., Vol. XV, 1846, p. 233.
[25] Ibid. p. 234.
[26] Ibid. p. 234.
[27] Ibid. p. 234.

Appendix Roshang - 12

Árakán Rájsabhây Bangálá Sáhitya   12

In the King's Court of Roshang during seventeenth century there were Muslim courtiers who appointed their own poets to uplift Bengali literature, the names of those Roshang Kings are as follows:

Arakanese Name	Name as adopted in Bengali literature	Reigning period
Thiri thu-dhamma Raja	Sri Sudharmma Raja	1622–1638 AD
Min Sani	x	1638 (28 days)
Narabadigyi	Nripatigiri, Nripagiri	1638 – 1645 "
Thado = Thado Mintar	Cadehu, Chado Umadar	1645 – 1652 "
Sanda Thudhamma	Chandra Sudharmma	1652 – 1684 "

Roshang King, Thiri thu-dhamma Raja (1622 – 1638 AD) was as greatly powerful as his father, Meng Kha Moung or Husain Shah (1612 – 1622 AD). He also used Muslim name as his father; unluckily that has not been deciphered. He ruled a vast area from Dhaka to Pegu[28]. During his rule, Poet Daulat Qazi, with orders from Ashraf Khan, while living in King's Court of Roshang, started witting the incomplete epic poem, "Satî Mainâ"[29]. The lineage, Dhamma [religion], religious practice, great power and justice of King Thiri thu-dhamma has been testified by Daulat Qazi as follows:

"To the east of the river Karnafuli there is a palace,
Roshang City by name – like the Heaven.
There rules the glorious king of Magadha descent a follower of the Buddha,
Name being Sri Sudhamma Raja, renown for his justice.
His power is like the morning sun, famous in the world,
Grooms the subjects like his own children.
Reveres the Lord [Buddha] and purely religious,
One's sins are forgiven when one sees his feet...."

{Cont: p-8}

---

[28] History of Burma – Lt. Col. A P Phayre, p. 177
[29] Sahitya Parisat Partika, 2nd issue, 1333 [Bengali era], p. 64.

Appendix Roshang - 13

13   *Arakanese Reaserch Journal. Vol. III*

Whoever extols the pious, famous and just king –
His poverty vanishes though born poor he is.
If by virtue of good deeds
One can see the King's face –
From hell (he's) delivered to heaven
A life of success.
Justice and peace prevail across the land
One needs not fear another, all (are) fairly treated
If the ants rejoice over honey-woods
The elephant doesn't cross them fearing the King.
Whoever hears and extols that virtue
His poverty vanishes though born poor he be.
The king also had vast number of soldiers and navy. The poet writes:-
"White, red, black – elephants of every hue
The sky is covered with colourful flags.
Millions of soldiers, and countless horses,
Who can tell the number of [war] boats?"

The "Laskar Uzir" or "War Secretary" was a Muslim – Ashraf Khan by name. He [the poet] wrote his poem by the order of Ashraf Khan. He was King's trusted favourite person. The King felt relieved by entrusting all the statecraft to him. The Queen also consider him to be more "worth and profoundly learned" than her own son[30]. This shows how much "authority, influence and control" the "Laskar Uzir"

---

30   "Chief Minister Srijuta Ashraf Khan,
          Of Chishti clan according to Hanih Mojab.
                    *   *   *
          (Who is) the most favouvite of the King,
          (He is) the Laskar Uzir – the Great Minister.
          Knowing his clean heart – the King,
          Handed over statecraft to him.
          Mahadevi [the Queen] knew for sure,
          More worthy and learned [he was] than her son.
          The King with satisfaction, as his own son,
          Made Ashraf Khan the Chief Minister."   (Satî Mainâ)

Appendix Roshang - 14

Arakán Rájsabháy Bangálá Sáhityu   14

wielded in Arakan. In fact he ran the country and was the supreme authority. No wonder, the influence and circumstances of the Muslims would flourish in such a country. Actually it was so. Countless number of Sheikhs, Syeds, Qazis, Mollahs, Alims, Fakirs, Arabians, Rumis, Moghuls, Pathans import to Arakan {cont: p- 9.} and Ashraf Khan took the responsibility to give accommodation in Roshang and service to them; he built mosques and dug ponds in many places. People who left their countries, people living abroad, travellers and merchants from Ashin (Achi, *Ache?*), Kuchin (Cochi), Maslipettan (Macilipatan) to Mecca- Medina praised his love of own nation and religion[31].

"Laskar Uzir" Ashraf Khan hailed from Chittagong. The remnants of his building at Charia village of Hathazari thana [in Chittagong district] can be seen even today. A pond in the village also carries his memories[32]. It can be heard that there are a number of monuments attributed to him in different places of Chittagong. Amongst them a large pond at Kadalpur village of Raozan thana is still renown as "Laskar Uzir's Pond"[33].

The influence and power of the Muslims that was established in the King's Court of Roshang increased day by day without any sign of lessening. For this reason we can see that the chief poets of Roshang kingdom [when vacant] were not filled without the Muslims. The

---

[31]   "Mosques, ponds and donations he made,
His fame spread to Mecca and Medina.
Syed, Quzi, Sheikh, Mollah, Alim, Fakir,
Looks after them as he would to his own body.
Foreigner, Arabian, Rumi, Moghul, Pathan,
Brings them up as he does to his own body.
          *   *   *
Exiles, locals, travellers, merchants,
Extols him in countries here and there,
To the north and to the south – Lands of
Achi, Cochi, Macilipatna – all."   (Sati Mainá)

[32] Sadhana, 2nd year, 8th issue, Agrahayan, 1327 [Bengali Era (BE)], page 303.
[33] Bangiya Musalman Sahitya Patrika, Magh 1325 [BE], p 284.

Appendix Roshang - 15

Muslims were without doubt skilled statesmanship. Or else the highest ranks in the Court would not been filled up by Muslims.

In 1638 AD Roshang King, Thiri thu-dhamma was assassinated. His son, Min Sani just after the twenty-eighth days of his incumbency and the Roshang throne was rendered vacant. The next King Narapadigyi (1638 – 1645 AD) was a minister of King Thiri thu-dhamma. After Min Sani, the Queen called on a meeting and put Narapadigyi [Narapatigri in Arakanese writing] in the throne.

The Arakanese Kings gave up Muslim names from his time onwards; there is no Persian script in coins he stamped in 1638 AD[34]. It is not right to guess that the Muslim influence died out in Roshang since his reign. From the last year of King thiri thu-dhamma's rule 1638 AD to the last year of Narapadigyi's reign {Cont: p- 10.} (1638 – 1645) extending these seven years saw a number of political strife and dissension in Arakan as a result Chittagong slipped out of Arakan kingdom in 1638 AD. That year the "Magh" ruler [governor] of Chittagong, Mengre i.e War-chief = commander-in-chief was compelled to hand over Chittagong to Islam Khan, representative of the Moghul Raj [empire]; this Mengre is renown as "Mukut Ray" in the Bengal history[35]. It is likely that the use of Persian language was banished from Arakanese coins for these political reasons[36].

Successor to the throne, Thado, Thado Mintar [Thado Mindara], was the son of King Narapadigyi's brother. He ruled from 1645 to 1652 AD. During Thado Mintar's (Chado Umadar in Bengali) reign the great epic poet Alaol wrote "Padmavati" – his epic poem[37]. It is surprising, Alaol mentioned Thado Mintar as

---

[34] J. A. S. B., Vol. XV, 1846, p. 234
[35] Ibid, - pp. 234-235,
[36] Ibid, - p,235,
[37] Sahitya-Parisat-Patrika, 2nd Issue, 1333BE, p.64.

Appendix Roshang - 16

Narapadigyi's son in his work[38]. Perhaps he did not know the real fact, or else, who knows history has not made a mistake by mentioning Thado Mintar as the nephew of Narapadigyi?

However, we know[39] from Alaol that the War Minister of Narapadigyi was Alaol's first protector and Muslim[40] Magan Thakur's father, "Sri Bara Thakur". During Sri Bara Thakur's lifetime, his son "Magan" was holding the post of a minister. King Narapadigyi trusted and loved Magan Thakur so much that, at the hour of his death he left his only daughter under Magan's custody. When this princess became the principal queen of Thado Mintar, she entrusted the post of the Roshang King's Chief Minister to Magan Thakur realising the guardianship she enjoyed in childhood[41]. {Cont: p- 11.} From this we know that though the Persian script was no more used in the coins since Nerapadigyi, the Muslim influences in Roshang did not diminish.

After the death of Thado Mintar, his son Sanda-thu-dhamma (1652 – 1684 AD) ascended the throne. None ruled for so long as he did; for thirty-two years as the longest ruling monarch he decorated

---

[38]   "When Salim Shah's lineage was ended
Nripagiri [Narapatigri] became the ruler of the country.
The luxury and happiness of the King – there is no match to it,
In opulence [he] spent the time.
A son and a daughter – fortunate and blissful,
The blessed King was born.
To go to heavens – gave the Kingdom to his son,
Indra [the king of gods] feel ashamed seeing him.
Chado Umadar by name, peerless in looks and excellence." – etceteras
(Padmavati)

[39] There is a lengthy description about Magan and his father in Padmavati of the footnote "4" above, which we think not necessary to be dealt here.

[40] Holders of the title "Thakur" – Magan and his father were Muslims, which we have dealt in the next chapter. [Editor: not within the scope of this journal]

[41]   "When the old King went to the heavens,
His daughter became the Chief Queen [of the new King].
Realising the affection she received in her childhood,
The Queen made him the Chief Minister.   (Padmavati)

Appendix Roshang - 17

17   *Arakanese Reaserch Journal. Vol. III*

the throne of Roshang. It is because he ascended the throne at a very young age. From Alaol's poem "Saiful Muluk"[42] it is known that when he ascended the Roshang throne he had not acquired the skills to run the country yet. Therefore the minor King's mother ruled as Regent by appointing Magan Thakur as the Chief Minister. Possibly Sanda-thu-dhamma took over the burden of government before Magan Thakur's death. After Magan Thakur, Solaiman – another Muslim – filled the position, that is, became the "Prime Minister" (chief counsellor/ courtier of the highest rank) of Roshang King Sanda-thu-dhamma. The treasury and general administration of the country was entrusted to this Muslim chief Minister[43]. During Sanda-thu-dhamma's rule the important posts of Roshang kingdom were given to the Muslims. Syed Muhammad was his "war minister" (armed force minister); Alaol got to write "Sapta Paykar" at his order[44]. Another Muslim named Majlis was "Navaraj"[*Nawa-raja* – young prince?] in the King's Court of Arakan; he is known as "Navaraj Majlis". Alaol translated "Sikandar Nama" – a Persian poem into Bengali by his order[45]. It seems that the civil and criminal courts were run by the Muslim Qazirs [judges]. It is known that during that period a man by the name of Saud Shah was a Qazi of Roshang – {Cont: p-12}

---

[42] Please see the next article on "Poet Magan Thakut" [in the Bengali book since it is not included in this Journal. Ed].

[43]   "Then the kingdom became prosperous again,
            Under Sri Chanda Sudhhama – the gerat King.
                *   *   *

            His chief minister Srimanta Solaiman.
                *   *   *

            Gold, silver, precious stones, the treasury,
            The King entrusted him with.
            Lakhs of employment in the Kingdom,
            All held under his authority.

[44] Sahitya-parisat-patrika, Issue 2, 1333 (BE), p. 68. And –
            The peerless King named Sri Chandra Sudhamma,
            Destroyed of the wicked, protector of the distressed.
                *   *   *

            Such great King's immerse wealth,
            His chief was minister is Syed Muhammad. (Sapta Paykar)

[45] Sahitya-parisat-patrika, Issue 2, 1333 (BE), p. 67.

Appendix Roshang - 18

Arakán Rájsabháy Bangálá Sáhitya 18

> "Syed Saud Shah, Qazi of Roshang,
> Agreed to [foster] me, finding in me a little learning..." (Sikandar Nama)

Another person, Sayed Musa, was a minister of Sanda-thu-dhamma. Alaol completed "Saiful Muluk" by his order[46].

The degree of the influence and presence of Muslims can easily be guessed in the King's Court where the Muslims prevailed. Of course, Sanda-thu-dhamma had a high esteem of the Muslims. Serious politics was behind the gruesome assassination of Shah Shuja by the King in 1660 AD. It does not prove the King's lack of love for the Muslims. Thus we see:

> "People from every country, hearing the magnificence of Roshang,
> Took shelter under the King.
> Arabian, Michiri [Egyptian], Shami, Turkish, Habsi [African], Rumi
> Khorachani and Uzbek.
> Lahuri, Multani, Sindi, Kashmiri, Dakkhini [Deccanese], Hindi,
> Kamrupi [Assamese] and Bangadeshi [Bengali],
> Ahopai Khotanchari (?), Karnali, Malayabari,
> From Achi, Kuchi[47] [Cochi] and Karnataka.
> Countless Sheik, Soiyadjada, Moghul, Pathan warriors,
> Rajput, Hindu of various nationals.
> Avai [Inwa], Burmese, Siam [Thai], Tripura, Kuki to name
> How many more should I elaborate.[?]
> Armenian, Olandaz [Dutch], Dinemar, Engraj [English],
> Castiman and Français.
> Hipani[c], Almani, Chholdar, Nachhrani,
> Many a races including Portuguese."   (Padmavati)

The Muslim poets in the Roshang Court, which itself was dominated by Muslim influence, nurtured Bengali literature in the 17th century AD. The outcome of the Bengali literature in Roshang Court was multifaceted and long-lasting. We will try to enumerate it slowly.

---

[46] Ibid.
[47] Achi, Kochi = Achin and Cochin country.

The end

Appendix-3

The Rakhine State Violence
Vol. 1: The Rakhaing Revolution

Table of Contents

Acknowledgement

Preface

Prologue 1-3

1. Our Demands 4-5
2. Colonialism and Decolonization 6-14
3. The Movement 15-19
4. The Case Against Separation of Burma from India 20-32
5. AFPFL 33-38
6. Kra Hla Aung 39-46
7. The Third Dimension 47-55
8. The Strategies and Tactics 56-71
9. Hidden Colony 72-85
10. The Prisoner of Mandalay 86-103
11. Democracy 104-117
12. Kingdom to Republic 118-126
13. ALD (in exile) 127-152
14. Arakan Army 153-186
15. Arakan Democratic Forces 187-217
16. The Rohingya 218-251
17. Solution or Illusion 252-269
18. Rohingya Persecution 270-281
19. Divide and Rule 282-291
20. Buddhist-Muslim War 292-313
21. Myanmar Apartheid 314-326
22. The Rising Sea 327
Epilogue 328
Appendix-1: ADF Manifesto 329-333
Appendix-2: Books by Shwe Lu Maung 334-339
Index to Vol.1 340-347

Appendix-4

Books by Shwe Lu Maung

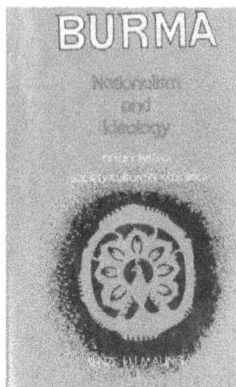

LC control no.:
89903911
Personal name:
Shwe Lu Maung.
Main title:
Burma, nationalism and ideology : an analysis of society, culture, and politics / Shwe Lu Maung.
Published/Created: Dhaka : University Press, 1989.
Description: xiii, 117 p. : maps ; 22 cm.

What happens in Burma has considerable implications for those who live in South and South East Asia. In this book a former Burmese guerrilla and a dissenter of the military regime, brings forth the complexity of Burma's present political and social dilemmas. He traces its roots in the historical and cultural diversities of Burmese people, in the feudal and colonial heritage of the country and in the stormy whirlwind of the modern political doctrines. It is the author's opinion that Burma today stands at the crossroads of socialism preached by Ne win, communism of the Burma Communist Party, democracy-based Federation of Burma and the disintegration of the present territory into feudal states. Shwe Lu Maung examines all the issues most succinctly and presents the readers with valuable information on Burma.
1999 re-publication:

- **Hardcover:** 117 pages
- **Publisher:** University Press Ltd. (July 25, 1999)
- **Language:** English
- **ISBN-10:** 9840511149
- **ISBN-13:** 978-9840511143
- **Product Dimensions:** 5.5 x 1 x 8.7 inches

****

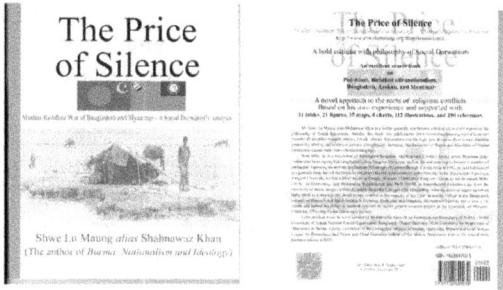

[US] Library of Congress
CALL NUMBER: DS528.8.B3 S48 2005

LC control no.:   2005906134
LCCN permalink: http://lccn.loc.gov/2005906134
Type of material: Book (Print, Microform, Electronic, etc.)
Personal name: Shwe Lu Maung.
Main title: **The price of silence : Muslim-Buddhist war of Bangladesh and Myanmar : a social Darwinist's analysis** / Shwe Lu Maung.
Published/Created: Columbia, Mo. : DewDrop Arts and Technology, c2005.
Description: 318 p.: ill., maps ; 27 cm.
ISBN: 9781928840039 (pbk.)
                1928840035 (pbk.)

The objective of this book is to find ways and means to stop the on-going Muslim-Buddhist War of Bangladesh and Myanmar. In view of this objective the book examines and gives detailed accounts of the causal factors that fuel the Muslim-Buddhist War. Three key contributing factors namely, 'Bangladesh Pan-Islam', 'Myanmar ultra-nationalism', and 'over-population' are thoroughly investigated.

The author tediously traced the historical events of Muslim-Buddhist War and rightly pointed out that today the war is simmering at Bangladesh-Myanmar border. The global warming and rising sea is gradually inundated the over-populated Bangladesh destroying the human habitat along the rivers and coastal area everyday. The agriculture and human habitat dwindles but the population grows rapidly approaching to the point of saturation at two hundred millions. At this point, Bangladesh will be swallowed by the chaos born of poverty, famine, and displaced people. Amidst the chaos and political instability, the Islamic Communes will emerge, in a similar style of the 1871 Paris

Commune, to tackle the situation. It will be the time when the chaotic movement of the people out of Bangladesh will take place, destabilizing the region and flaring up the Muslim-Buddhist War of Bangladesh and Myanmar.

The author supports his presentation with 31 tables, 21 figures, 15 maps, 8 charts, 112 illustrations, and 280 references. The reader can listen to his videos at Amazon author page or at his website http://www.shwelumaung.org.

****

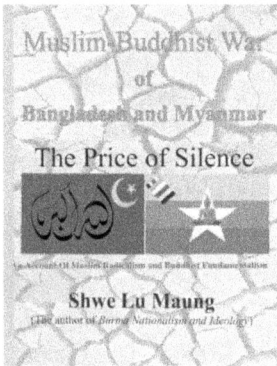

This ebook (ISBN 13: 978-1-928840-04-6) is the digital version (Kindle) of the physical book The Price of Silence: Muslim-Buddhist War of Bangladesh and Myanmar, 2005, ISBN-13: 978-1-928840-03-9, Library of Congress Control Number: 2005906134, Library of Congress Call Number: DS528.8.B3 S48 2005.

- **File Size:** 12520 KB
- **Print Length:** 455 pages
- **Publisher:** Shahnawaz Khan (May 31, 2011)
- **Sold by:** Amazon Digital Services, Inc.
- **Language:** English
- **ASIN:** B005GFJ3W0
- **Text-to-Speech:** Enabled ☑

****

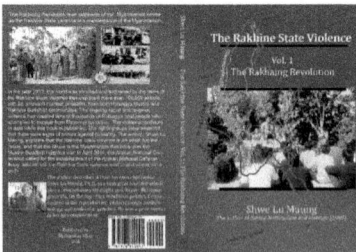

The Rakhine State Violence by Shwe Lu Maung
(in 2 volumes, total 622 pages)
Library of Congress Control Number: 2014902841

Vol. 1: The Rakhaing Revolution
ISBN 13: 978-1928840-09-1
ISBN 10: 1-928840-09-4
341 pages

Publisher: Shahnawaz Khan, USA, 2014

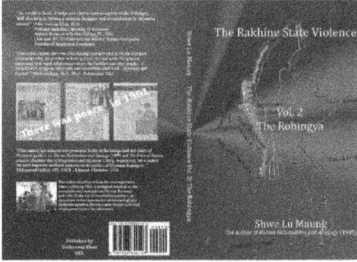

Vol. 2: The Rohingya
ISBN 13: 978-1928840-10-7
ISBN 10: 1-928840-10-8
281 pages

Publisher:
Shahnawaz Khan, USA, 2014

Description of the book
This is a very important book in view of Myanmar's transition to a democratic civil society.
On the Rakhine State violence:
"The Rohingya are reduced to dire stateless, homeless, landless, destitute refugee status, and the Rakhaing are transformed into blood-thirsty racist-religionist monsters, a disgrace to humanity. The Burman ruling class is the only beneficiary of the Rakhine State violence; even the Burmese Nobel Peace Laureate is trying to make a political profit out of it, rather than stopping it."
On the Rakhaing Revolution:
Shwe Lu Maung explains that Rakhaingpray (Arakan) is a hidden colony. The philosophy of the Rakhaing Revolution is 'we-the-people' (ရို့ပြည်သူ), and its strategy is "Decolonization of Burma" in favor of an equitable United Republics of Burma, in which the Rakhaingpray will participate as a People's Republic of Rakhaingpray (ရခိုင်ပြည်သူ့ သမတ နိုင်ငံ).
Rakhaing-Rohingya relationship:
The author also describes Rakhaing-Rohingya relationship with the declassified personal and official documents in this volume, whereas the Vol. 2: The Rohingya deals with the Rohingya crisis in depth.
His solution for Burma:
"Myanmar crisis is so complex, delicate, sensitive, and volatile that only a Geneva Convention on Myanmar Crisis will lead to a lasting peace and prosperity to the people of Burma and the region."
The *Rakhine State Violence* is a *reflection* of Shwe Lu Maung, Ph.D., a cadre of the Rakhaing Revolution since the 2nd March 1962, the day General Ne Win seized power in Burma. He is a revolutionary strategist and theoretician. In this book, he candidly presents the theories, strategies, and tactics from days of King Bering Resistance (1784-1815) to date. On the top of his rebellious politics, Dr. Maung, a biological scientist, specializes in the reproductive endocrinology, biotechnology, and molecular genetics. He was a gene-hunter in his last employment.

****

Is Suu Kyi a racist?
Shwe Lu Maung

ISBN 13:978-1-928840-11-4
ISBN 10:1-928840-11-6

Publisher:
Shahnawaz Khan, USA, 2014

Description of the book

Since Suu Kyi is working hard to become the president of Myanmar the world needs to know the answer.

There are three main reasons why the question of Suu Kyi racism arises. These are (1) the Rohingya issue, (2) the Kachin War, and (3) the Bama Supremacy.

These issues are examined and analyzed in light of common humanity, Universal Declaration of Human Rights, and Aung San Suu Kyi's politics in Myanmar. The scientific view of racism is also weighed in.

The big question is–
Why shall not we openly discuss these thorny and sensitive racial issues?
By keeping these issues suppressed and prohibited, as taboos behind closed doors, we are simply brewing jungle fires, and we are seeing the jungle fires in the Rakhine State, Mandalay, Meiktila, and in all conflict zones around the borders of Myanmar.

In the eyes the world, Suu Kyi is the only qualified Myanmar person to lead Myanmar into openness. When she is silent, conserved, reserved, or calculating at a time of dire need for openness and transparency a legitimate question arises.

Based on his own experience, the author digs Myanmar culture and politics in search of the answer. Shwe Lu Maung, Ph.D., is a biological scientist who is also a revolutionary strategist and former Burmese guerrilla. On the top of his rebellious politics, he specializes in the reproductive endocrinology, biotechnology, and molecular genetics. He was a gene-hunter in his last employment.

Index to Volume II

Index   Page

Index	Page
969 movement	185
A girl who is like water	170
Ahmed, Wakil	151,157
Ahsan, Syed Mohammad Kamrul	135
Alaol (poet)	173-174
Alaungsithu, King	81
Al-Hanafiya, Imam Muhammad	151,155
Ali, Hazarat	151,155
Ānandachandra Stone Inscription	101
Ānandachandra, King	101,102
Anawrahta, King	81,87,93,94,96,101
Aristotle	9
ASEAN	205
Asian rice, *Oryza sativa*	119
Aung, Bogri Kra Hla	187,188
Aung, Htin	80,94
Aung, Nga	87
Aung, San Tha	107,109
Aung, Ye Myint	85,109,135,222
Aurangzeb, Emperor	195
Autosomes	117
Bangladesh Institute of Research and Rehabilitation in Diabetes, Endocrine and Metabolic Disorders (BIRDEM)	143
Banyan tree	87
Bayinnaung, King	82
Bengali Kala	78
Bin, Min, King	197,198
Brahmaputra Civilization	101
Buchanan, Dr. Francis (1799)	172,173,175
Burman-Muslim riot	84
Cakravartin, meaning	198
Chandra Dynasty	101
Chindwin	59

Chittagong Ethnological Museum	7,58
Chittagong University Museum	7,58
Chromosome	117
Citizenship Act 1982, Burma	12,13,57, Chapter 5,84,186
Cohen Johnathan.	61
Cole, G.D.H.	186
Collis, Maurice	103,109,198,199,200,201
Darwin, Charles	5,9
Dhamma Cariya	181-182
Einstein, Albert	220
Einthi, Shwe	80
Eukarya or eukaryote	113
Ficus benghalensis	87
Firdaus, Dr. Muhammad	171
Fish, Jefferson M.	77,78
Fourth World people	141
Franklin, Rosalind Elsie	115
Funan, Kingdom of	96,98,99
Ganga-Brahmaputra Basin	74
general relativity	76
Genes	117
Genographic project, National Geographic	120
Graffin, Roger	184
Grantha alphabet	96,97
Great Image, The Land of the	103
Gutman, Pamela	197
Gyi, Aung, Brigadier General	Chapter 4, 31,144,193
Hall, Daniel George Edward	101,109
Hamza, Syed	151
Hanifa O Kaiyapuri	151
Harikela	193
Hasina, Sheikh, Prime Minister of Bangladesh	206,214
Heraclitus (*Herakleitos*)	219
Himalayan Belt	74
Hla, Narameit, King	201-202
Hlaing, Kyaw	107,188
Homo sapiens	9
Horst, J.	112

HUGO, SNP Consortium	5,132,134
Ibrahim, Dr. M.	143
Indian Genome Variation Consortium	5
International Crimes Tribunal (ICT), Bangladesh	171
Irrawaddy, river	59,92
Islam, Nurul (ARNO)	144
Johnson, Gary	4-5
Johnston, E.H.	101
Kala (meaning)	79
Kala-kya-min, King	82
Kam, Nga Raman	94,95
Karnaphuli River	59
Kha, Maung Maung (Rector)	107
Khan, Enayetullah	3,143
King of Pattikera	81
King-Bering	83
Kissapanadi	59
Kula Thamaga	79
Kyansittha, King	79,80,81,94-96,100,101
Kyaukpyu Kala Paikseik	181
Kyaw, Aye	107,164,165,166
Kyaw, Bonpauk Tha	187
Kyi, Aung San Suu	164,185
LaPolla, Randy J.	99,100,101,109
Laws of Manu	67
Laymro River	59
Leik, Sai Khum	70
Lizard eggs	87
Macrohaplogroup, M	133
Magadha (language)	110
Magwe College	59
Mainamati Museum	58
Manrique, Augustinian friar Sebastião	200
Mârayo (Marayu)	89 (73,90)
Marayu (Mârayo)	73, 90, (89)
Maung, Chairman Khin	188
Maung, Oo Khin	182

Maung, Shwe (Abdur Razak)	51-56
Maurya Empire	72
Mauryan Empire	90
Maw, Sai Saing	70
Mayu River	59
Meiktila	192
Meru, Mount	63
Min, Kyaw (DHRP)	107
Min, Kyaw (ICS)	103,107,109,190-192,193,204
Moni, Dipu, Dr.	59
Most recent common ancestor (MRCA)	135
Mount Radwa	156
Mt. Popa (Mt. Puppa)	92
Mujahid rebellion	84
Mwan, Mun Saw (Narameit Hla)	82, 201-202
Myanmarism	78
Myazedi Stone Inscription	100
Myedu	192
Naaf River	59,179
Narathu, King	81
National Institutes of Health	119
National League for Democracy (NLD)	11
National Museum, Dhaka	58
Naungdaw Chay	147
Naungdaw Gri	147
NCBI (National Center for Biotechnology Information)	122
Negrito	5
Neolithic Age	74
Ni, Maung	63
Nigger (cf.Kala)	11
Nu, U	35,161,204
Nu-Attalee Agreement	10,185
Nucleus	114
Nyunt, Chairman Maung Sein	188
Obama, Barack, US President	160
Ogre-nymph	88,90,92
Oo, Kyaw Kyaw	31

Oo, Major (retired) Tun Kyaw	188
Oryza rufipogon	120
Pākārama	87
Pallava dynasty	96
Panthwar	93
Pattikera Prince	80,81
Pearn, Bertie Reginald	83
Phayre, Arthur Purves	62,65,72,81,83,95,96,100,109
Preamble of the US Constitution	186-187
Pyu	193
Qanungo, Suniti Bhushan	196
Qazi, Daulat (poet)	172, 173
Race and human genomic diversity	136
Rahman, Nayak Mizanur	216,
Raza Kumar	80,100
RazaGri, King	82
Red Comrades	182
Responsibility to Protect	145,162
Rhee, Chairman Kyaw Zan	187,188
Rhetoric	134
Rousseau, Jean Jacques	186
Saffron Revolution	185
Sai, Sai Htee	70
Samatata	193
Sambul (Thambula)	80,94
Sawlu, King	94,95
Sein, Thein, President of Myanmar	168,206,209,210
Seinda, U	187
Shah Barid Khan	151
Shah, Sultan Ghiasuddin Azam	202
Shin Nagainda Mawgwun	70,106
Śilāmegha, King	101,102
single nucleotide polymorphism (SNP)	121
special relativity	76
Śrīvatsa	193
Subhaplogroup	133
Sultan Jalaluddin Muhammad Shah	82

Talaings	95,96
Telingâna	95,96
Tennyson, Alfred	219
Tha, ACP Chairman Shwe	181-182,188
Thaw Kaung	88,92,93
The Grand Central	134
The time to the most recent common ancestor (TMRCA)	120
Thikya Religion	81
Thikyamin	81
Thiri Thu-Dhamma Raja, King	173
Thudhamma, Sanda, King	195
Time travel	76
Tribal belt	177
Tsandaya, Tsu-la-taing, King	196
Tun, San Kyaw	107
Twelve Nobel Peace Laureates	167
Uddin, Sultan Jalal	202
Ugly as ogres	85
Union Solidarity and Development Party (USDP)	11
United Nations Charter	13
United nations Refugee Agency	12
Universal Declaration of Human Rights (UDHR)	13
Varendra Museum	58
Vedic Religion	66
Vedic Religion	66,67
Veisali	193
Venezuela	104
Vesālī (Vaisali, Weithali)	101
Vietnam	96
Vijaya, Prince	91
Watson and Crick	114-115
Wheeler, L. Kip	134
Wilkins, Maurice Hugh Frederick	115
Win, Khin	203
Win, Ne	35,Chapter 5,164
Wunthanu rakkhita taya (Patriotic Defense Principles)	164-165

Ye Kyun (island)   147-148
Young Men Buddhist Association
(YMBA)   163-164
Yunus, Dr. (RSO)   144

Notes